THE
BATH
BOOK
OF
DAYS

D.G. AMPHLETT

The History Press

To Beth, for her love and support.

First published 2014

The History Press
The Mill, Brimscombe Port
Stroud, Gloucestershire, GL5 2QG
www.thehistorypress.co.uk

© D.G. Amphlett, 2014

The right of D.G. Amphlett to be identified as the Author
of this work has been asserted in accordance with the
Copyright, Designs and Patents Act 1988.

British Library Cataloguing in Publication Data.
A catalogue record for this book is available from the British Library.

ISBN 978 0 7524 7016 0

Typesetting and origination by The History Press
Printed in India

– January 1st –

1825: During the eighteenth and nineteenth centuries, a network of turnpike roads were developed throughout Britain. On this date, John Skinner, rector of Camerton in Somerset, drove to Bath to attend a turnpike meeting in order to discuss whether Radstock Hill should become a turnpike road, given the volume of traffic. In his diary he wrote: 'Sir J. Hippisley in the chair, and such a chairman never before did I witness. Instead of hearing calmly and impartially what each side of the question had to say, he got up and advocated the cause which he had espoused. Indeed, that the said Baronet did not possess the same upper stowage as Solomon [Old Testament king famed for his wisdom] it would have been clearly ascertained at this exhibition, where the worthy gentleman gave us all to understand that he was *Asinus Maximus* [Latin: Biggest Ass]. Old Thomas, the Quaker, spoke good sense, "Let us first," said he "consider the state of our funds, whether we are able to spend any money whatever in improvements; if not let us wait til we have the power, and then see the best means for employing it." I left the meeting fully resolved not to visit such a motley assembly again where men seem openly advocating their private interests, under the specious name of consulting for the common public good.' (John Skinner, *Journal of a Somerset Rector*, Howard Combes & Arthur N. Bax (eds), John Murray, 1930)

~ January 2nd ~

1810: Henry Clark was convicted at the Old Bailey of robbing a mail coach of bank notes belonging to the Wotton Basset Bank. The notes, totalling the not inconsiderable sum of £1,825, were placed in a parcel and addressed to Mr Large of Bath. On this date, in 1810, the parcel was delivered to the coach office of the Swan Lane Two Necks in Lad Lane, London. It was never fully ascertained quite how the parcel was stolen, although it is quite likely it was taken from the coach offices. Three £10 notes were traced to Clark. In his defence, Clark stated he found them, but he could offer no proof of this. It was also demonstrated that Clark had used a fictitious name rather than his own. The jury did not take long to find Clark guilty and he was sentenced to death. (*Newgate Calendar*)

1904: The first regular electric tram service started in Bath. Trams ran in Bath until 1939. (David and Jonathan Falconer, *A Century of Bath*, Sutton, 1999)

‒ January 3rd ‒

1871: Excitement was caused in the district when a double wedding took place involving couples who were deaf and unable to speak. Mr W. Cox was married to Miss Sarah Weir, matron of the Deaf and Dumb Institute that existed in Walcot Parade, and Mr H. Rudkins was also married to Miss M'Cabe, a staff member of the same institution. Canon Bernard, officiant at the wedding and president of the Institute, ran his fingers along the print of the prayer book so those taking part could follow the service. When the couples were required to give their consent to the all-important question 'Wilt thou have …?' the couples simply nodded their assent. In the afternoon, after the wedding breakfast, the couples left to begin their honeymoon in Clevedon. The Victorian period witnessed the growth of institutions and schools for those with disabilities. The majority, like the Deaf and Dumb Institute in Walcot Parade, were charitable institutions, as local authorities were not empowered to make any educational provision until the 1890s. (*Western Mail*)

~ January 4th ~

1928: An article in *The Times* stated: 'The Great Western Railway Company ran an experimental excursion to Bath on Wednesday to visit the Roman baths and other attractions. The result was so successful that an official of the company stated that further conducted educational excursions to other places of interest in the West would be run. The train, which carried two restaurant cars, ran from Paddington to Bath in 1 hour 55 minutes, arriving at 1.30 p.m.' Today the journey can be made in around one and half hours. The article continues, stating that 'the return journey, which was also non-stop, was made in 4 minutes under the scheduled time, and Paddington was reached shortly before eight o'clock. The party, on arrival at Bath, were conducted to the Roman Bath, where the whole course of curative treatment was demonstrated and the history of the bath explained. Afterwards the excursionists visited the printing and publishing works of Sir Isaac Pitman and Sons at Bath, and were entertained at tea by Messrs Pitman.' Sir Isaac Pitman was the inventor of a system of shorthand. A long-term resident of Bath, he had established a printing works in the centre of the city, which by the 1880s was using steam-powered printing presses on an industrial scale. (*The Times*; *Oxford Dictionary of National Biography*)

~ JANUARY 5TH ~

1842: 'A most diabolical attempt was made on Wednesday night to cause a further accident on the Great Western line. The mail train was on its way from London, and when within about three miles of Bath, the signal was given by the engine driver of something wrong, and the train was stopped with all possible dispatch, on investigation it appears that some monster had placed two large stones (one on each rail) with a view of sending the engine off the line, but which providently did not take place. One of the stones was crushed into a thousand atoms, and flew over the driver and stoker without doing them any serious injury; the other stone was forced on one side by the sword, or guard, which is placed before the wheels, but both the guards were put out of their place, and much bent and twisted. The stone that was turned off the rail by the sword, or guard, and which was brought to Bristol by the driver, would be about 40lbs in weight.' (*Ipswich Journal*)

JANUARY 6TH

1865: At the Bristol Quarter Sessions, James Redan, aged 27, an ivory turner, was indicted for stealing a horse valued at £25. The brown mare was stolen from Elm Tree Farm, Bedminster, the property of William Wakefield, on 26th October. PC William Membray, stationed at Twerton, saw Redan riding the horse along the turnpike road and stopped him. He was given seven years' imprisonment, as he already had two previous convictions, one of which was for stealing a horse in Cardiff. (*Bristol Mercury*)

2008: A collection of scripts and other theatrical memorabilia of the late Arnold Ridley were made available online on this day. Ridley was best known for his portrayal of Private Godfrey (who often asks to be excused) in the television comedy *Dad's Army*. Ridley is also noted for his play *The Ghost Train*, conceived as Ridley was waiting for a train at Mangotsfield station. The collection, given to the University of Bristol in 1984 by Ridley's son following his father's death, includes thirty original scripts, programmes, handbills, posters, newspaper cuttings and production photographs. (www.bbc.co.uk; www.bristol.ac.uk)

1859: *The Times* newspaper reported 'a most heartless case of robbery, attended, it would seem, with the most disastrous result to the health and even lives of a number of those poor unfortunates, pauper lunatics, came before the Bath Winter sessions, just held. John Cave, the attendant in the male lunatic's ward at the Bath Union Workhouse, was indicted for stealing beef, mutton, butter, and cheese, the property of the guardians of the Bath Union; and Benjamin Skeates, of Combe Downe, was indicted for feloniously receiving the same knowing it to have been stolen. The prisoner Cave, as the principal attendant of the lunatics, had daily to serve out to them their rations, but, instead of faithfully performing that duty, he appears to have stinted them of their food for a considerable period, and to a great extent. The master of the workhouse, Mr Eaton, suspecting something of the kind from the altered appearance of the unfortunate lunatics, set a watch upon the prisoner Cave, and on the 5th and 6th December he was observed to secrete meat which ought to have been distributed to the lunatics in a drawer in his room. The rations of the inmates, by the prisoner's heartless conduct, were reduced to less than half the workhouse diet.' Both the defendants were found guilty; Cave was sentenced to eighteen months, and Skeates to twelve months, with hard labour in each case. (*The Times*)

⏤ JANUARY 8TH ⏤

1913: The mystery of who was responsible for the robbery of Miss Edith Wheelwright, a leader of the suffrage movement in Bath the preceding September, was resolved in a statement issued by her solicitor on this day. The assault had taken place when Edith had been walking home, at dusk, when she was attacked from behind by an assailant who placed a chloroformed handkerchief over her mouth and rendered her 'insensible'. Whilst in this condition, the perpetrator stole her pearl and emerald ring. Edith had her suspicions of Miss Emily Jane Beatrice Manning, a nurse, whom she thought was responsible for writing a number of libellous letters and forging documents. Emily, therefore, employed a female detective to keep watch on her. After a time, the detective was able to accompany the nurse to a solicitor's office where she made a full confession. She stated that her intention had only been to scare Miss Wheelright and only took the opportunity to attack Edith when she saw her walking home. However, as Emily was ill, Miss Wheelright did not press charges and Emily died in a Dublin hospital aged 39 on December 23rd 1912. The ring was recovered. (*The Times*; *The British Journal of Nursing*; Elizabeth Crowford, *The Women's Suffrage Movement: A Reference Guide 1866–1928*, Routledge, 2001)

— JANUARY 9TH —

1842: A letter of this date, published the following day in *The Morning Post*, reports 'a tremendous and most singular occurrence that has just taken place in the neighbourhood of our city.' The published letter goes on to state: 'Between 4 and 5 o'clock this evening, and when almost twilight, the entire surface of a very large piece of ground more than seven acres, at Combe-Down, gave way, owing to the workmen having conducted their excavations in a stone quarry far beneath an angle, or rather street, of that populous village, of which above 18 houses, with its beautiful new church, school-house, &c, were instantaneous subsiding of their foundations, involved in ruin; and multitudes in the buildings and accidentally assembled on the spot have perished. Though late when I write, the various avenues in the outlets of the city are thronged with anxious thousands crowding towards the scene of desolation. The bells of the Abbey and other churches are ringing violently, and the authorities are hastening to Combe to render what assistance they can to the surviving sufferers.' On January 11th, the letter was again published, but the editors of *The Morning Post* prefaced it stating that they believed the letter to be a hoax since *Keene's Bath Journal* made no mention of the alleged events and no confirmation of the statement had been received at Paddington station. The letter was, indeed, a hoax. (*The Morning Post*)

~ January 10th ~

1893: A fire occurred at the Albion Cabinet Works in Upper Bristol Road, the property of Messrs F. and A. Norris. This was the third fire to occur at the premises within a few years. The blaze originated in the packing room and carving shop. This section of the works was 'almost a separate building', with an iron fire door which ran the width of the building and separated this section from the rest of the works. The door had been installed following the two previous devastating fires at the works. At times, this iron fire door glowed red hot during the blaze, but nevertheless helped to save the rest of the building from the fire. The firemen responsible for putting out the blaze experienced difficulty in tackling it since the fire hydrants were found to be frozen. They were thawed by burning a quantity of paraffin near them. (*Bath and Wilts Chronicle & Herald*)

1956: Gusts of up to 50mph hit Bath and the surrounding district. In Bathford, a 40ft walnut tree was blown across the vicarage path from the adjoining property, just before the Revd Kenneth Flenley and his wife retired to bed. The tree narrowly missed the house, although the outermost branches succeeded in bringing down the gutter. The winds also brought down a 20ft elm tree in Winifred's Lane. It was broken up by members of the city's engineering department the next day. (*Bath and Wilts Chronicle & Herald*)

~ January 11th ~

1885: An accident occurred on the Great Western Railway at Limpley Stoke, near Bath, which caused two men to lose their lives. The railway company was relaying a double line of rails between Bathampton and Bradford-on-Avon and, as part of the improvement works, a goods shed was being erected at Limpley Stoke. Behind the shed, but on lower ground, was a stable belonging to Mr G. Holbrow, a timber merchant. The space between the goods shed and the stable had been filled with loose stones to a depth of 7ft and it was reckoned that the weight of these stones was about 100 tons. During the night, two labourers, George Marment (30) and Arthur Mustye (50), slept in the stables, along with eight horses. The following morning, the weight of the stones forced the stable wall to collapse and the roof buried the sleeping men and horses. Assistance was called for at once, but both men were found crushed to death, along with six of the horses. (*Manchester Times*)

~ JANUARY 12TH ~

1867: The unfortunate death of a 'newsman' took place and is described in the following account. (A newsman, in this context, was simply someone who delivered newspapers.) 'On Saturday evening an old newsman named Knight, was frozen to death not far from Bath. He was returning from his round to that city, where he resided, and had gone as far as Englishcombe, when he endeavoured, during the hail and sleet, to reach the main road from Wells to Bath by a short cut through the fields. One of those fields is on the incline, and it is believed that his hat was blown off, that in endeavouring to regain it he fell down, and, from the effects of the weather and exhaustion was not able to regain his feet. He was found the following morning, quite dead, by a shepherd. The poor man was in his eighty-fourth year and had been a newsman for nearly half a century.' (*Trewman's Exeter Flying Post*)

～ January 13th ～

1794: At the Quarter Sessions held at Bath, George Wilkinson was accused of making seditious expressions that supported France, with which Britain was, once again, at war. Wilkinson was alleged to have wished 'success to the French and down with the allies' and that 'the King and his ministers are villains'. Wilkinson offered no defence except to say that the words were those of a 'thoughtless young man' and that there was no malice in his remarks. For this crime, he was sentenced to four months in prison and fined 20*s*. (*The Times*)

———

2006: The inauguration of the University of Bath Spa was celebrated in Bath Abbey. The university gained its new title (it had previously been known as Bath Spa University College) after an application to gain full university status was approved in August 2005 by the Department for Education and Skills. Senior academic staff and the Mayor of Bath, Cllr Peter Metcalfe, formed a procession from the Guildhall to the abbey. As part of the celebrations, an honorary fellowship was awarded to Jason Gardner, an Olympic gold medallist in the 400m relay, who graduated from the University College in 2003. (Bath Spa University website)

~ JANUARY 14TH ~

1878: At Bath Police Court on this day: 'Frank Skinner, a boy of 11 was summoned for breaking a pane of glass, value 6*d*, at East Walcot on the 9th inst. – The bench reprimanded the lad and fined him 1*s* and costs, or 3 days imprisonment.' (*Bath and Cheltenham Gazette*)

1882: Mary Williams and Catherine Reeves, of No. 3 Avon Street, appeared before Bath magistrates charged with stealing a pair of boots valued at 7*s* 6*d*. The boots were stolen from William Henry Holland's residence in Pulteney Bridge and the pair were each given a one month sentence with hard labour. They were also charged with stealing a pair of trousers from No. 1 Kingsmead Square, the property of Sidney Baxter. Reeves was also convicted of this offence and was given a further month's imprisonment. (*Bath and Cheltenham Gazette*)

1893: A rugby match between Bath and Bristol took place at Bath. The game was affected by a heavy snowstorm, during which 6in of snow fell over the city. Bath was only able to put up a team of thirteen men to Bristol's fourteen and conditions were described as 'near impossible'. Amazingly, 200 to 300 people stayed until the end to watch the match. Bristol won the game 13–5. (Kevin Couglan, Peter Hall, Colin Gale, *Before the Lemons: A History of Bath Rugby Football Club 1865–1965*, Tempus, 2003)

~ JANUARY 15TH ~

1840: Frances (Fanny) Burney was born in King's Lynn, Norfolk, on June 13th 1752. She is best known as a writer, and her first novel, *Evelina*, was published amidst great secrecy from her family members in 1778. It gained critical acclaim and many theories were voiced as to the identity of the author. Another successful book, *Cecilia*, followed in 1782. The success of her novels brought her a modest financial income, and she also accepted the £200 per annum post of Second Keeper of the Robes to Queen Charlotte. However, she was not happy in the role, which simply involved helping to dress the queen. Her unhappiness was exacerbated by her anxiety about protocol. Eventually she petitioned the queen to be released from her duty on health grounds on July 7th 1791. She married Alexandre D'Arblay, a French émigré, on July 28th 1793, much to the consternation of her family. The couple lived in France from 1802, but came back to Britain in 1815 and settled in Bath. *Camila* was published in 1796 and was Burney's most successful novel, the first edition having sold out within six months. In 1818, her husband died and Burney shunned Bath after that to avoid any further distress, moving to London. She suffered the loss of her son in 1837 and she died three years later, on January 6th 1840. She was buried on January 15th alongside her son at St Swithun's in Walcot, Bath. (*Oxford Dictionary of National Biography*; Clare Harman, *Fanny Burney: A Biography*, HarperCollins, 2000)

– January 16th –

1867: Aeronautical engineer Percy Sinclair Pilcher was born in Bath. He started his career in the Navy, which he entered in 1880. He resigned in 1887 and was apprenticed to the engineering department of Randolph, Elder & Co. Shipbuilders of Govan. After stints as a marine engineer, in 1891, Pilcher accepted the post of Assistant Lecturer at the University of Glasgow in Naval Architecture and Marine Engineering. Soon afterwards he began researching birdlike gliders. In 1895, he built his first glider, the *Bat*. His second glider, *Hawk*, which had the world's first sprung-wheeled undercarriage, was built 1896-7. With *Hawk*, Pilcher was able to reach a record glide of 750ft. The contraption was raised by the drawing of a cord by men or horses. In 1896, Pilcher filed the first patent for a powered aeroplane. By 1899 he had built a tri-plane and had tested a 4hp engine, which weighed only 40lb, to power his plane. On September 30th 1899 he demonstrated *Hawk* at Stanford Hall in Market Harborough. The plane was raised in the usual way, but a crossbar snapped, causing the wings to fold up and collapse. *Hawk* crashed to the ground and Pilcher died from his injuries two days later. Some historians believe that if Pilcher had lived, he would have achieved the first powered flight. (*Oxford Dictionary of National Biography*; *The Times*)

─ January 17th ─

1775: Richard Brinsley Sheridan was born in Dublin in 1751. His family moved to Bath in 1770, and two of Sheridan's poems, 'The Ridotto of Bath' and 'Cleo's Protest or, The Picture Varnished', were published in the *Bath Chronicle*. Sheridan is particularly well known for his comic play *The Rivals*, which was set in Bath and first performed at Covent Garden, on this date, in 1775. One of the play's characters, Mrs Malaprop, habitually confuses long words and her name has entered the English language to describe the confusion long words. Famous examples of malapropism include 'the very pineapple of politeness' instead of 'the very pinnacle of politeness'. Sheridan's marriage to Elizabeth Ann (Eliza) Linley, a great beauty with a wonderful soprano voice, was controversial. Eliza's parents thought that Sheridan would squander Eliza's wealth, whilst Sheridan's father thought that Eliza was too low in social standing. Retiring from singing, Eliza withdrew to a convent in Lille, France. Sheridan, acting as her escort, proposed to her en route and the couple were married by a Roman Catholic priest in a village near Calais. On Sheridan's return to England, he found that a married pursuer of Eliza, Captain Matthews, slandered Sheridan in the *Bath Chronicle*, calling him a 'L[iar] and a treacherous S[coundral]'. In the resulting duel, Sheridan won. The couple were married in England on April 13th 1773. Sheridan died on July 7th 1816. (*Oxford Dictionary of National Biography*)

~ JANUARY 18TH ~

1888: A robbery occurred on this day at No. 7, The Crescent, the residence of Sir Edward and Lady Russell. The jewellery of Lady Russell and a friend, amounting to between £200 and £300, was stolen between eight and nine o'clock in the evening. The thief entered an empty property, No. 2, The Crescent, and walked along a parapet between the two houses. 'So silently was it carried out that the inmates of the house heard nothing of it.' (*Bristol Mercury*)

1892: The hazards of electrical generation and supply to the city's streets are shown by the following newspaper extract: 'Thomas Inker, aged 29, an employee at the Bath Electric Light Works, was cleaning out a boiler, on Saturday, when the foreman, unaware of Inker's doings, let off the steam. Inker was frightfully scalded, but lingered at the hospital until Monday [January 18th 1892], when he died. Another employee of the company, while re-carbonating a lamp, fell a considerable distance, and received serious injuries to a head.' The Bath Electric Light Works was located on Dorchester Street and supplied electricity for the city's street lights, which had come into operation on June 24th 1890. (*Hampshire Advertiser*; William E. Eyles, *Electricity in Bath* 1974)

– JANUARY 19TH –

1884: George Herman, aged 19, died shortly after the conclusion of a rugby match between Oldfield Park and Bristol University College. The match was described as rough, with many disputes. Herman was tackled several times but was always able to get up. About 5 minutes before the end of the game he was feeling unwell and left pitch, unaided, but collapsed miuntes later. At the inquest, the cause of death was given as apoplexy. The foreman of the jury stated that the jurors wished to express their condemnation of football as played under the rugby rules, considering it 'most dangerous to life and limb'. (*Bristol Mercury*)

1889: 'Hugh Walker, while marking at the Bath Volunteer range, about thirteen years ago, was accidently shot in the back of the shoulder by a bullet, which passed through a slit in the marker's mantlet. In the Western Infirmary he was under treatment for nearly two months, but the surgeons failed to find the bullet. Some months later a splinter of the bullet was extricated after which the wound healed. Recently a slight swelling appeared at the lower part of the chest, where a small opening had formed like a pin-hole. On an incision being made a folded flattened piece of the lead bullet was removed, weighing nearly a quarter of an ounce.' (*Berrow's Worcester Journal*)

~ January 20th ~

1972: *The Times* reported on the recent excavations of a new group of Roman baths which included an oval bath, small treatment baths and a well-preserved hypocaust system. It was the first time that these Roman remains had been seen in nearly 100 years. The excavation was made possible following the demolition of the Victorian douche and massage baths, erected by Major Charles Davis in 1886, which had become derelict. The Victorian additions to Bath were not without controversy. J. Henry Middleton, the secretary to the Gloucester branch of the Society of Antiquities, thought that Major Davis' scheme should have placed greater emphasis on saving the Roman remains rather than building over them. He considered that Davis' building would cut through the hypocaust and destroy it. Excavations nearly 100 years later show that Davis was careful in the preservation of the Roman remains and ensured its survival when building the Douch and Massage Baths. The time of Davis' construction marks a turning point in the preservation of antiquarian interests, when, compared with a century previously, when no one raised any objections to the construction of the Duke of Kingston's Baths. (*The Times*; Barry Cuncliffe, *Roman Baths Discovered*, Tempus, 2000)

~ JANUARY 21ST ~

1766: Actor James Quin died in Bath on this day. He was born on February 24th 1693 in Covent Garden, London. His father was a lawyer who married Elizabeth Grindall in 1690. In 1701, it was revealed that the marriage was bigamous, as Elizabeth was already married. It was this revelation that allowed his uncle, John Quin, and a cousin, William Whitehead, to prevent James from inheriting his father's fortune when he died in 1710. Quin joined Drury Lane Theatre Company around 1715, and transferred to John Rich's Company at Lincoln's Inn Fields Playhouse. Remaining there for the next fifteen years, he became a leading actor of his day, starring in both comedies and tragedies. He had a fiery reputation and was convicted for the manslaughter of William Bowen following a brawl in a tavern. He was sentenced to be branded on the hand but the punishment seems never to have been carried out. He retired in 1751, after reputedly being paid £1,000 for his final season. During a visit to his actor friend David Garrick, one of his hands became inflamed and he quickly returned to Bath, where he died. He was buried in Bath Abbey on January 25th 1766 and Garrick composed his epitaph, part of which reads: 'That tongue which set the table in a roar, And charmed the public ear is heard no more, Closed are the eyes, the harbingers of wit, Which spoke, before the tongue, what Shakespeare writ.' (*Oxford Dictionary of National Biography*; Geoffrey N. Wright, *Discovering Epitaphs*, Shire, 1996)

— January 22nd —

1825: The *Morning Post* stated that Princess Caraboo was now exhibiting at Bath. Princess Caraboo was 'found' wandering the streets of Almondsbury, just to the north-west of Bristol, wearing a black turban and speaking an unknown language. Her striking appearance added weight to her claim that she had been kidnapped by pirates from her homeland of Javasu and escaped from them by jumping into the Bristol Channel. Elizabeth Worrell, the wife of the Town Clerk of Bristol, took sympathy on her and allowed her to stay at their home of Knowle Park. During that summer, she provided written examples of her language, Javasu, performed an exotic war dance, showed off her archery skills and even swam naked in the lake. Eventually, she was exposed as a fraud. Caraboo's actual name was Mary Wilcocks, the daughter of a Devon cobbler. After her exposure as a fraud, Elizabeth Worrell paid for her passage to America. Here she exhibited herself as 'Princess Caraboo', although the show was of limited success. She returned to England in 1824 and again exhibited herself as Princess Caraboo in New Bond Street, London. Afterwards she seems to have toured Britain with her act, including shows in Bath. She married a Richard Baker of Bedminster, in 1828, and spent the rest of her life supplying leeches to the Bristol Infirmary. (*The Morning Post*; *Oxford Dictionary of National Biography*)

⁓ January 23rd ⁓

1844: The consecration of the abbey cemetery took place on this day, followed, on February 12th, by the first burial. The cemetery was laid out by the celebrated horticulturalist, John Claudius Loudon (1783–1843). From 1798 until 1802, he studied at the University of Edinburgh, whilst working part-time as an apprentice to Dickson & Slade, nurserymen. His first publication was a translation of the life of Abelard for an encyclopaedia. In 1806, Loudon moved to London and by 1809 he had established a small agricultural college at Great Tew, Oxfordshire. Loudon published frequently on horticultural matters, including *Hints on the Formation of Gardens and Pleasure Grounds* (1812) and *Encyclopaedia of Gardening* (1822). Loudon also published magazines on the subject, establishing and editing *The Gardener's* magazine (1826–43) until his death. One publication, *Aboretum et Fracticetum* (1838) led Loudon into debt. It was an ambitious book that aimed to survey all the species of trees grown in England. His first cemetery, with architect Edward Buckton Lamb, was at Histon Road in Cambridge and was characterised by a grid layout with evergreen shrubs and trees evenly arranged. Financial difficulties led Loudon to accept two further cemetery commissions at Bath and Southampton. He died on December 14th 1843 before either could be completed. The mortuary chapel in the Abbey Cemetery was designed by G.P. Manners. (Bath Abbey website; Widcombe Association website; *Oxford Dictionary of National Biography*; Nikolaus Pevsner, *The Buildings of England: North Somerset and Bristol*, Penguin, 1958)

— January 24th —

1873: Shortly before dark, four students from Somerset College in Bath took a rowing boat and travelled upstream towards Bathampton. On arriving at the weir at Bathampton, the boys amused themselves by rowing in the rough water near the weir. Their actions could only end in tragedy and the boat was drawn into an eddy and capsized. The two eldest youths, Edward Moscardi and Charles Seagrain, drowned. One of the students, named Goehr, was able to swim ashore and the other, the younger brother of Edward Moscardi, was saved by a man named Allen, who was brother to the MP Major Charles Allen. (*Birmingham Post*)

———

1962: The coldest day in Bath was recorded with a temperature of -5°C. The day was part of a prolonged cold spell of weather that had begun on Boxing Day of the previous year and continued until the following February. The cold weather caused the River Avon to freeze at Bathwick and, owing to the number of cancellations at the Theatre Royal, the production run of the pantomime *Mother Goose* was cut short. (David and Jonathan Falconer, *A Century of Bath*, Sutton, 1999)

~ January 25th ~

1991: The Bath Assembly Rooms were reopened by the Duchess of Kent following a £2 million restoration. Four years previously, the Assembly Rooms had shut after part of the ceiling in the ballroom had collapsed. A further £200,000 was spent on the restoration of the large Georgian chandeliers, for which the building is well known. The Assembly Rooms were designed by John Wood the Younger and completed in 1771. Assembly buildings were constructed to allow people to meet, dance, play cards and listen to music. There are four main rooms: a ballroom, a tea room, an octagon room and a card room. John Collett of London built five chandeliers for the ballroom. Shortly after opening, one of the arms of the chandeliers broke loose and nearly hit the artist Thomas Gainsborough. A new set of chandeliers were ordered from William Parker of London. Collett was allowed to salvage the rejected chandeliers in order to use the parts to create one large chandelier for the ballroom. The assembly rooms suffered significant damage when they were hit by a bomb in 1942. The building was then restored by Sir A. Richardson and reopened in 1963. Fortunately the rare Georgian chandeliers were removed from the building following the outbreak of war and consequently suffered no damage. (*The Times*; Nikolaus Pevsner, *The Buildings of England: North Somerset and Bristol* Penguin, 1958; www.nationaltrust.org.uk; www.museumofcostume.co.uk)

~ JANUARY 26TH ~

1816: *The Times* newspaper reported a case of 'female heroism at Bath'. The article goes on to say: 'There happens to have been at Bath, for some time past, and still to remain there, a Lady of rather diminutive stature whose principal amusement in the morning is á promener á cheval [to ride a horse] about the streets of Bath.' On one occasion, however, two men appear to have forgotten their manners and, by their looks and gestures, the lady assumed that they were quizzing [mocking] her. At the time she took no notice. However, the next day she rode as usual, this time equipped with a horsewhip. On seeing the two men in Milson Street, described as 'the most fashionable promenades in Bath', she proceeded 'san acremonie [without acrimony], to chastise them for the liberties in which they had indulged themselves the day before at her expense, by horsewhipping them the whole length of the street, from the part where she met them, to the great mirth of the company who happened to be present at the time'! (*The Times*)

~ January 27th ~

1539: Prior Holloway of Bath surrendered the abbey to Tregonwell and Petre, King Henry VIII's representatives. The prior signed the surrender, as did the sub-prior of Dunster and the eighteen monks who made up the community. The prior was given an £80-a-year pension and a house in Stall Street and the sub-prior was given £9 per annum. The monks got pensions of varying amounts, ranging from £4 13s to £8 depending on the length of service. Since Bath Abbey was the second richest monastery in Somerset, this apparent generosity was easily afforded. Many of the monks were still alive in 1553 and one monk, William Clement, had become vicar of St Mary de Stalls. In the years following the Dissolution, John Leland, travelling through Bath in the 1540s, noted that the recent rebuilding started in the 1490s, stating that 'Oliver King, Bishop of Bath, began of late days a right godly new church at the west part of the old church of St Peter and finished a great piece of it. The residue of it since made by the priors of Bath and especially by Gibbs, the last prior there, that spent a great sum of money on the fabric.' (Peter Davenport, *Medieval Bath Uncovered*, Tempus, 2002; Bath Abbey website; John Leland, *John Leland's Itinerary: Travels in Tudor England*, Sutton, 1999)

— January 28th —

1899: Domestic violence in the Victorian period seems to have been an all too common occurrence, perhaps owing to entrenched social attitudes and a court system of limited effectiveness. One such case took place, on this date, at Bath Police Court. The previous evening, PC Crane was called from the Central Police Station to the Milsom family home, where he found Annie Milsom, a small girl aged 13, bleeding profusely from a head wound. He found the girl's father, Sampson Milsom, on the premises and asked that he accompany him, with the girl, to the hospital, which he did. The girl stated that she had received the head wound after a plate had been thrown at her. The girl's father was charged with maliciously wounding her and claimed that it would not have occurred if the children had been home at the proper time. Annie had been out with her mother visiting her grandmother when they returned home together. Sampson had thrown a number of objects at the mother before hurling the plate. Sampson pleaded guilty to throwing the plate, but not at the child, stating that he was aiming at his wife. The clerk replied that he was still guilty of assault and sentenced him to two months' hard labour. Mrs Milsom asked the court for an order of separation, but was told by the court that if Mr Milsom's behaviour did not improve when he was released then she should apply for the order. (*Bath Journal*)

— JANUARY 29TH —

2004: An unusual Anti-Social Behaviour Order was served on a homeless man who habitually dined extravagantly in Bath's posh restaurants despite being unable to pay the bill; when he finished his meals he either admitted that he could not pay or just ran off. Mr Hughes, aged 58, was given the ASBO, normally reserved for teenage delinquents and drunks gathering in parks, which banned him from all the restaurants in Bath. In recent months, Hughes failed to pay his bill no less than fifty-nine times. He was caught after visiting a Café Uno. The owner became suspicious when Hughes entered and ordered a pizza and a couple of beers. While staff were busy, Hughes slipped out but the manager, who noticed Hughes was missing, went out and managed to catch him around the corner. His last assault upon Bath's restaurants was at the Fishworks Restaurant. Commenting at the time, the restaurant's chief executive stated: 'The trouble is that with it happening so often, there is obviously a concern that he will carry on in this way.' As well as being given the ASBO, Hughes was fined £50. (*Western Daily Press*)

~ January 30th ~

2001: David Hempleman-Adams, adventurer and explorer, was awarded one of the highest accolades in ballooning. The British Balloon and Airship club bestowed their gold badge with three diamonds on Hempleman-Adams of Box, near Bath, after he met the requirements for the award. The requirements test a balloon pilot's abilities in distance, accuracy, duration and height for hot-air ballooning. Hempleman-Adams met the altitude requirements by flying over the Andes in a 120,000ft^3 balloon constructed by Cameron, a Bristol-based balloon company. The duration requirements were met with a balloon flight to the North Pole and the distance requirement from a balloon trip to Canada. In addition, Hempleman-Adams also needed to have flown for a distance of 300km at an altitude of 6,000ft and drop a small marker on an agreed target to obtain the gold badge. The scheme had been running for ten years before Hempleman-Adams became the first person to gain this accolade. (*Western Daily Press*)

— January 31st —

1881: At Bath Police Court, two dairymen were fined £5 and £7 10s respectively for selling adulterated milk, to which had been added 17 per cent and 40 per cent of water respectively. In their defence, both defendants claimed that they had bought the milk from the same farmer and that they had retailed the product as bought. (*Berrow's Worcester Journal*)

2012: It was reported that a dog owner from Bath, who eight months previously had lost his Staffordshire Bull Terrier, was surprised to be told that it had turned up in London. The dog, called Fido, went missing from the family home in Lower Bristol Road and was found wandering the streets of Kensington, 120 miles away. It was taken to Battersea Dogs Home where it was scanned for a microchip. Staff were then able to contact the owner, Chris Eyles, who went immediately to London to retrieve his dog. During 2011, Battersea Dogs and Cats Home took in almost 6,000 dogs, of which 28 per cent were microchipped. Had it not been for the microchip, it was almost certain that Fido would not have been able to be rehomed. (www.bbc.co.uk)

~ February 1st ~

1945: A plan for Bath was presented to the people of the city at an exhibition opened by Mr W.S. Morrison, government minister for Town and Country Planning. The plans were drawn up by Sir Patrick Abercrombie in an attempt to provide a framework in which the city could expand. More housing was envisaged, but not on the city's hill crests, to retain a visual link with the countryside. *The Times* stated that the 'most striking feature of the internal road plan is an inner circle for traffic' which aimed to relieve traffic in the city centre. However, large-scale demolition of Kingsmead was also proposed, involving the demolition of several Georgian buildings, including the baroque Rosewell House. The plan was not followed through in the main, but Cuncliffe notes that 'nonetheless the plan was a valuable exercise, and even though little of it had been realised, it had the effect of focusing peoples' attention on Bath, as a developing organic whole, in a way that had never been attempted.' Sir Patrick Abercrombie was a leading town planning consultant in the UK and abroad and was knighted in 1945. During the war, when his London offices were bombed, Abercrombie braved the wrath of the air-raid wardens to retrieve a casket of vintage claret from the cellar. He served it immediately to his fellow workers to boost their morale. (*Oxford Dictionary of National Biography*; *The Times*; Barry Cuncliffe, *The City of Bath*, Sutton, 1986)

~ February 2nd ~

1847: Elopement stories were of great interest to the newspapers of the period and such cases were told and retold in newspapers around the country. 'Like Miss Burdette Coutts [a well-known heiress of the period, thought to have been the richest woman in the country after Queen Victoria] she was pestered with lovers; but had her face and form been her only dowry she might have been deemed a noble prize, for in the exclusive circles of the provincial town, she was universally known to be the belle of Bath.' She went missing from her home on this date, and it was reported that she had been married, in Exeter, to a tailor, two days later. (*Preston Guardian*)

1963: *The Times* announced that, at the end of March 1963, Bath Oliver biscuits would cease to be made in Bath. Produced in Bath since 1735, the biscuit is thought to have been invented by Dr William Oliver for his patients. They were produced by Cater, Stoffell & Fortt Ltd, a subsidiary of Harveys of Bristol, at their Manvers Street premises. Production of the Bath Oliver biscuit would transfer to a larger factory in Reading. The move was put down to the difficult production and distribution conditions experienced by a small firm at that time. (*The Times*; *Oxford Dictionary of National Biography*)

— February 3rd —

1878: 'Some strange proceedings took place … at Salem Chapel, Englishcombe, near Bath, in connection with the H.J. Brown, a solicitor of Bath, was in possession, acting as pastor, and when about to give out a hymn at the commencement of the service, the trustees entered the chapel with the avowed intention of turning him out. Mr Brown maintained his position in the pulpit during a long altercation, during which he expelled the trustees by freely brandishing his umbrella in their faces. After an hour's interruption during which abusive language was copiously poured forth on either side, the trustees quitted the chapel discomfited. Mr Brown then preached. The dispute will probably be settled in the police court.' (*Lancaster Gazette*)

1896: Henry Williams, a painter of Brentwood, Essex, appeared in a Bath Police Court charged with breaking into Kelston Church. Shortly after 2 a.m., Richard Vowles, a farmer who was looking after his ewes during lambing, noticed a light on in the church. On reaching the building he saw a broken window and an intruder inside, who moved towards the window as if to escape. Vowles shouted out to him that he would not be able to get out that way. Williams then attempted to leave by the vestry door but was caught by Vowles. When questioned, Williams stated that he was looking for a few coppers because he was hungry. He was remanded into custody. (*Nottinghamshire Guardian*)

~ February 4th ~

1845: A 'frightful coal-pit accident' occurred at Timsbury, 8 miles south of the city, in which eleven people lost their lives. The accident occurred at the Hayeswood Coalpit, where the mine was extending towards a disused but flooded mine working. The first indication of possible water ingress was an apparent dampness of the coal, but this was by no means uncommon. At 5.30 a.m. on this date, miners noticed a sudden rush of air throughout the pit, followed by an inundation of water, some having to wade through water up to their chins to get to safety. (*The Bristol Mercury*; *The Standard*; *The Morning News*)

1953: Bath Abbey Church House, which is used for the church's secular activities, was reopened and rededicated, after an air raid damaged the building during the Second World War. The building was rededicated by the Rt Revd Dr H.W. Bradfield, Bishop of Bath and Wells, following a reopening ceremony undertaken by the Mayor of Bath, Alderman A.W.S. Berry. Abbey Church House was built as a mansion house for Sir Walter Hungerford in 1570. Dr Robert Baker rebuilt the house in the 1590s. Later, the building was used as a shop for wines and spirits, groceries and cabinet making. The building was also used as an office and as a club. From 1888, it was let to the Rector of Bath. It is Bath's only Elizabethan mansion, noted for its Elizabethan panelling and elaborate chimney piece. (*The Times*)

~ February 5th ~

1895: A huge fire destroyed the Fernleigh Temperance Hotel which stood in North Parade. The fire started in the stockroom and spread quickly. Several people had narrow escapes. One man is reported to have left the hotel as the stairs behind him collapsed. Some servants, who were sleeping in the basement, escaped through grating in the road outside the hotel. Happily, no fatalities were reported. (*Berrow's Worcester Journal*)

2001: Two artists from the West, who were told that their nude portraits were not suitable and consequently banned from an exhibition at Bath Library, were today told that their paintings could now be displayed after all. The debate over whether the paintings were too risqué had started when a library member stated they would have to ask senior officials whether the paintings were appropriate for the venue. The head of Arts and Libraries for Bath and North-East Somerset Council, Ms Jacqui Campbell, said, 'We like to cast our eye over whatever goes up because we do have families coming in, but we certainly have no policy banning material like that. We have worked for years to try and overturn the image of libraries being dusty, prudish places and this does not do the old stereotype any good.' (*Western Daily Press*)

— FEBRUARY 6TH —

1900: At the monthly meeting of Bath City Council the following letter was read out:

Sir – With reference to your letters of the 27th and 29th December last I am directed by the Secretary of State for War to accept with thanks the patriotic offer of the City of Bath to grant free use of the waters of Bath to officers and men invalided from South Africa. As you were informed in the letter from this office on 30th ultimo the offer was transmitted to the Soldiers' and Sailors' Help Society and it is understood that arrangements have already been made by the society in conjunction with the military medical authorities to send to Bath case likely to be benefitted by taking the waters. It is also likely that some men on the furlough may avail themselves of the generous offer. I am to add that the Corporation will be surely informed of any men sent, but it is not possible to give any information as to probable numbers at this present stage.

I have the honour to be sir,

Your obedient servant,

(signed) G. Fleetwood Wilson

The war referred to in the letter is better known as the Second Boer War which was fought in South Africa between 1899 and 1901. (*Bristol Mercury*)

– February 7th –

1903: Mr Percy Fitzgerald, President of the Dickens Fellowship, unveiled a tablet at No. 35 St James's Square, Bath, in honour of Charles Dickens. The tablet bore the simple inscription 'HERE DWELT CHARLES DICKENS, 1840'. Some, however, claim that Dickens never spent a night there. The house belonged to his close friend, Walter Savage Landor, and Dickens would return to the York House Hotel after taking dinner there. (*The Times*; Andrew Swift & Kirsten Elliott, *Literary Walks in Bath*, Akerman Press, 2012)

2009: The seventy-fifth anniversary of the Bath Preservation Trust was celebrated. The trust campaigns to protect the city's heritage and unique character. The Bath Preservation Trust also operates a number of the city's museums. These include the museum at No. 1 Royal Crescent; the Countess of Huntingdon's Chapel, run as the Building of Bath Museum; and Beckford's Tower. Established in 1934, the Trust fought a number of campaigns including the defeat of a 1930s scheme to extend Milsom Street through Edgar Buildings to the Assembly Rooms; the launch of a campaign to protect the greenbelt; and persuading the government, in the 1970s, to intervene in order to prevent the demolition of Bath's historic buildings. (*Bath Chronicle*)

~ FEBRUARY 8TH ~

1796: After receiving a university education at Oxford, John Sibthorp went to Paris to study botany with Antoine Laurent de Jussieu at the Jardine des Plantes, as well as a further ten months' study with Auguste Brissonet at Montpellier University. He took his MD at Oxford in January 1784 and was made Sheridan Professor in March of that year. It was whilst in Vienna, during the autumn of 1785 with Nikolaus Joseph von Jacquin, that he saw a copy of the *Materia Medica*, the work of first-century Greek army surgeon Padacius Dioscorides. Sibthorp resolved to visit Greece to study the botany and find the 700 plants given in the *Materia Medica* and ascertain their medicinal value. In September 1787 he was forced to leave Greece owing to the growing political unrest and the plague in Thessaly. He returned to England with 2,000 plant specimens. For the next few years, Sibthorp lectured and added many specimens to the Sheridan herbarium, as well as publishing the *Flora Oxoniensis*, a student's guide to 1,200 plant species of Oxfordshire. He longed to return to Greece and did so in 1794, but this journey had many problems including bouts of illness and the death of his assistant, Francis Barone, who died in a sleepwalking accident. Sibthorp returned to England in July 1795 suffering from tuberculosis. He died in Bath on this date in 1796, aged 37, and was buried in Bath Abbey. His plant collections are still retained at Oxford. (*Oxford Dictionary of National Biography*)

— February 9th —

2002: Police launched an investigation into claims that traffic wardens left their patrol cars on double-yellow lines all day whilst booking other motorists. It was alleged that traffic wardens left laminated cards on their car dashboards to ensure that they were not booked by other wardens or police officers. The scam came to light when a television reporter followed wardens from their illegally parked cars to the police station where they attired in their distinctive yellow and black uniforms. The local authority, Bath and North-East Somerset Council, had recently imposed tighter parking restrictions in the city in order to deter visitors arriving to the city by car and to persuade people to use public transport alternatives. The chief traffic warden and five other wardens were disciplined. Traffic wardens were introduced to Bath in 1967, seven years after the very first traffic wardens were introduced in London. The chief constable of the Somerset Constabulary at that time described the wardens as a 'courtesy to other motorists' and warned them 'it is not your job to be a damn nuisance to the motoring public'. (*The Times*)

— February 10th —

1873: Cases involving the family were often dealt with in the local Police Courts. Two such cases were heard on this date, in 1873. The first concerned Thomas and Selina James. Thomas had been arrested under warrant for failing to appear before magistrates the preceding week to answer the charge that he had assaulted his wife. The case was a trumpery one since Thomas' wife, Selina, failed to prove that Thomas had hit her and so this charge was dropped in favour of using threatening language, to which Thomas pleaded guilty. He was ordered to keep the peace towards his wife for three months and to be bound over, himself in £10 and two sureties of £5 each. The second case concerned Michael O'Neill, who was summoned to show if he had any reason to deny his former partner, Eileen Flaherty, a contribution towards the support of an illegitimate child they had together. They had been living on the New Quay. He was ordered to pay 2s 6d each week, plus the cost of the hearing. (*Bath and Cheltenham Gazette*)

— February 11th —

1877: 'A scandalous incident' took place during the funeral of William Cunningham, who was well known as a prize fighter. About 500 people attended the funeral. Immediately after the conclusion of the burial service, a man made his way to the grave and, standing at the edge, drank a pint of beer from a bottle. The man claimed that he had acted in this way to fulfil a promise he had made to Cunningham fifteen years earlier. (*Birmingham Post*)

1896: James Harrison, aged 30 and described as 'a well-dressed young man', appeared before Bath Police Court, charged with breaking into a house in Oldfield Park and stealing £22 10s. A servant saw the prisoner and an accomplice loitering outside the house before the pair entered. An off-duty police constable, who also happened to be passing at the time, had his suspicions and, after ringing the bell of the house, went around to the back of the house, when the men got through a window and tried to make off. A chase ensued, during which several garden walls were scaled. It was reported that a 'jemmy' [crowbar] was thrown at the police constable, but PC Dury was able to ward it off with a stick and eventually caught the prisoner. Four skeleton keys and £4 17s were found on the prisoner and he was remanded for a week. (*Berrow's Worcester Journal*)

— FEBRUARY 12TH —

1877: Charles John Parsons and William N. Morgan were caught in Glasgow with stolen jewels. They were stolen from the Midland railway station at Bath (Bath Green Park). The jewels, consisting of watches, lockets and rings, were sent by Mr Meyer of Blackensee, Birmingham, to Mr Vokes, watchmaker and jeweller of Southgate Street, Bath. The parcels were entrusted to a guard named Snell, who handed them to Morgan at Mangotsfield station for their safe delivery to Bath. Morgan later claimed that the parcel for Vokes had not arrived at Bath. In Glasgow, one of the pair entered a pawn shop on Bridge Street, gave his name as Arthur Lloyd and said he wished to pawn a large ring set with turquoise and diamonds. The owner of the pawn shop, John O'Hara, asked how he came by the ring, which appeared very new. 'Lloyd', appearing timorous, stated that the ring had belonged to his father. Further enquiries found that 'Lloyd' was staying a nearby hotel, in the same street as the shop. O'Hara became suspicious and sent his assistant to find a police officer. Police involvement led to the arrest of Parson and Morgan, and a large quantity of jewellery was recovered from their luggage. (*The Glasgow Herald; The Birmingham Daily Post*)

~ February 13th ~

1829: A by-election with two candidates took place in Bath. The candidates were George Charles Pratt, Earl of Brecknock (1779–1866) and General Charles Palmer (1771–1851). The result of the vote was a tie. *The Times* stated: 'In other cases, when a double return has taken place, a scrutiny has invariably awarded the seat to one of the members; but in this case such a proceeding is rendered unnecessary, as the validity of every vote is unquestionable.' Nevertheless, despite the unquestioning validity of the votes cast, the election was re-run, and after a fiercely fought contest, the earl was declared the victor. (*The Times*; www.historyofparliamentonline.org; *Oxford Dictionary of National Biography*)

1875: George Price, George Alsopp, and Thomas Flynn were brought before Bath Magistrates charged with desertion from the army. The men were discovered sleeping in a shed by two police officers. One of the men tried to escape but fell into a pond with one of the arresting officers. A number of leave passes were discovered in the men's possession. It was discovered that these passes could be obtained four-a-penny in some regiments' canteens. The soldiers were required to fill them in and have them signed by an officer. The magistrates condemned the practice as it was unlikely that a policeman could tell if the officer's signature in the leave pass was genuine or fake. (*York Herald*; *Liverpool Mercury*; *Worcestershire Journal*)

~ FEBRUARY 14TH ~

1951: The last goods train ran on the Camerton Railway branch on this date. The Camerton branch is best remembered as being the setting for the film *The Titfield Thunderbolt*. The line ran just south of Bath from Limpley Stoke via Monkton Coombe and Camerton to Hallatrow. Services began on March 1st 1882. The passenger service on the line ran until 1925 and normally only one carriage was sufficient for this purpose. Ealing Studio's production of *The Titfield Thunderbolt* is thought to take inspiration from the Tallyllyn Railway, which was taken over and run by the line's supporters. In *The Titfield Thunderbolt*, a small branch line is threatened with closure and a group of locals take over the running of the line. 'Titfield Station' is, in fact, Monkton Coombe station and the train in the film, The Titfield Thunderbolt itself, was *Lion*, a locomotive built for the Liverpool and Manchester Railway in 1838. *The Titfield Thunderbolt* was not the only film that used the Camerton branch. In 1931, *The Ghost Train*, based on the play by Bath-born actor and playwright Arnold Ridley, was filmed at Camerton. (Vic Mitchell & Keith Smith, *Frome to Bristol: Including the Camerton Branch and the 'Titfield Thunderbolt'*, Middleton Press, 1996)

— February 15th —

1856: The inquest concluded its investigation into the mysterious death of Thomas Spiller, librarian of the Bath Athenaeum. Spiller left the Athenaeum on the evening of February 7th intending to go to Twerton, as he was to receive some money there. However, his body was discovered near the mill-head of the Swinford copper works the following morning. Injuries were sustained to Spiller's face, the front of his shirt was torn, his necktie missing and no money was found on his person. The verdict of the coroner was wilful murder by persons or persons unknown. The case was widely reported, but the author has not has not found any contemporary reports to suggest that the case was ever solved. (*The Times*)

1897: At Bath Police Court, James M. Marsh, aged 26, was charged with the stealing two Post Office bags containing letters and other valuables. On the evening of Saturday, February 13th, Marsh was discovered opening letters in the third-class carriage of an empty train standing at Bath station. The discovery was made when the guard of the up-train that was just leaving the station, saw that two bags were missing and stopped the train. A railway servant went to the carriage where Marsh was. On being captured, Marsh placed a letter in his mouth and tore it up with his teeth. On being remanded for a week, the prisoner became violent. (*The Times*)

⹁ FEBRUARY 16TH ⹁

2003: Channel 4's popular archaeological television series *Time Team* was aired. This particular episode was filmed in Bath and featured the first ever archaeological dig to have taken place in the Royal Crescent. The dig also looked at a triangular green to the west of the Royal Crescent where St Andrew's Church had once stood, until it was bombed during the Second World War. The programme makers were invited by the Bath Archaeological Trust to find evidence of Roman activity in and around the vicinity of the Royal Crescent. The episode featured *Time Team* regulars Tony Robinson, Mick Aston and Phil Harding. On the first day of the dig, 'scorch marks' in the parkland beside the Royal Crescent were investigated. *Time Team* found nothing and it was concluded that the marks were due to natural formations. However, a substantial Roman Road was uncovered, and was enough to have possibly been part of the Fosse Way, whose precise route through the city remains unknown. The archaeological teams also uncovered some Roman sarcophagi and evidence of an expanding Roman city in the trenches that were dug on the site of St Andrew's Church. (www.channel4.com)

— FEBRUARY 17TH —

1761: The funeral of Richard Nash, also known as Beau Nash, took place at Bath Abbey. Nash was born in Swansea on October 18th 1674, educated at Carmarthen Grammar School and later went to Jesus College, Oxford with a view to take a career in the law. However, aged 17, he was dismissed from the college after an intrigue with a local woman. After a brief spell in the army, he became a student at the Inner Temple. Despite his limited finances, he gained a reputation as a man about town, presenting himself as elegant and refined. In 1695 he supervised a pageant at Inns Court in honour of William III. It was his move to Bath, in 1705, that established his reputation and celebrity, and it was not long before Nash was made Master of Ceremonies. Nash was then able to enhance the reputation of Bath by building a community and establishing some rules, including ensuring that all dances ended before 11 p.m. and banning the wearing of swords. (Nash's predecessor was killed in a duel.) Nash was not without his critics, including John Wesley, whom Nash tried to stop preaching (*see* June 6th) and those who resented that a man whose life was dedicated to pleasure and triviality should have some much influence. Nash died on February 12th and, two days later, Bath Corporation agreed to contribute 50 guineas towards his funeral expenses. (*Oxford Dictionary of National Biography*)

— February 18th —

1851: 'On Tuesday evening last a woman named Clark, residing at Lampard's buildings, Bath, came by her death through the violence of her husband, Joseph Clark, a carpenter. The woman, it appears, was of intemperate habits, and Clark, having been out of town to work during the day, returned about eight o'clock in the evening and found her in a state of intoxication which so exasperated him that he beat her with great violence with a stick, till she fell down in a state of insensibility. Alarmed at the consequence of his ill-treatment, he called to the other inmates of the house to come to his assistance. They found the woman sitting on the floor, apparently dying, and supported by Clark, who was endeavouring to rouse her to consciousness, but without effect … As soon as the parties entered the room, Clark made the exclamation, "I have done it!" A stick, broken into several parts, was found on the floor, one part of which was clotted with blood and hair. Surgeon Mr Hunt was sent for, but the woman was dead before his arrival. A policeman charged Clark with killing his wife, upon which he replied, "I am the cause of her death, I first pushed her down [pointing to the foot of the bed, where there was a pool of blood], and afterwards beat her with a stick." At the subsequent inquest, it was judged that Clark had wilfully murdered his wife.' (*Bristol Mercury*)

~ February 19th ~

1827: Reverend John Skinner, rector of Camerton, received a summons to the Court of Requests in Bath by his 'worthless tenant', a man named Lewis. The summons was for the hire of the rector's own horse! As Revd Skinner explains in his journal, the horse was given to Lewis' care in order that it could be used for small tasks around the farm and give assistance to Revd Skinner's own horse on some occasions. One such occasion had arisen and Lewis had sent him the bill on February 1st for upwards of £7 – Revd Skinner simply ignored it. Two days after receiving the summons, he drove to Bath to attend the hearing. On arrival at court, the presiding judge, Mr Golden, 'called to me in a stentorian voice, "Mr Skinner, you are late, we have settled the business as you did not appear to answer the charge."' Skinner replied that the case should have been heard later since living out in the country, he had further to travel. He succeeded in having his case heard and the court ruled in Revd Skinner's favour. He was, however, disappointed that the judge threw back the bill to Lewis without any comment on his conduct. (John Skinner, *Journal of a Somerset Rector*, Howard Combes & Arthur N. Bax (eds), John Murray, 1930)

~ February 20th ~

1844: A father and daughter were reunited following the daughter's disappearance from Bath on February 5th. Two days later, a girl, about 14, was overtaken on the road between Buckland and Stanford-in-the-Vale, both in Oxfordshire and about 50 miles from Bath. She was found in a state of great exhaustion and cold. She was brought to the Parsons at the Packhorse Inn, Wantage, where she gave a vague account of herself and was detained. The following day, Mr William Ormond and the Revd J. Hewlett of Letcome Regis 'took considerable pains' to find out who her friends were. It appears that this young girl set out from Bath on Monday, February 5th with a small bundle of accessories and walked to Chippenham. She caught a luggage train to Wootton Bassett and from there she continued on foot. She slept in crop fields in what were very cold conditions. Her 'interesting person and manners' seem to have given her a host of friends. Mr Ormond and the Revd Hewlett were able to trace her friends back to Bath. On this date, her father, described in the report as a 'respectable clergyman', came to collect her from Wantage and take her back to Bath. (*The Times*)

— February 21st —

1896: An unknown man gave a parcel to a railway tout at Bath with instructions to give it to a man named Drake. On opening the parcel, Drake discovered a tin canister which exploded, injuring him to the extent that he needed hospital treatment. Drake suffered facial injuries but went on to make a full recovery. Another parcel bomb was sent to Drake's brother-in-law, a man named Crisp, by way of a tout. However, this tout became suspicious and placed the parcel in a field, out of harm's way. The parcel was then taken to a police station and immersed in a pail of water, where it exploded within a few minutes. The trigger for both bombs was a spring attached to the string used to tie up the parcel. Alfred Hawkins, aged 27, was arrested in Cardiff a couple of days later. At his residence similar materials, namely tins, tacks, a wire spring and some string, were found, which had been used to make the bombs. Hawkins also kept a dagger and a loaded pistol. It would appear that Hawkins had got into a disagreement with Drake and Crisp, and the bombs were his way of solving his problems with the two men. Hawkins was remanded in custody and was later sentenced to ten years' imprisonment. (*The Standard*; *The Times*; *Bristol Mercury*)

~ FEBRUARY 22ND ~

1846: 'Early on Sunday morning [February 22nd] some villains made a forcible entrance into the dwelling house of Thos. Bunn, Esq., attorney, of From[e], and took away various silver and plated articles, to the value of £50. The thieves made themselves "at home" with such wine &c, as they found, and actually lighted a fire by which to regale themselves. Mr Bunn's servants were awoke about two o'clock by the smell of smoke proceeding from the fireplace, the thieves having neglected to raise the damper. An alarm was instantly raised, and Mr B. (a hale gentleman of eighty years) rushed down stairs, sword-in-hand; but the birds had flown! On searching the premises, it was discovered that an entrance had been effected through the drawing-room window, which opens into the garden. The dining and drawing rooms, office, and even the kitchen and cellars, had been ransacked, with the result to the plunderers already stated. Two men, named William and Ward alias Cress, were apprehended about half-past nine, on the morning of the robbery, on the platform of the Twerton railway-station. On Monday, they were brought up at Chandos-house, before G. Blathwayt, Esq, and the Rev. G. Rous, when the evidence was fully gone into, the property found in the possession of the prisoners identified as belonging to the prosecutor, and the men committed for trial.' (*Bristol Mercury*)

⁓ February 23rd ⁓

1936: On this day, Citizen House, a mansion built by the Duke of Chandos, was destroyed by fire. The fire broke out on a Sunday evening and the fire brigade was alerted at 9.43 p.m. On arriving at the scene, Chief Officer Hurst was told that there were people trapped inside the burning building. He ordered that an extendable ladder be put against the building and Hurst ascended the ladder to rescue the two children of Mr and Mrs Peter King from a top-floor window. Hurst again went up the ladder to rescue Miss Jean Scott, who was paid to look after the children. In less than an hour, thirty fire officers attended the scene and Citizen House was surrounded by fifteen jets of water. The rescue effort was later recognised in a ceremony held in the Guildhall on June 9th of that year. The mayor, Dr J.C. Carpenter, presented Chief Officer Hurst with a silver medal from the Society of Protection of Life from Fire. Station Officer Fear and Fireman Henry Hanney also received bronze medals from the society. A few months later the society awarded a certificate to Jean Scott for her part in helping to save the children. (*The Times*; Dennis Hill, *Bath Fire and Ambulance Service: 1894–1974*, Millstream Books, 2003)

~ February 24th ~

1829: A meeting of clergy of the Archdeaconry of Bath took place at Weymouth House. The Venerable Archdeacon Moysey chaired the meeting. A petition against Catholic emancipation was agreed upon, with over forty of the clergy present agreeing with the petition and only one dissenting hand. It was resolved that the petition should be presented to the House of Lords by the Bishop of Bath and Wells and to the House of Commons by Sir T. Lathbridge. Catholics achieved emancipation only three years later, following the passing of the 1832 Reform Act by Earl Grey, the then Prime Minister. (*Bath Journal*)

———

1898: Robert Rankin, 17, who described himself as a sailor, was charged at Bath Police Court with stealing over 10*s* from the contents of a contribution box from the Church of St Mary, Bathwick. The previous day, the verger saw the accused in church and noticed that the box had been broken open. He caught the prisoner and held him until a policeman could be sent for. The money was found in the accused's pocket, but none of the witnesses called were able to prove whether the money belonged in the box, as nobody knew its contents. Nevertheless, Rankin, who had been in a reformatory, was sent to prison for three months with hard labour. (*Bristol Mercury*)

~ February 25th ~

1728: John Wood the Younger was born in Bath and on this date he was baptised at Bath Abbey. Like his father John Wood, he became an architect and was responsible for many of the buildings in Bath. It seems likely that the younger John Wood was trained by his father and his contribution to Bath's architecture included completion of The Circus, the Royal Crescent (1767–75) – a large half-ellipse which faces a grassy slope – and the New Assembly Rooms. He was a pioneer of the neo-classical form of architecture, which took its inspiration from classical Greek architecture, as evidenced by the Old Royal Bath. Other notable buildings outside of Bath include Buckland House, Buckinghamshire (1755–58), the Corn Exchange, Bristol (1743) and All Saints' Church, Woolley (1761), a few miles to the north of Bath. Wood also used other styles in his work including the castellated façade of the General Infirmary, Salisbury (1767–71) and Tregenna Castle, St Ives, Cornwall (1773–74). He married Elizabeth Brook in 1752 or 1753 and together they had at least ten children. In his later years, Wood's lived in Eagle House, Batheaston. It was here that he died, deeply in debt, on June 16th 1781. He was buried with his father in the chancel of St Mary's, Swainswick. (*Oxford Dictionary of National Biography*; Nikolaus Pevsner, *The Buildings of England: North Somerset and Bristol*, Penguin, 1958)

~ February 26th ~

1938: It was reported that Miss Alloway, a florist's assistant of Fairfield Park, Bath, received a cornea transplant. The donor cornea came from a child's eye, which was removed following several attempts to repair the damage to the eye, inflicted after being pierced with the stalk of a flower. Miss Alloway had been blind for fourteen weeks and partially blind for two years before receiving treatment at the Bath Eye Infirmary. After receiving treatment, Miss Alloway found that she could see slightly. Her sight improved to the extent that she could see as well with her left eye as before she went blind. The first cornea transplant was carried out by Dr Eduard Zirm on Alois Gloger, a 43-year-old farm labourer, in 1905, in Olomouc, now in the Czech Republic. Zirm transplanted the corneas into both of Gloger's eyes using strips of conjunctura (the lining of the white of the eye) to tape down the new cornea. He then stitched down the patient's eyelids to allow the strips to knit together. After ten days, Zirm unstitched Gloger's eyes to find he was successful in attaching the graft to Gloger's left eye. There was a view that Zirm's success would be hard to replicate and, consequently, the first British cornea transplant did not take place until 1930. Today, around 2,500 cornea transplants take place in the UK each year. (*Bath Chronicle and Weekly Gazette*; www.news.bbc.co.uk)

~ February 27th ~

1770: A peal of Plain Bob Major was rung in 3 hours and 35 minutes at St James' Church, Bath. A contemporary newspaper states that it was 'an extraordinary performance and first ever in these parts'. In bellringing, a peal refers to a specific type of performance where the bells are rung to complete at least 5,040 changes. Change ringing was developed in the sixteenth century when bells began to be rung using a full wheel, giving greater control over the bell. This allowed sets of bells to be rung in continuously changing patterns known as methods. Plain Bob Major is a method for eight bells. (*Bath Chronicle*)

1927: Severe flooding affected Bath. The River Avon rose over 3ft overnight, leaving forty people cut off. The flooding particularly affected those living the Dolmeads area of the city. Many of those affected were taken away in boats to the homes of relatives. Police were also using boats to supply those affected with food and drink. Green Park was described as a 'lido', with water levels reaching up to halfway up the net posts on the park's tennis courts. (*Bath Chronicle*)

— February 28th —

1925: A memorial tablet for seventy previous students of Bath College, who fell during the First World War, was unveiled in the War Memorial Chapel of Bath Abbey. A large attendance of ex-students and friends of the school attended. The memorial was unveiled by Mr C.T. Carr, an ex-student of the college, and dedicated by the Archdeacon of Bath, the Ven. S.A. Boyd. In the evening a large party of 'old boys' attended a dinner at the Grand Pump Room Hotel. (*The Times*)

1928: Fire broke out early in the morning at the Briars, Entry Hill, a private nursing home run by Mrs Harding. The entire household was alerted and managed to escape the building, though many were dressed in their night attire. Mrs Harding was woken up by her barking dog and went downstairs to let the animal out. Mrs Harding opened the kitchen door, where the dog was located, but was met by thick black smoke and tremendous heat. She called the dog but to no avail. She realised that she must alert the residents and closed the kitchen door. The fire brigade were called and quickly responded. Sadly the dog did not survive. (*Bath and Wiltshire Chronicle & Herald*)

⁓ February 29th ⁓

1804: John Howlett (1731–1804) was an economist and writer whose works were especially concerned with the poor and the effect that rising food prices had on this group. During the famine of the 1790s, Howlett advocated financial compensation for those affected by the loss of common lands, owing to enclosure and minimum wages. His work also showed that the population of England and Wales was rising during this period, which countered alarmist reports that suggested that the population was falling. He died on this date whilst visiting Bath. (*Oxford Dictionary of National Biography*)

1928: George Cave (1856–1928) was a lawyer and politician. He was called to the bar in June 1880 and practiced at chambers in Lincoln's Inn. He was elected MP for Kingston-upon-Thames in 1906 and later served as Home Secretary and as a law lord during the Conservative government. He was Lord Chancellor from 1920. He became ill in February 1928 and elected to have surgery, on this date, in Bath, so he could convalesce in the country. The surgery proved unsuccessful and he died exactly one month later. (*The Times*; *Oxford Dictionary of National Biography*)

~ MARCH 1ST ~

1917: 'Five Bath tradesmen were fined yesterday for infringing the Potato Order. They declared that they could not sell at the fixed price without a loss. One defendant, Frank Lawrence, who was fined 40*s*, said when he sold potatoes at 1¹/₂*d* per lb. poor people came from all parts of the city and cleared him of his stock. He did not cater for the poor, but dealt the best potatoes only. Some potatoes were rubbish, and it was absurd to fix a uniform price. He charged 2¹/₂*d*. The other defendants, one of whom sold potatoes as seed, were fined 20*s* each.' But what was the 'potato order'? The potato orders were part of a set of food pricing control orders introduced in 1914 when the government set retail prices following the outbreak of the First World War, which led to a sharp increase in the cost of food. The control orders also gave the government a degree of control over demand and supply, to try to ensure that food shortages did not materialise. Food supplies, in 1917, were running short and the need to economise was stronger than ever. Despite government efforts, rationing was introduced to Britain by the end of 1917. (*The Times*)

~ MARCH 2ND ~

1950: Princess Elizabeth visited Bath as a part of a three-day visit to the West of England. Despite heavy rain, large crowds greeted her when she visited the city. After luncheon in the Guildhall, the princess toured the Dutchy of Cornwall estate at Newton St Loe. At Newton Park, she opened a teacher training college for women. She complimented Bath City Council for their enterprise in providing a training college, and it is reported to have said that 'students were fortunate in making teaching their career because they would avoid that hard conflict between the calls of a profession on the one hand and marriage and home upon the other which beset so many professional women. A teacher need fear no conflict in preparing herself for work with children for bringing up a family was in itself a form of teaching as well as being a real education for the mother.' The college now forms part of the University of Bath Spa and trains both men and women. (*The Times*)

~ March 3rd ~

1857: A well-dressed young man, who gave his name as Thomas Wright, was brought before Bath Magistrates. He was charged with stealing a gold watch and assaulting a police officer. A pigeon shooting match was taking place at the Folly Tavern, Bathampton, and large numbers of people were in attendance, a great many of whom were strangers to the area. The prisoner snatched a gold watch belonging to a Mr Green of the Exeter Inn, Bath. However, the defendant was immediately seized, thrown down to the ground, and the watch was returned to its owner. One of the prisoner's friends handed him a large knife and Wright was able to make his escape through the crowd. He was pursued and made his way to the River Avon. Here he plunged in and swam to the other side. Coincidence allowed the prisoner to be brought to justice, for Superintendent Wright of the Chippenham Police was driving alongside the London Road and could see clearly the events occurring on the opposite side of the river. He alighted and ran down the field, just in time to meet the prisoner as he emerged from the water. Although almost exhausted and shivering with cold, he put up a desperate fight in which Superintendent Wright was assaulted and received a cut to his cheek which required hospital attention. With the help of some labourers, the prisoner was bound and conveyed to Bath Police Station. (*The Times*)

1876: A freight train, of mixed goods and forming part of the London goods train, caught fire near Bath at daybreak. The engine driver stopped the train and ensured that no other trains could pass along the line. He detached the truck which was on fire and this ran on to Bath, where the fire was extinguished. However, the engine, whilst running up the down-line to fetch the remainder of the train, knocked down two men and seriously injured them. The men were named as Brewer and Lawrence, permanent way staff who were proceeding to their work. The fire is thought to have originated from some combustible articles that were being transported. (*Huddersfield Chronicle*)

1915: *The Times* reported that the Bath Corporation had placed the bathing waters at the disposal of the War Office and the Admiralty for injuries sustained during the First World War. The article states that many officers are making use of the baths and a great many others had sufficiently recovered to allow them to return to active service. (*The Times*)

- MARCH 5TH -

1773: Francis Phillip was born in Dublin on July 19th 1708, and, although ordained into the Anglican Church, his interests lay in translating and writing. He is best known for translating *Horace* into English, which was published in four volumes between 1742 and 1746. He was also a playwright, but does not seem to have a great deal of success. His first play *Eugenia*, performed at Drury Lane in 1752, was unsuccessful. Another play, *Constantine*, produced two years later, was even less successful. In 1767, he moved to Bath as his health deteriorated and he suffered a paralytic stroke in 1771. He died on this date, in 1773.

1853: *The Bristol Journal* reported on the following: 'Not withstanding the many failures of the steam-carriage on common roads, it has again made its appearance between Bath and Bristol; and this time owning to several most ingenious improvements in the machinery employed, has thoroughly realized the expectations of its projectors. The rate of travelling is about twelve miles an hour, and the cost is most trifling – say 6d for the journey.' The historian John Latimer could find no further references for this venture and consequently concludes that, like so many steam-carriage businesses, this failed. (John Latimer, *Annals of Bristol*)

— March 6th —

1926: The Mayor of Bath took part in an elaborate prank on the city's inhabitants in order to raise funds for Bath's hospitals. Crowds turned out to see the mayor welcome an Indian prince and his retinue. The mayor delivered a welcoming speech, followed by a reply from the colourfully dressed prince. Then suddenly, a number of policemen burst out from the Pump Room and arrested the prince. The 'chief constable' told the mayor that the prince was an imposter. The mayor feigned surprise and demanded to know what the policeman's authority was, whereupon the 'chief constable' produced a warrant 5ft long, complete with oversized seal. The mayor attempted to intervene, but in vain as the prince and his retinue were bundled into waiting police cars. Then a group of Klu Klux Klansmen appeared and arrested two Bath councillors, Aldermen Sir Harry Hall and Mr Percy Jackman. The two councillors were handcuffed together and auctioned. The bidding started at 3*d* and reached £20, at which point the mayor ordered their release, instead of the alternative of a 'night on the quod, with a fish-and-chip supper and a glass of beer.' Processions and torchlight tattoos continued proceedings into the night. A considerable sum was made by the collection. (*Bath Chronicle and Weekly Gazette*)

~ MARCH 7TH ~

1820: Thomas Baldwin, architect and property developer of Bath, died on this day. He began his career as a clerk to the Palladian local architect, Thomas Warr Atwood. In 1775, Atwood was awarded the contract to build the city's new Guildhall, but in November of that year he died. As his clerk, Baldwin presented his own designs for the Guildhall, which were accepted by the council. In 1776, Baldwin was appointed city architect and surveyor and used this position to establish a successful practice to execute public building works. Baldwin's other works in the city include: the Cross Bath (*c.* 1784); Pump Room (1789–99), which was finished by John Palmer; Union Street, laid out in 1789; and Bathwick, which originated as a New Town following Baldwin's broadsheet publication of 1788 in which he outlined his plans. However, in 1796 Baldwin was dismissed from his official positions after false accounting and his subsequent bankruptcy came to light. Baldwin continued to work after bankruptcy, rebuilding Hafod House in Cardingshire for Thomas Johnes in 1807, and building the Town Hall in Devizes, Wiltshire, in 1806–08. He is buried in St Michael's Church, Bath. (*Oxford Dictionary of National Biography*; Nikolaus Pevsner, *The Buildings of England: North Somerset and Bristol*, Penguin, 1958)

— MARCH 8TH —

1935: An unusual case was heard in Bath when remarkable evidence was given concerning the criminal activities of a gang of children known as the 'Black Clan'. Two members of the gang, a boy of 14 and another of 12, appeared at the Juveniles' Court, charged with stealing money, chocolate and cigarettes to the value of £9. The elder was also charged with stealing £5 from a doctor's house in Larkhill, and a rug from a car. The elder boy admitted entering the house, going into the bedroom where the doctor's wife was sleeping, taking her handbag and going downstairs to open it in order to steal the money, before returning the handbag to the side of her bed. When the elder was asked why he committed these crimes, he said that he had no explanation to give, and when asked 'What made you do it?', the boy replied, 'The pictures.' The gang used a cave along one of Bath's hillsides where twenty youngsters were found by police, together with a quantity of stolen goods. The boys had been missing from their homes for about a week. Magistrates adjourned the case for the elder boy whilst the younger boy was given two years' probation on condition he disassociated himself from the other children. (*Bath Chronicle*; *Western Daily Press*)

— MARCH 9TH —

1863: John Gully, prizefighter, racehorse owner and politician was born at the Crown Inn, Wick, 4 miles east of Bristol. During Gully's childhood, the family moved to Bath, where his father became a butcher. Business did not go well after his father's death and Gully became an inmate of the King's Bench, a debtor's prison. In 1805, he received a visit from pugilist Henry Pearce, known as the 'Game Chicken'. The men fought, and Gully impressed a number of prize-fight promoters who paid his debts. After some training a more serious match took place at Hailsham in Sussex on October 8th 1805. Seventy-seven minutes and sixty-four rounds later, the fight was over. Gully had given up, as he was nearly blinded. Another fight took place on October 14th 1807 with Bob Gregson. This fight, which was noted for its brutality, was won by Gully in thirty-six rounds, after a blow to Gregson stopped him from continuing. Gully also won another fight with Gregson, this time after twenty-seven rounds. Following his retirement in 1808, Gully bought a pub, the Plough Inn in Carey Street, Lincoln's Inn Fields, and in 1812 became a racehorse owner. Here he made a greater fortune and was able to buy Ackworth Park near Pontefract, standing as MP of that pocket borough between 1832 and 1837. Gully also invested his winnings, buying collieries in the north of England. He died on March 9th 1863 and is buried in Ackworth. (*Oxford Dictionary of National Biography*)

~ March 10th ~

1821: William Meylor was born in Newborough, Anglesey, on December 13th 1755. He was educated at the Free Grammar School in Marlborough, where his uncle, Revd Thomas Meyler, was master. Afterwards he was apprenticed as a bookbinder to Andrew Tennent, a prominent bookshop owner in Bath. Although apprenticed, Meylor wrote poetry and gained a good reputation as an amateur actor. His literary output gave him connections with Bath's leading literary figures, which no doubt contributed to his success with his later business activities. After his apprenticeship, he established his own bookshop. In 1792, he launched *The Bath Herald and General Advertiser*. He managed to buy out his partners in the newspaper business three years later and the newspaper remained in the family until the 1880s. His success allowed Meylor entry into the city's civic life, becoming elected to the city council in 1801. Here he served as Constable and Bailiff. In 1818 he became a JP. Afterwards, his health deteriorated and he died, on this date, in 1821. He is buried in Bath Abbey. (www.coalcanal.org)

～ MARCH 11TH ～

1912: Sir William Ramsay, the most eminent physical chemist of his day, gave his findings on the chemical composition of the mineral water at Bath to the city council and a number of physicians at the Pump Room. In particular, Sir William spoke of the gases given off in the mineral water, but also concluded that the mineral content of Bath's water was similar to that of other hot springs. The chemical properties of Bath mineral water have been analysed on a number of occasions. Responsibility for the spring water now lies with Bath and North-East Somerset Council, who cite a more recent study which shows that the thermal waters are rich in sodium, calcium, chloride and sulphide ions. Three natural springs deliver over 1 million litres of water at 45°C to the surface each day. Bath has had responsibility for the hot springs since Elizabeth I granted a royal charter in 1591. The speaker at the 1912 meeting, Sir William Ramsay, was particularly noted for his work on inert gases having, with J.W. Strutt, discovered argon and, with Morris W. Travers, discovered neon, krypton and xenon. Ramsay also categorised the properties for a new eighth group in the periodic table. (*The Times*; *Oxford Dictionary of National Biography*; www.bathnes.gov.uk)

— MARCH 12TH —

1984: Arnold Ridley, actor and playwright, died on this day. Ridley was born on January 7th 1896 at No. 4 Pera Place, Bath. His first stage appearance was at the Theatre Royal, Bristol, in a production of *Prunella*. He joined the Somerset Light Infantry in 1916 but was discharged a year later after sustaining injuries that left him prone to blackouts – it was his war wounds that led him to start writing. He achieved success with the play *The Ghost Train*, which was first performed at the Theatre Royal, Brighton, in 1925 and subsequently at many London theatres. The play, a comic thriller, was allegedly inspired after Ridley was forced to wait four hours for a train at Mangotsfield Junction station. A number of his plays became films, including *Third Man Lucky*, *Beggar My Neighbour* and *Easy Money*. However, Ridley is perhaps best known for playing Private Godfrey, a doddery man of questionable continence, who was a member of the fictional Warmington-on-Sea Home Guard in the television comedy *Dad's Army*, which ran for eight years between 1969 and 1977 and has been frequently repeated. He was awarded an OBE in 1982. (*Oxford Dictionary of National Biography*)

‒ March 13th ‒

1781: William Herschel (1781–1822) discovered the planet Uranus from his Bath observatory. On this date, Herschel decided to study the constellation Gemini when he noticed a heavenly body that he remarked as curious. A few days later he looked again and found that the body had moved. Herschel concluded that it was probably a comet. He told fellow astronomers Maskelyne and Hornsby, and Maskelyne was able to confirm that Herschel had in fact discovered a new planet. Herschel called the planet *Georgium Sidus* (George's Star) after the reigning monarch, George III. However, other astronomers settled on Uranus which is named after the *Urainia*, the ancient Greek patron goddess of astronomy. It was the first planet to be discovered using a telescope which Herschel had built himself. Uranus is the seventh planet from the sun and a cold gas giant, taking eighty-four years to complete an orbit of the sun. An unusual feature of the planet is the axis of rotation, which is tilted 98°. The tilt creates extremely long seasons, for each pole receives forty-two years of sunlight followed by forty-two years of darkness. (*Oxford Dictionary of National Biography*; *Manchester Times*; Carole Stott & Clint Twist, *Space Facts*, Dorling Kindersley, 1995)

~ March 14th ~

1840: A memorial signed by members of the Church of England was presented to the Archdeacon and Clergy of Bath, calling upon them to remove from their church anything that was considered Roman Catholic, particularly images. Generally, those who held 'high church' views advocated a moderately reformed church that was closer to the Roman Catholic Church. Other Anglicans advocated a 'low church', or a more Protestant outlook. The high church had been increasingly vocal during the 1830s, through the publication of *Tracts for the Times* which advocated high church views that although, known amongst the clergy had been largely forgotten by the laity who, with some clergy, associated them with Roman Catholicism. Consequently, ritualist controversies persisted within the Church throughout the nineteenth century. (*Bath Chronicle*)

1920: Of interest to the early motorist were reliability trials, usually involving some considerable distance, to test the reliability and performance of motorcars and motorcycles. One such was the 'light motor reliability trial' finished on this date in 1920. Nineteen competitors set off the previous day from Bath to Land's End, with the return journey to be completed on the following day – the round trip making over 400 miles. Only four cars on this occasion returned on schedule, those driven by Messrs Victor Smith, E. Colmer, E. Kirkham and C.M. Harvey. Large crowds welcomed them as the returned to Bath including Revd R. Garfield Waterbury, president of the Bath and West of England Motor Club. (*The Times*)

— MARCH 15TH —

1847: 'A foot-race took place on Landsdown, for £10, between the celebrated Robert Inwood of Tooting, near London, and Charles Usher, of Weston, near Bath. The former, who is just in his prime, gave thirty yards start out of one hundred to the latter, who is nearly sixty years of age. The race was won by Usher, in gallant style, by one and a half yards. Inwood, when about seven yards from home made a desperate spring, and, finding himself short, made another, but he jumped against a boy about a yard beyond the handkerchief, which threw him down. Both umpires declared that Usher had fairly won; yet, after some time, the backer of Inwood desired the stakeholder not to give up the stakes.' (*Bristol Mercury*)

– MARCH 16TH –

1845: *The Era* newspaper, then noted for its sporting coverage, reported an amazing feat of shooting accuracy that was alleged to have taken place: 'At Bath, some years since, an officer of rank made a bet with another officer, of a ball and supper for one hundred ladies and gentleman, that he drove fifteen bullets, at as many shots, through an orange, in the same room in which they sat, at the distance of sixty feet. Not to incommode the ladies, he chose an air-gun, and the first shot passed through the very centre of the orange. The second, from some unknown cause, varied about a quarter of an inch, the ball taking an oblique direction and he consequently lost the bet. The experimenter, however, was so certain of his aim, that he afterwards laid 500 guineas to 400 that he drove nineteen balls out of twenty through an orange, at the same distance; and this he performed, to the great astonishment of the beholders.' (*The Era*)

~ March 17th ~

1764: Dr William Oliver (1695–1764) is best remembered as the inventor of the Bath Oliver Biscuit. He was born in Ludgvan, Cornwall, on August 4th 1695 and was admitted to Pembroke College, Cambridge, on September 17th 1714. He completed his medical training at Leiden University. In 1725 he settled in Bath and soon had a leading practice in the city. Dr Oliver also contributed brief papers to *Philosophical Transactions of the Royal Society* and wrote *A Practical Essay on the Use and Abuse of Warm Water Bathing in Gouty Cases* in 1751. In 1760 he put together a collection of *Cases of the Persons Admitted into the Infirmary at Bath under the Care of Doctor Oliver*. As a philanthropist, Dr Oliver raised a number of subscriptions to found the Bath Mineral Water Hospital. Although it cannot be known for certain, towards the end of his life, Dr Oliver is said to have confided the recipe of the savoury Bath Oliver Biscuit to his coachman, Atkins, giving him £100 and ten sacks of wheat flour. Atkins set up shop in Green Street and soon acquired a large fortune from the sale of the biscuits. The biscuit continued to be manufactured in Bath by Fortt and Son until the 1960s, when production of the biscuit was transferred to Reading. (*Oxford Dictionary of National Biography*)

— MARCH 18TH —

1706: Thomas Guidott (1638?–1706), physician and writer, was buried at Bath Abbey. He was educated at Oxford and by 1667 had come to Bath. With the help of established physicians, which included John Maplet and Samuel Bave, he was able to build up his own practice. He published widely on the subject of Bath and its hot springs, beginning with a third edition of Edward Jorden's *A Natural Discourse of Natural Bathes* which he supplemented with his own appendix. Between 1673 and 1676, Guidott published several treatises on the properties of the bath's mineral water, the antiquities, the baths as a place of therapy and biographies on the lives of its physicians. His final work, published in 1705, criticised Sir John Floyer's advocacy of cold water bathing and defended the use of hot mineral springs, such as those at Bath. He died the following year. (*Oxford Dictionary of National Biography*)

1746: John Bowdler, Church of England layman and religious writer, was born in Bath. He was a High Churchman who emphasised apostolic succession in the Anglican Church. He was an outspoken stern moralist, emphasising the need for strong Sabbath observance and stating that adulterers should be barred from marrying or inheriting land. Bowdler also supported parity for the disestablished Church of Scotland and the building of new churches to cope with the increase in population. To this end, he raised £1 million for the Incorporated Church Building Society founded in 1818. (*Oxford Dictionary of National Biography*)

~ MARCH 19TH ~

Roman Times: The Romans dedicated the springs to Sulis Minerva, goddess of wisdom. The Romans celebrated her festival for five days, beginning on March 19th. The festival was called Quinquatria.

2005: It was reported that lollipop men and women in Bath were to swap their yellow high-visibility jackets for orange ones. The reason: swarms of insects were attracted to their yellow jackets. It was hoped that the change of colour would help and a trial would begin over the next few months. (*Western Daily Press*)

2006: A record number of runners took part in Bath's half marathon, with 10,000 people taking part. The course is popular since it takes place over relatively flat land between Bath and Keynsham. On this occasion, Simon Kasimili ran the quickest time for the men, in 1:04:08, and Cathy Mutura completed it in 1:12:45 for the women. Both athletes are from Kenya. The Bath Half Marathon has been running since 1981. (*Western Daily Press*)

~ March 20th ~

2003: Elite commando units were in Iraq at the forefront of the second war against the Iraqi dictator, Saddam Hussain. The 40 and 42 Commando Units, both based in the west, were the first to cross the border into Iraq at the start of the war. Meanwhile, in Bath, 300 protestors stormed the Guildhall, setting fire to both the Stars and Stripes and the Union Jack. The protestors disappeared by the time the police had arrived on the scene. (*Western Daily Press*)

———

2008: HRH the Duke of Gloucester visited the Victoria Art Gallery and the Building of Bath Museum. At the art gallery, in Bridge Street, he was shown around the 'Blue and White Show', an exhibition inspired by the 2,000 items of nineteenth-century transferware belonging to the Hickman family of Cornwall. Three contemporary artists – Kaffe Fassett, Candace Bahooth, and Carole Waller – also displayed work inspired by the blue and white china. By the time of the Duke's visit, 25,000 people had visited the exhibition which had been open since January of that year. The Duke, who was himself an architect, also requested a visit to the Building of Bath Museum, where he met trustees, staff and volunteers. (*Western Daily Press*; www.victoriagal.org.uk)

~ MARCH 21ST ~

1881: At Bath City Police Court, two police constables, John Staines and William Hudd, were sent to prison for an assault on James Williams. The latter had been trying to enlist with the Majesty's Regiment of Guards but was told he was of 'insufficient stature'. However, the recruiting sergeant told him to go to the GWR station and wait for a recruiting sergeant for the Royal Artillery who would be arriving shortly. Whilst at the station, he was approached by Police Constables John Staines and William Hudd, who asked him what he was doing. James Williams replied that he had been sent to the station by an enlisting sergeant and was waiting to be enlisted. Then, for no obvious reason, Staines struck Williams, hitting his left ear and knocking him to the ground; Hudd also struck Williams across the back with a stick. Williams picked himself up and ran in the direction of Manvers Street, followed by the two constables. He was chased into Stanley Road when the constables caught up with him. Staines then grabbed him by the ear and said, 'Let's have a look at his face.' Staines again knocked him to the ground whilst Hudd struck him across the forehead with a stick. Two bystanders then helped Williams to the nearest police station. Staines was sentenced to a month's imprisonment with hard labour and Hudd received six weeks' imprisonment with hard labour. (*Bristol Mercury*)

━ MARCH 22ND ━

1875: Mary Davis, described as 'an aged gypsy woman', was convicted of 'unlawfully telling fortunes' and sentenced to three months' imprisonment at Bath Police Court. Mary Davis, under the guise of being a repairer of wares, offered to tell two servant girls their fortunes. The girls, Elizabeth Milson and Emily Garland, gave Davis a shilling and she examined the lines on their hands. Davis then produced a pack of cards, saying that she would also be able to 'rule their planets', and invited the girls to cut the cards. (As this part of the story was retold in court, a question from the Bench asked whether she had turned up a knave from the pack of cards, which caused those present to laugh.) Davis then told the girls that their fortunes were positive, but that she would only give definite information on payment of a further fee. Milson gave 6s and was told that she would be sought by a fair, well-to-do man. Garland handed over 7s and was told that she would meet a dark man – an engineer. The Bench then asked whether they believed what they had been told. The witnesses replied that they did at the time, but as the prophesy had not come true, they no longer believed. Again the court was left in hysterics. At the end of the proceedings the Bench congratulated the girls on having lost their money in such a manner and suggested that the incident would be a valuable lesson to them. (*Reynold's Weekly Newspaper*)

~ March 23rd ~

1867: Reading material for patients at the Bath Mineral Water Hospital was provided in the following novel way: 'There has just been erected at Bath railway station a receptacle for such newspapers and periodicals as travellers by trains have no further use for, which newspapers and periodicals are daily sent for the use of the patients in the Bath Mineral Water Hospital.' (*Bristol Mercury*)

———

1960: Queen Elizabeth the Queen Mother visited Bath, following a £100,000 restoration of the abbey. After the service at Bath Abbey, the Queen Mother walked to the Guildhall for luncheon with the mayor and civic guests. During the afternoon, thousands of schoolchildren lined the Royal Crescent as the Queen Mother was driven to Sion Hill Place in order to open a college of domestic science. The tour of the newly opened college by the Queen Mother had to begin with a climb up some stairs as the lift was thought to be out of order – though it later emerged that someone had just pushed the wrong button. The college was merged to form part of the Bath College of Higher Education in 1975. Today, the college is known as Bath Spa University. (*The Times*)

— MARCH 24TH —

2010: Bath FM Radio, which had been broadcasting since November 1999, closed on this day. The reason for the closure was that the parent company, Your Media, was unable to secure a licence from OFCOM, the government regulator for broadcasting, telecommunications and postal services. Bath FM had got off to an embarrassing start, according to contemporary newspaper accounts. The radio station had organised a champagne breakfast for the launch of their 7 a.m. show at Bath's Weston Hotel. The launch was attended by Bath's great and good, including the Chief of Police. Unfortunately, no one seems to have informed a police sergeant who, on his way to work, noticed that a party was in full swing at the Weston Hotel. Apparently, he rushed into the police station in Manvers Street, donned his uniform and returned in a panda car, but he was brought up short when he noticed that his boss, the Chief Superintendent, was there enjoying himself along with several prominent Bath citizens. The sergeant went back fuming to the station. (*The Guardian*; *Western Daily Press*; *Bath Chronicle*)

~ March 25th ~

1899: At Weston (Bath) Police Court, John Brook, aged 26, and William Rawlings, 21, appeared before the magistrates charged with robbery against Alfred Henry Fry of Midsomer Norton. Fry had first met the two men whilst he was at the New Inn, Southgate Street. He told the two men of the sale of his trap and even treated the defendants to a quart of beer. Brook and Rawlings followed Fry out of the pub, stating that they were 'going up on the hill'. Fry climbed upon his pony, at which point Brook grabbed his shoulders, pulled him back and forced him to the ground. Brook put his hand in Fry's pocket, which contained money. During the course of the scuffle, the pocket was torn and the money spilled upon the ground. Brook responded 'You ******, I am going to have your money.' Whilst Fry lay on the ground, Brook and Rawlings picked up the money before running off. Rawlings pleaded guilty and was sentenced to three months' imprisonment with hard labour. Brook, however, pleaded not guilty, and was sentenced to six months' imprisonment with hard labour. (*Bristol Mercury*)

— March 26th —

1804: Richard Pepper Arden, 1st Baron Alvany, was born on May 20th 1744, in Cheshire. He was educated at Cambridge where he distinguished himself, gaining an MA in 1769. Also in that year, he was called to the bar and travelled the Northern Circuit, where his family connections were strongest. Family connections may have helped him to secure the position of Recorder of Macclesfield and, in 1776, he secured junior Welsh judge. In 1780, he became bencher for the Middle Temple. Friendship with William Pitt, the then Chancellor of the Exchequer, as well as a barrister at Lincoln's Inn, brought Arden into politics and may have helped him gain the position of Solicitor General from March 1782. He was MP for the Isle of Wight from January 1783. He supported Pitt during his time in opposition and became Attorney General in 1784, when Parliament was dissolved. In the new parliament, he was MP for Aldborough, and from 1794 he represented Bath, until elevated to the judicial bench. He was active in legal matters, but never presided at a major state trial. He had an amiable character but attracted criticism as someone who had gained his positions by patronage and by not bringing sufficient dignity to his judicial roles. He died on March 19th 1804 and was buried on this date at the Rolls Chapel, Chancery Lane. (*Oxford Dictionary of National Biography*)

— MARCH 27TH —

1839: The Court of Requests in Bath summoned the mother of an apprenticed tailor, aged 17. She was summoned for £4 9s – the cost of clothes supplied to her son. The mother argued that she had supplied the requisite clothing as far as her circumstances would allow. The plaintiff argued that he had given credit to the apprenticed tailor on the basis that another apprentice had assured him that his parents were 'respectable'. The majority of the commissioners sided with the mother, arguing that due caution had not been used, since the plaintiff, in a few hours, and for the cost of 4d postage, could have obtained the necessary information that would have prevented the plaintiff issuing credit. (*The Times*)

1994: Protestors converged on the fountain of Laura Place to demonstrate against the building of the Batheaston to Swanswick bypass. The road passed through a scenic valley and a long-running protest camp was established against the development at Solsbury Hill, which stood next to the route of the bypass. During the protest, two policemen walking up Solsbury Hill asked to speak to the camp's leaders. They were told, 'You must speak to Aqua and Sulis. You'll recognise them because they're both black.' The officers continued to the top of the hill and enquired for Aqua and Sulis. They were taken to meet two black piglets which were kept as pets at the camp. The protest was ultimately unsuccessful and the bypass built. (*The Guardian*; www.bathintime.co.uk)

— MARCH 28TH —

1828: Frances Burney (1776–1828), governess and poet, died from jaundice at her mother's home in King Street, Bath. She was the niece of novelist Frances Burney (1752-1840) (*see* January 15th). Her parents, despite being talented musicians, were poor, and in 1794 Francis took up her first post as governess in Lord Beverley's household. Family connections helped to secure other governess positions at other prominent households. Despite ill health and the gruelling nature of her profession, she built up a considerable library with books in French, German, Italian, Latin and Greek. In 1818, she published *Tragic Dramas: Chiefly Intended for Representation in Private Families to Which is Added, Aristodemus, a Tragedy from the Italian of Vincenzo Monti*. The title, showing that the plays were for private performances only, hints at Frances' concern about the impropriety of the stage, especially for women – a concern that her grandfather, Charles Burney (1726–1814), also shared. The plays themselves were overblown and melodramatic. Indeed, the opening lines from *Fitzmorond* are indicative:

> Hail, solitary shades of silent woe,
> And deep, and mournful meditation made.

At her death, she was said to be 'wasted to a skeleton'. She was buried on April 4th at Batheaston Church. (*Oxford Dictionary of National Biography*; Frances Burney, *Tragic Dramas*, 1818)

— MARCH 29TH —

2006: A violent robber, who escaped from a prison van after threatening the guards with a razor blade, was recaptured after a dramatic police chase. Sean Baker, 20, was being transferred to HMP Erlestoke when the van was stopped at a lay-by in Claverton, near Bath, and Baker escaped with a quantity of cash. He threatened the driver of a nearby bus, before running to a parked Renault Megane Scenic. The owner had parked the car in order to buy a newspaper, and when he returned, he found Baker inside. The convict threatened the owner and made away with his car. A police chase ensued and Baker was caught four hours later in the Brislington area of Bristol. (*Western Daily Press*)

—

2007: Protestors gathered outside council offices and presented the council with a petition in order to save Churchill House, a building dating from the twentieth century and styled with a mix of Georgian and Art Deco features. Ultimately, the protestors were not successful. The demolition came as part of the Southgate Shopping Centre scheme, and the architecture is seen by some as being out-of-keeping with the Georgian architecture of Bath. (*Western Daily Press*)

~ MARCH 30TH ~

1898: 'At Bath city police court, before the Mayor, Major Simpson, and Colonel Vaughton, John Cowan, 49, moulder, of the Engineer's Arms, was charged on a warrant with maliciously wounding William Goodson on the 28th of March, and also with assaulting him at the same time and place. The prosecutor was in a public house with a friend when the prisoner came in and drank the contents of their glasses, after the landlord had refused to serve him. The prisoner poured out more of their beer, and the prosecutor went to take the glass out of his hand when he turned round and hit him with a broken glass, causing four cuts, which could not have been done by one blow, in the region of his left eye. The Bench treated the case as one of common assault and sentenced the prisoner to a calendar month's imprisonment with hard labour.' (*Bristol Mercury*)

~ March 31st ~

1788: The foundation stone of Laura Place was laid amidst much celebration. Laura Place was the first of an extensive plan by Thomas Baldwin, city architect, to develop the area on the Bathwick side of the River Avon. Bells were rung for the occasion and guns in Spring Gardens were fired. The local populace were also treated to plenty of strong beer. An inscription was placed on the foundation stone, reading: 'This corner stone of Laura Place was laid on the 31st day of March 1788; when the New Town of Bath was begun to be built on the estate of Henrietta Laura Pulteney, daughter of William Pulteney Esq M.P. and Frances his wife, the cousin and devisee of the estate of William late Earl of Bath the building of this New Town was the consequence of the exertions of William Pulteney Esq M.P. who obtained authority from Parliament for building a new bridge, and opening a communication to this ground, and for granting building leases of the ground for 99 years; which he carried, in some degree, into execution during the minority of his daughter. The plan and designs were made by Mr T. Baldwin, architect and city surveyor.' Development of Bathwick was heralded by the erection of Pulteney Bridge in 1770, by Sir William Pulteney to the design of Robert Adam. However, it was Baldwin's publication of the plans to develop the area in a broadsheet in 1788 that kick-started building in the area. (*The Times*; Nikolaus Pevsner, *The Buildings of England: North Somerset and Bristol*, Penguin, 1958)

~ April 1st ~

1852: Mrs Shele, living at Box Hill, walked to Box station intending to take the train to Bath. However, as the 10.15 a.m. from London passed through Box station at speed it 'so alarmed her that she fell down insensible. Mrs Shele was removed to the Station Inn and put to bed. The shock, however, was too great for human skill to alleviate, and she expired at midnight.' (*Bath Gazette*)

1974: Avon's first citizen was born at St Martin's Hospital Bath. The county of Avon came into being at midnight and Peter Calver was born at 25 minutes past midnight. His mother, Brenda Calver, stated at the time that he has not made a noise since he was born. The child's grandfather was John Connell, founder of the Noise Abatement Society, and the family used to joke that he founded the society because of his experience with babies. (*Bath and West Evening Chronicle*)

1996: The county of Avon was abolished and Bath became part of Bath and North-East Somerset. Heather Gilling, the new county's Information and Communications Manager, stated that they were treating the day like any other. Bath's muted response to the abolition of the Avon was in marked contrast to Bristol (which also regained its county status), whose mayor, Joan McLaren, celebrated by riding through Bristol in a carriage drawn by two shire horses. (*Bath and West Evening Chronicle*; D.G. Amphlett, *The Bristol Book of Days*, The History Press, 2011)

‑ April 2nd ‑

1839: On April 1st, Henry Vincent, a chartist and radical, was attacked by a mob in Devizes. Rumours soon spread that he had been killed. Vincent recorded that afterwards his party 'then rode on to Bath, reaching the city in safety, at twelve o'clock. The most intense excitement prevailed in Bath; the news of our deaths having reached the city, large numbers threatened to march to Devizes that night. The news of our arrival soon spread, and we retired to rest, much fatigued, about eleven o'clock. Thus ended a day which the Chartists must never forget.' On this date, Vincent stated: 'At 7 o'clock an immense concourse of people assembled in the Abbey Green, to congratulate myself and [W.P.] Roberts, a fellow chartist, on our escape. We went to the meeting, and were received with tremendous cheering. Roberts delivered a soul-stirring speech, and was received with every demonstration of enthusiastic delight. He told the people the Devizes affair would do more towards aiding the Chartists than any other event which had occurred during our whole progress. I then addressed them, and was received with reiterated bursts of cheering.' Vincent was later arrested, in May 1839, for a 'riotous assemblage' that he held in Newport in April of the same year. It earned him a spell in prison. After his release he married Lucy Chappell and the couple settled in Bath. He remained active, lecturing on a variety of social and historical matters. He died on December 29th 1878. (*Western Vindicator*; *Oxford Dictionary of National Biography*)

– April 3rd –

1730: David Roberts was born in Chepstow, Monmouthshire, and was a joiner by trade. His first wife died in childbirth and he spent the majority of her £300 fortune. He moved to Southwark, entering into a partnership with his brother, a carpenter. Despite making good money, including a £300 profit on one particular job, Roberts was reluctant to pay his creditors. He became involved in a long-term relationship with Sarah Bristow, but the couple never married. He left for Bristol, where he furnished an inn on credit. His London creditors caught up with him, and indicted him to stand trial. Roberts was released owing to a technicality in the writ. Thinking it unwise to remain, he moved away, eventually ending up in Coventry, where he again resided until pursued by creditors. However, it was Roberts' early attempt at coin clipping that led him to being arrested. He attempted to pass off the clipped coins at an inn, and some of the dust lingered on the proprietor's hands, who commented, 'What have we got here? The fellow who filed these guineas ought to be hanged for doing his business in so clumsy a manner.' Although arrested, Roberts was released but soon his name was on an advertisement. He attempted to leave the country, but returned and once again took lodgings in Bath, where he continued to file coins. For this he was brought to trial at the Old Bailey and sentenced to death. The sentence was carried out on this day. (*Newgate Calendar*)

— APRIL 4TH —

1716: William Oliver was born in Launceston, Cornwall, the son of the rector of Launceston in 1658. His medical studies in Leiden were interrupted when he took part in the Duke of Monmouth's rebellion against James II. He served as one of three surgeons. Following the Duke's defeat on the battlefield, he rode to Bath and took refuge amongst friends until the end of the Bloody Assizes, which purged the supporters of the rebellion. Oliver then made his way to the Continent to complete his medical training at Leiden. In 1688, Oliver accompanied William III to England as an officer in the army, and he was soon rewarded for his services. He qualified as licentiate of the Royal College of Physicians on September 30th 1692. Between April 27th 1693 and 1702, he was physician to the Red Squadron. Between 1702 and 1709, he lived in London and Bath, although it is probable that he did not practice in Bath. He did, however, write on the medicinal uses of Bath's waters. In 1704, he produced a practical essay on fevers containing remarks on the hot and cold methods of this cure, which included a dissertation on the hot waters of Bath. Between 1709 and 1714 he was a physician at Chatham Hospital for Sick and Wounded Seamen, and lastly from 1714 he became a physician at the Royal Hospital Greenwich. He died at Greenwich on this date. A memorial to William Oliver was also erected in Bath Abbey. (*Oxford Dictionary of National Biography*)

— April 5th —

1852: Edward Mahoney was brought before Bath Magistrates, charged with stabbing William Tuckey. Mahoney had been drinking in the Seven Dials pub in the company of a woman, with whom he had quarrelled. Infuriated, Mahoney stated that he would stab the first person that apprehended him. In a lane outside the pub he plunged a knife into the unfortunate William Tuckey. Blood poured out and Tuckey was taken to the United Hospital. Sadly, Tuckey died a few days later from his injuries. Newspaper reports began to emerge that Tuckey provoked Mahoney and that Mahoney acted in self-defence. He was tried for murder but was found guilty of manslaughter. The judge passed a light sentence of one month's imprisonment. (*Bath Chronicle*; *Morning Chronicle*; *Bristol Mercury*)

1897: The foundation stone was laid for Weymouth School House. A time capsule was buried underneath the foundation stone which contained copies of *Keene's Bath Journal* for May 2nd and 9th 1896, a portrait of the Marquis of Bath, two Victorian coins and a diamond jubilee medal of Queen Victoria. The school was demolished in 1961 and the site purchased to enable a large retail development by Marks & Spencer and Woolworths. (David and Jonathon Falconer, *A Century of Bath*, Sutton, 1999)

~ April 6th ~

1817: The Bristol mail coach journeying towards London was robbed of a parcel containing £80 in silver. 'The person to whose care the package was entrusted, left Bristol by the mail on Sunday evening, having placed the parcel in the seat-box of the coach. On arriving at Bath, he looked in the place, and at that time the parcel was perfectly safe. He gave himself no farther concern about it, until the coach stopped at Hounslow, when he again examined the seat-box, and, to his great consternation, discovered that the package was gone ... A man who came inside from Marlborough to Newbury is suspected to be the person by whom the robbery was committed.' (*The Times*)

2013: The grand opening of the Greenway Cycle Path took place. It involved a mass cycle, with 2,000 people taking part. The route opened a former railway tunnel, built as part of the Somerset and Dorset Railways extension into Bath. The new route, from Bath to Midford, now possesses the longest cycling tunnel in Britain – a distance of 1,829 yards. When constructed, the tunnel was the longest railway tunnel in Britain without intermediate ventilation. The smoky conditions in the tunnel could cause havoc on the footplate and, on November 20th 1929, the driver and fireman of a freight train passed out as the train passed through the tunnel with fatal consequences (*see* November 20th). (www.bbc.co.uk/news; *The Guardian*; www.forgottenrelics.co.uk)

‒ April 7th ‒

1849: Henry Marchant, who lived at Angel Buildings, Bath, was a worker in the local quarries. He arrived home on March 31st and his wife, Charlotte, made him a cup of tea. Soon afterwards he fell ill with stomach pains and nausea. After several days of sickness, he died on April 7th. After only three days, his merry widow married again! This time it was to a 'man of property' called Harris, who was considerably older than her. She was 32, he was 70. Unsurprisingly, tongues soon started wagging and suspicion fell on Charlotte. Henry's interred body was dug up and traces of arsenic were found. Charlotte was arrested on a charge of murder. Six or seven weeks before Henry's death, Harris had offered to marry Charlotte, observing that it would be good thing if she was a widow. At her trial, the jury found her guilty of murder. Normally, she would have been executed, but Charlotte pleaded 'the belly' – that she was pregnant. For women who were found guilty of capital crimes 'pleading the belly' was a common defence. The judge could postpone a death sentence, commute a death sentence to transportation or issue a reprieve. In Charlotte's case the sentence was respited. (Nicola Sly & John van der Kiste, *More Somerset Murders*, The History Press, 2011)

~ April 8th ~

2003: David Hempleman-Adams became the first person to reach the geomagnetic North Pole alone and unsupported. The explorer, who lives in Box, near Bath, dedicated his achievement to Terry Lloyd, an ITN News reporter killed whilst covering the Iraq war. Lloyd and Hempleman-Adams had known each other for fifteen years and Lloyd had covered the explorer's previous expeditions. Hempleman-Adams had suffered a 20ft fall from a glacier a week previously and had to struggle over icy terrain with a badly bruised leg. The expedition began on March 17th from Ellesmere, west of Greenland, with Hempleman-Adams averaging 10 miles per day during the polar trek. He stayed close to the coastline in order to avoid glaciers as far as possible and was gradually able to make his way to the Darling Peninsula where the geomagnetic North Pole is located. Hempleman-Adams failed to reach the geomagnetic North Pole four years ago in a similar expedition and he wanted to return to try again. As he put it: 'I hate failure. The only person who fails is the person who knows he can do it, but does not do it. I knew in my heart I could.' Hempleman-Adams also did not tell his family and friends that he was undertaking the expedition. They thought he was taking part in the polar race. Hempleman-Adams admitted, 'I'm in big trouble with my wife.' (*Western Daily Press*)

~ April 9th ~

1999: *The Times* reported that a duck called Beatrice, together with her mate, Arthur, caused problems for the Bath Spa building project. Council chiefs wanted to press ahead with the works but Beatrice, a mallard duck, laid eggs in the famous Cross Bath. Under the Wildlife and Countryside Act, a wild bird's nest may not be disturbed without a licence. Volunteer workers for the Springs' Foundation wanted the nest left in place, whilst the duck reared her chicks. Bath and North-East Somerset Council wanted to move the nest in order to move in heavy machinery, as well as carry out tests on the water to see if it could be made safe for drinking and bathing. The presence of the ducks and their faeces would contaminate the results. Animal activists were thought to be involved earlier that year, when netting to stop Beatrice, who was a regular visitor to the pool, was slashed. Despite £2,000 worth of replacement netting, the duck still managed to find a way into the baths. Just over a week after the story was reported, it was decided that work was to continue around the ducks. (*The Times*)

~ April 10th ~

1881: 'Walter Gladstone and Thomas Knee were charged with obstructing the thoroughfare in Grove Street, on the 10th inst. The defendants were engaged in preaching, which caused some disturbance as well as annoyance, and they were taken to the police station to obtain their names and addresses. They refused to leave the station until they were bailed out. The Bench now discharged them. A man in the court came forward and complained that he had taken the Corridor room to hold Salvation [Army] services in, but that the constable, with the assistance of some policemen had prevented the people from attending. The Clerk explained that, the Corridor being private property, the Bench could not interfere. The remedy was in the County Court. Other preachers had complained that they were also molested whilst they were preaching in the Dolmeads, and asked for more police officers to be placed there. The Mayor replied that the applicant could apply to the police on the beat, or they could summon the persons who annoyed them. The parties then left the court.' (*Bristol Mercury*)

~ April 11th ~

1685: Dr Peirce gave this account of finding a shell in the kidney of a 'gentle-woman of about 28 years of age, very fat and corpulent' in a letter to the Royal Society on this day. The woman suffered from severe vomiting, from which she died. Dr Peirce then performed a post-mortem examination, and an ulcer in the pancreas is given as the cause of the vomiting. Dr Peirce looked at her kidneys, noting that 'they were covered with a prodigious quantity of fat; which removing with my hand, and reaching one of the kidneys I felt something prick my finger in the lower part of the kidney where the ureter is inserted: I presently concluded it to be a stone, and kept hold of it till I made my way to it with my knife and took it out (with an abundance of mucous bloody matter about it) and laid it by in the window; opening the kidneys, I found not so much as gravell (much less any stone) in either of them: upon further examination of this matter (supposd to be a stone) by washing off the mucous that was about it I found it to be a small shell, very finely wrought; in the hollow of it there was a mucous slimy matter, not at all unlike the substance of a snail as to consistence; but of a bloody colour.' (*Philosophical Transactions of the Royal Society Vol. 15*, 1685)

~ April 12th ~

1881: A singular case of horse theft occurred at Twerton, Bath. A cart mare, with the value of £40, belonging to William Wenmouth Salmon, was left in a stable overnight on March 8th 1881. However, twelve hours later, the horse was stolen and offered for sale 40 miles away in Gloucester. It is assumed that the thieves rode the horse that distance in those twelve hours. A Gloucester police sergeant found two men trying to offer the horse for sale and the men were arrested. The men were Richard Thompson, 26, and Henry Hughes, 18, both from Bath. On this date, they were charged with the theft and committed for trial at the next Somerset Assizes. Both men pleaded guilty to the charge. Thompson received eighteen months and Hughes received nine months as the judge felt that he had acted at Thompson's instigation. (*Bristol Mercury and Daily Post*; *Jackson's Oxford Journal*)

2012: BBC News reported on a club for men with the most impressive moustaches, who held their annual general meeting at a hotel in Bath. The Handlebar Club, founded in 1947, now has over 100 members. Members are strictly vetted and beards are not allowed. (www.bbc.co.uk)

~ APRIL 13TH ~

1896: Albert Millson and Henry Fowler were arrested for the murder of Henry Smith at Muswell Hill, North London. The arrests took place in Bath with the assistance of the local constabulary. The Muswell Hill murder was well documented in the press. Millson and Fowler entered the property of Henry Smith, an 80-year-old retired engineer, in the early hours of February 14th, robbing and murdering him. Both Fowler and Millson were known to the police and suspicion fell on them when they suddenly appeared to have acquired a considerable sum of money. The men went on the run and were eventually traced to Bath, where they had taken lodgings above a confectionary shop in Monmouth Street. Whilst in Bath, they could be frequently found in the local public houses. The arresting officers were Chief Inspector Marshall of Scotland Yard and Detective Inspector Nutkins of the Highgate Police. Both police officers were armed with revolvers at the time of the arrest. Nonetheless, Fowler strongly resisted being arrested and aimed a blow for Insp. Marshall's head, smashing his hat. Fowler fought desperately and tried to retrieve a revolver he had hidden underneath a sofa. By the time he was subdued, the furniture had been scattered and broken. Both men were found guilty of the murder of Henry Smith and were executed. (*The Times*)

~ April 14th ~

1809: In a murder trial lasting eight hours, James Taylor was found guilty for the killing of John Dyer. Taylor had got into a gambling dispute with three other men, Johnson, Guyon and Dyer. Taylor then ran upstairs to find his gun and shot Guyon in the face before shooting Dyer, who died instantly. In his defence, Taylor claimed that he heard his mother screaming and thought that her life was in danger. He lost control and, in a moment of frenzy, he committed the fatal deed, which he now deeply regretted. The court, however, decided that the fact he went upstairs to fetch a gun showed premeditation. Consequently, Taylor was found guilty and sentenced to be hanged and dissected. At this time, the only legal source of cadavers for medical dissection was the convicted criminals sentenced to death. The 1752 Murder Act permitted judges to allow condemned felons to be used by the medical establishment in this way. Dissection was also thought to increase the deterrent effect of the death penalty, adding to the humiliation of those convicted. (*The Times*)

~ APRIL 15TH ~

1863: The following article was reported in the *Bristol Mercury*, but the story was reported widely in other newspapers also: 'An awful instance of the uncertainty of human life occurred at Twerton, on Wednesday last. It has been the custom hitherto for the guardians of that union, with their officers, to dine together the first meeting after the annual elections, and on the day above-named they met for that purpose. After dinner, the chairman, the Rev. J.P. Sydenham, after other toasts, proposed the health of Mr James Wood, who had been clerk of the board for many years. The toast having been drunk, Mr Wood rose to return thanks, and had just used the words that he hoped to meet them on many such occasions, when he fell on the floor, gave a deep sigh, and instantly expired. The cause of death was disease of the heart.' However, the melancholic event, as described, never actually happened. Another newspaper, *Lloyd's Newspaper*, helps to clear up the matter: 'We are informed that it was Mr James Wood, the clerk to the Tiverton board of guardians, who died suddenly in his chair, after having dined with the guardians at Tiverton, a few weeks since. This has no doubt been confounded with Twerton in Somersetshire, and caused the mistake alluded to in the Bath papers and noticed by us.' (*Lloyd's Newspaper; Bristol Mercury*)

― April 16th ―

1770: James Calderbank (1770–1821) was born on this date in Liverpool. In 1787, he entered the English monastery of St Laurence at Dieulouard, Lorraine. He received a classical education and made his profession in 1792. He was ordained a priest on December 21st 1793. However, the French Revolution of 1794 caused the monks to seek refuge in different parts of Europe. He then started his pastoral ministry in England, including the congregation at Bath between 1800–05 and 1809–17. In 1814, Calderbank published observations in a series of letters in answer to certain questions relating to various subjects of religion, proposed by a clergyman of the established church to a Catholic convert, where he showed himself to be a gentle controversialist. Calderbank was secretary of the General Chapter of the English Benedictines from 1802 to 1814. He died on April 9th 1821 and was buried at St Peter's Church, Seal Street, Liverpool. A memorial tablet was erected at the Bath Chapel in Pierrepoint Street. (*Oxford Dictionary of National Biography*)

— April 17th —

1608: The consecration of James Montague (1568–1618) as Bishop of Bath and Wells took place at Lambeth Palace. James Montague was born in Broughton, Northamptonshire, to Sir Edward Montague (*c.* 1532–1602) and his wife, Elizabeth. James Montague matriculated from Christ's College, Cambridge, in June 1585. His great-aunt, Frances Radcliffe (née Sidney), left in her will funds for the establishment of Sidney Sussex College, Cambridge. The principal executors of her will chose James Montague to be the first master of the college. Given Montague's young age, this was unusual. Nevertheless he oversaw the building of the college until its completion in 1602 and remained master until 1608. After the ascension of James I, he was appointed to the deanery of the Chapel Royal on Christmas Day, 1603. This appointment has been seen as James' way of countering the influence of Scottish Presbyterianism since he was a staunch Calvinist and a committed Episcopalian. As Bishop of Bath and Wells, he visited his diocese annually between July and September and was an effective administrator, paying strict attention to Sunday Observance, excommunication and keeping the observances of the Gun Powder and Gowry Plots. He also spent some of his wealth on the repair of Bath Abbey roof and restoring the Bishop's Palace at Wells. He was transferred to the diocese of Winchester on July 3rd 1616. He died on July 20th 1618 and was buried in the nave of Bath Abbey. He left £300 for his monument in the hope that it would encourage more benefactors to the abbey. (*Oxford Dictionary of National Biography*)

‒ April 18th ‒

1881: 'For a long time past there has been considerable discussion as to who was the best long-distance runner in the Bath district, and the various aspirants to the honour of champion never had a change of an even all-round competition. It was some few weeks since mutually arranged that a level race of 10 miles should be engaged in to determine the question, and the race took place on Monday [18th April], some thousands of persons assembling to see the race between Bath and Keynsham. The distance was 5 miles out and 5 miles back from Locksbrook, Bath, to Keynsham and back. The starters were Webb, Weaton, Bath; Wright and Gray, Bath; Hamilton, Bath; Eades, Bath; Mitchell, Bath; and Gray, Bath. Eades was the general favourite, but there were sections of the public who had their special favourites. The evening was not favourable for racing on the roadway, as there was plenty of wind and dust and the many vehicles added to the general disturbance of the dust. The race occupied exactly one hour, Mitchell winning easily by 300 yards, and Eades was second, and Hamilton a close third.' (*Bristol Mercury*)

~ April 19th ~

1012: St Alphege (*c.*953–1012) was a monk of Deerhurst, Gloucester, but later became a hermit in Somerset. Archbishop Dunstan of Canterbury made him Abbot of Bath, and in 984 Bishop of Winchester. In 1005 he succeeded Aelfric as Archbishop of Canterbury. Alphege was much loved for his generous almsgiving and his austere life. In 1011 the Danes overran south-east England and, owing to the treachery of his Archdeacon Ælfmaer, Canterbury was besieged and Alphege captured. The Danes demanded a £3,000 ransom, but Alphege refused to let anyone pay for fear that raising the money would further impoverish the ordinary people. The Danes kept him prisoner at Greenwich for seven months before murdering him using oxen bones on this date. Consequently, this day is kept as his feast day. He was buried at St Paul's Cathedral, London, but was translated to Canterbury in 1023 by King Canute. St Thomas à Becket, in his last sermon before he was martyred at Canterbury in 1170, dedicated his life to God and St Alphege as the first martyr of Canterbury. Tradition has it that Archbishop Lanfranc once tried to suggest that Alphege did not die for the faith, but St Anslem reputedly scorned him, stating that to die for justice was tantamount to martyrdom. (David Farmer, *Oxford Dictionary of Saints*, OUP, 1997; Simon Kershaw & Br Tristran (eds), *Exciting Holiness*, Canterbury Press, 2007; Henry Sebastian Bowden & Donald Attwater, *Miniature Lives of the Saints*, Burns & Oates, 1959)

~ APRIL 20TH ~

1848: The *Bath Chronicle* reported on a 'singular application of chloroform'. Mr Bond, a tanner of Twerton, wished to slaughter one of his pigs but wanted the deed done so that the cries of the dying animal would not awaken his neighbours. Mr Bond also wanted it to die in a more humane manner. Mr Bond asked his neighbour Mr Harding, a druggist, to make the necessary preparations for the chloroform, whilst the butcher woke the pig. The animal was then given 'a good sniff' of the chloroform, which deprived the animal of sensation and motion. The butcher was then able to inflict the fatal wound without the animal squealing in distress. (*Bath Chronicle*)

─ APRIL 21ST ─

1841: Isambard Kingdom Brunel, who was responsible for the building of the Great Western Railway, was probably also responsible for the design of Bath Spa railway station. He left some of the actual building work to an employee named Fripp, whom Brunel found to be ineffectual and increasingly exasperating. In a letter, dated April 21st 1841, Brunel wrote the following to Fripp: 'A long time ago I gave you instructions respecting certain details in the rooms at Bath station. Notwithstanding this I have to attend to every detail myself. I am heartily sick of employing you to do anything that, if I had ten minutes to spare, I would do myself. If you go over to Bath on Friday and can be ready with the outlines of the finished rooms you may save me some trouble – if you wish to do so. If not pray keep out of my way or I will certainly do you a mischief you have tried my patience so completely.' The reason why Brunel was not able to fire the hapless Fripp could be due to a William Fripp, who was on the city council at Bristol and a director of the Great Western Railway; probably a relation. (Adrian Vaughn, *Isambard Kingdom Brunel*, John Murray, 1993; Nikolaus Pevsner, *The Buildings of England*, Penguin, 1958)

~ April 22nd ~

1899: Sir Robert Bull unveiled a bronze memorial plaque to William Herschel, a musician and astronomer, at his former Bath residence of No. 19 New King Street. William Herschel was born in Hanover and came to this country in 1762. He quickly gained a reputation as a musician and by 1766 had been offered a position at Halifax Church, which he declined in favour of becoming organist at the Octagon Chapel, Bath. Whilst at Bath, Herschel taught himself astronomy and building telescopes. From the 1770s, Herschel was able to construct his own bigger and more powerful telescopes, and when local founders were not able to construct a large enough telescope, he converted the basement of his Bath home into an observatory. Using one of his own telescopes, Herschel was studying the Orion Nebula when, on March 13th, he noticed a 'star' whose appearance was curious. A few days later he observed the 'star' in a different position. Initially he thought that the body may be a comet, but consulted Nevil Mansdyke, the Astronomer Royal, who calculated its orbit and concluded that it was in fact a planet. Following the discovery, Herschel was offered a Royal pension that enabled him to devote more of his time to studying the night sky and went towards new premises in Windsor. Today, Herschell's former residence, No. 19 New King Street, is home to the Herschel Museum of Astronomy. (*The Times*; *Oxford Dictionary of National Biography*; www.bath-preservation-trust)

~ April 23rd ~

1702: Bath's celebrations for the coronation of Queen Anne are described by travel writer Celia Fiennes: 'Companyes of the town being assembled at Mr Majors [the Mayor's] house begin to proceed with their officers masters and wardens and each Company with their flag after marched the troupe the Maides of the suburbs.' The 'Citty Maides' came 'with their Majoress [Mayoress] Generall with their plummes of feathers with a wreath of gilded lawrell like a crown on top with all sorts of pretious stones the Jewellers shops could supply them with, and were guarded with young men.' Also in the procession were a Company of Grenadiers and 'four couple of Maurice [Morris] dancers with their prancing horses, in Holland shirts with laced hats ribined, and cross swashes and garters with bells, with their two antiques drest in their formalityes, with hankerchiefs in their hands dancing all the way.' After the Morris dancers came the clergy and the mayor. Then 'thus as they [the procession] repaired its way to the Cathedrall [Bath Abbey]; the granadeers salutes them just as they enter with a volley of shott and there they have a sermon and as they come out of the Cathedrall the Company of artillery salutes them againe with another volley; so in the same order they return to their Guild Hall where there is a sumptuous feast with Musick and danceing which ends the solemnity with binfires as usual.' (Christopher Morris (ed.) Celia Fiennes, *The Journeys of Celia Fiennes*, Cresset Press, 1949)

~ April 24th ~

1990: An unusual and colourful protest was held in Bath's normally quiet streets when 100 shops owners closed their shops in order to protest against the introduction of a new uniform business rate. The protest involved BARB (Business Against Rate and Rent Increases in Bath) who organised a mock funeral procession, complete with an undertaker dressed in eighteenth-century costume and dark glasses, which walked in front of a 1966 Austin Princess hearse. The hearse contained a coffin symbolising the loss of Bath businesses. A 'counter-demonstration' was held by members of the Bath Natural Theatre Group. Three members, two men and a woman, dressed in pinstripe suits and bowler hats, waved placards with slogans saying 'Get Back to Work' and 'Poll Tax Payers Say Yes'. They also 'protested' outside a tapestry shop shouting, 'Essential services should remain open'. The nature of the protest in Bath prompted a *Times* journalist to state: 'It was a yuppy's nightmare. For most of the morning it was impossible to purchase such essential goods as futons, whirlpools and oriental rugs.' The Bath Natural Theatre Company has been producing its surreal and delightfully absurd brand of street theatre since 1970 and describes itself as 'UK brand leader' in this field of enterprise. (*The Times*; www.naturaltheatre.co.uk)

~ April 25th ~

1942: Bath was hit during a night-time bombing raid by the Luftwaffe (which also continued the following night). The raid killed 417 people, destroyed 1,000 buildings and damaged 2,000 others. The Assembly Rooms were gutted and part of Queen's Square was destroyed, along with some buildings along Julian Road. Individual buildings were burned in the Circus and the Royal Crescent. Despite this, the damage to Georgian Bath was relatively slight, and it is suggestive of the relative weakness of the German Luftwaffe at that time. The raid was part of a series of attacks known as the Baedeker Raids. It is thought that these were initiated following the bombing of the historic port of Lübeck by the RAF on March 28th. Incensed, Hitler ordered that reprisals be made on Britain's historic cities and Exeter was the first city to be affected on April 23rd. The following day, Baron Gustav von Sturm, a Nazi propagandist, claimed that the Luftwaffe would work through the Baedeker tourist guides of Britain. Other historic cities affected during the Baedeker raids were Norwich, York and Canterbury. (Barry Cuncliffe, *The City of Bath*, Sutton, 1986)

‒ APRIL 26TH ‒

1912: Mr Percy Fitzgerald unveiled a memorial to novelist Jane Austen (1775–1817) in the Pump Room. The memorial consisted of a bust of the author; Fitzgerald was not only the artist who made the bust; he was also the donor. Although familiar with Bath from her visits to the city, Jane Austen spent most of her life in Steventon, Hampshire. Her father, George Austen, a clergyman, decided to retire and move the family to Bath. They arrived in May 1801 and took lodgings at No. 4 Sydney Place. They stayed there for three years and moved to No. 3 Green Park Buildings (since demolished). The death of her father in 1805 meant that the family were now in somewhat straightened financial circumstances, and a move to a cheaper property at No. 25 Gaye Street was needed. Jane Austen remained with her mother and sister until the 'trio' left Bath in July 1806. Jane Austen eventually settled in Chawton, Hampshire, in 1808. At Chawton, she was able to revise her earlier novels for publication and write new ones. All of her novels mention Bath and two novels, *Northanger Abbey* and *Persuasion,* are set in the city. These two novels were both published after her death. (*Oxford Dictionary of National Biography*; www.seekingjaneausten.com)

~ April 27th ~

1942: The second night of an air raid on Bath caused loss of life and considerable damage to St John the Evangelist's Roman Catholic Church and the presbytery. Father Sheridan, the housekeeper and three members of the Sweet family, who were sheltering there after a previous air raid, were killed, and the south aisle of the church needed to be demolished.

The foundation stone of the church was laid by the Bishop of Clifton on July 25th 1861, who stated: 'The church when completed will be in every respect worthy of the wealth and influence of the Catholics of Bath.' The church was completed two years later and consecrated in October 1863, when Dr Clifford, Bishop of Clifton was assisted by Dr Ullathorne, Bishop of Birmingham, Dr Vaughan, Bishop of Plymouth and Dr Morris, Bishop of Troy. Thirty Benedictine monks and twenty secular clergy were also in attendance. The ceremony lasted five hours and Hayden's *Number One Mass* was played with full orchestral accompaniment. The church was designed by C.J. and E.J. Hansom and is, as the architectural historian Nikolaus Pevsner puts it, 'a demonstrative proof of how intensely the Gothicists hated the Georgian of Bath'. (*Daily News*; *Bristol Mercury*; Nikolaus Pevsner, *The Buildings of England: North Somerset and Bristol*, Penguin, 1958).

~ April 28th ~

1814: Stories that hinted of supernatural intervention for persons seen as wicked were popular in most British nineteenth-century newspapers. This short extract from the *Bath Herald* is typical: 'The two unfortunate lads, Beard and Moon were hung at Ilchester on Wednesday 28th ult. For ill-treating a person named Wyatt, near this city some months ago. A person of the name of Lewis was also concerned in the affair, but he turned King's evidence, and escaped. Soon after the assize, on his return to Shepton, he and another worthless character hung Beard and Moon in effigy! A few days after, Lewis was seized with an inflammation of the brain, which, it is supposed was partly brought on by some "compunctious visiting of conscience", and expired about half-past twelve on Wednesday, being near the time that his two unfortunate companions were executed.' (*Bath Herald*)

2013: A service was held to remember the 417 people killed in the Bath Blitz. The event took place at the Victoria Park War Memorial and was organised by the Bath Blitz Memorial Project. Nine victims of the blitz remain unidentified. A few years previously, in 2008, Willi Schludecker, a Luftwaffe pilot who flew in the raids, attended the service to offer his apologies to the city. (www.bbc.co.uk)

⟶ APRIL 29TH ⟶

1856: A co-habiting couple, George Popjoy and Harriet Trueman, were charged at Bath Magistrates for assaulting William Harding, who was robbed of a gold watch and chain, a knife, a bunch of keys, a lobster and some lozenges. Harding was returning home after spending the evening in Bath and was passing through the Prior Park Estate at about midnight when he was attacked by Trueman, who pushed Harding against the wall, holding him by the neck. She told Harding that if he 'squeaked' it would be the worse for him as she had two men behind her. Harding was 'rendered almost insensible by the pressure on his throat and begged the woman not to kill him, if she meant to rob him'. Trueman was able to wrest the items off Harding before running from the scene of the crime with Popjoy. Harding returned to Bath to raise the alarm with the police. Two hours later, the police returned to the scene of the crime and found Trueman and Popjoy with a candle searching the ground. As the police approached them, the pair blew out the candle in order to conceal their presence. Nevertheless, the felons were arrested. Lozenges and the stolen knife were found in Trueman's pocket, whilst more lozenges and part of a lobster were found at the home of Popjoy and Trueman. Despite a search of the crime scene the watch and chain remained missing. The pair were remanded in custody. (*The Times*)

— APRIL 30TH —

1839: A meeting of Chartists was held at Weston, Bath, who were said to be 'armed and with the worst kind of feeling towards the inhabitants.' The Chartists were met by three magistrates, two high constables, and many inhabitants of Weston, who were well prepared to deal with any trouble. Contemporary newspaper reports were not always sympathetic to Chartism. Chartists were a very diverse group of working-class people with differing grievances. The newspaper report goes on to state that the 'deluded Chartists' paraded the village of Twerton 'uttering the most savage yells, brandishing bludgeons in defiance, and firing off pistols.' The Chartists left Twerton, following a full-scale riot, at around 10.30 p.m. (*The Standard*)

———

1942: An ARP warden was sifting through the debris, following a Luftwaffe air raid on Bath three days previously. He noticed a black cat vanishing into a hole in the rubble and put his hand into the hole, hoping to rescue the cat. Imagine his surprise when a tiny hand grabbed his fingers. A rescue party was called out and after several hours, a 7-year-old child was pulled out alive from the rubble. (*Western Daily Press*)

- MAY 1ST -

1766: The *Bath Chronicle* announced the publication of a new work by poet Christopher Anstey (1724–1805). That work was *The New Bath Guide*, a satirical take on life in Bath. It was Anstey's first major work and proved very successful; Bath was at the height of fashion and the poems imitated local celebrities. *The New Bath Guide* ran to forty editions over the following fifty years and was much imitated. Anstey was born on October 31st 1724, the third child of Christopher Anstey (1680–1751), vicar of Brinkley, Cambridgeshire, and Mary Thompson, daughter of a squire. He was educated at Eton College and King's College, Cambridge, where he was admitted a fellow in 1745. However, in 1748 he was suspended after mocking the rules that the senior fellows followed in making a Latin declamation. On January 20th 1756 Anstey married Ann, the third daughter of Felix Calvert of Albury Hall, Hertfordshire. He and Ann went on to have thirteen children, of which eight outlived their father. A recurring fever caused Anstey to visit Bath annually until 1770, when he moved to Bath permanently. He was one of the first to move into the Royal Crescent. Anstey died on August 3rd 1845 and was buried at St Swithin's Church, Walcott, Bath. A monument was also placed in Poet's Corner, Westminster Abbey. (*Oxford Dictionary of National Biography*; Arthur L. Salmon, *Bath and Wells*, Blackie and Son, 1914)

~ MAY 2ND ~

1844: Born on September 29th 1760, William Thomas Beckford was the only legitimate son of William Beckford, a sugar plantation owner in Jamaica. He was born into a great deal of wealth, which he inherited in September 1781. In May 1783, he married Lady Margaret Gordon, aged 21, the daughter of an impoverished earl. Scandal broke out in 1784 when he was accused of having an affair with Louisa Beckford, wife of his cousin, Peter Beckford, and daughter of George Pitt MP, whilst at the same time being enamoured with William Courtenay, who was regarded as particularly handsome. The scandal caused Beckford to go abroad with his family. Beckford is best known for the novel *Vathek* (published 1787) and his travel writing. Beckford spent much of his life travelling and completed a grand tour of Europe before he became of age in 1780. On returning to England in 1796, Beckford was responsible for the building of Fonthill Abbey, a vast gothic structure with a tower designed by James Wyatt and hastily constructed. However, the abbey tower was never structurally sound and collapsed on a couple of occasions. In 1822, Beckford was forced to sell Fonthill Abbey, owing to the declining price of sugar. He moved to Bath where he constructed Beckford Tower, which stands to this day. It was completed in 1825 by Henry Edmund Goodridge and has a 120ft-high tower with commanding views of the countryside. Beckford died on May 2nd 1844 in Bath and he is buried in Lyncombe Cemetery. (*Oxford Diction of National Biography*; Bath Preservation Trust website; www.personal.psu.edu)

— MAY 3RD —

1844: It was reported that John Hancocks, a quarryman of Combe Down and measuring no more than 4ft in height, carried 3cwt of stone over a distance of 3 miles. He started from St Mary's Church, Bathwick, went up Bathwick Hill, over the Down to the White Hart at the foot of Widcombe Hill, completing the whole journey within half an hour. Hancocks, described as a 'rigid teetotaller', won a wager of half a sovereign. His preparation before the event was to eat 2lb beef, bread and drink two quarts of coffee for breakfast. (*The Standard*)

2012: Five hundred and fifty pounds was paid for giants' underwear at Tennants Auctioneers in Leyburn, North Yorkshire. The underwear belonged to Fred Kempster who lived in Bath and Wiltshire in the years prior to the First World War. At age 15, he was slightly taller than average, but grew to 7ft 11in by the age of 19, when doctors measured his height. Consequently, he was known as the Bath or Avebury Giant. His full height has never been confirmed, but it appears he continued to grow after doctors measured his height. He died aged 29 from pneumonia. His undertaker measured him at 8ft 4in and made a 9ft coffin for him. (*Bath Chronicle*)

~ MAY 4TH ~

1877: *The Times* reported on a 16-year-old boy, Charles Bolwell, who had tried to emulate Thomas Fellows, a celebrated tree climber in the Bath district, with near-fatal results. Fellows had climbed a tall poplar tree and affixed a bell to the upper branches, and Bolwell attempted to carry out a similar feat, selecting another tall tree. Like Fellows, Bolwell had a bell in his pocket to tie to one of the upper branches so that it would ring in the wind. He had climbed high into the tree, when he slipped and fell. His fall, however, was broken when his left arm became caught in a forked branch. Bolwell was left dangling in that position for over an hour while his rescuers searched in vain for a ladder that was tall enough to reach him. Several other boys climbed the tree to sustain his weight and so relieve the tension on his left arm. Eventually, it was decided to tie Bolwell to the tree, to relieve his left arm, and cut the tree down around him. At this time, Thomas Fellows appeared on the scene and climbed the tree, up and above Bolwell, eventually succeeding in freeing him. Bolwell's left arm was bruised and very swollen, and a subscription was raised for Fellows. (*The Times*)

⌐ MAY 5TH ⌐

1921: On September 7th 1855, William Green was born in Bristol. He became famous for developing motion pictures and as a photographer. He was first introduced to photography when apprenticed aged 14 at the studio of Maurice Guttenburg. Four years later he had his own studio and married Victoria Mariana Helena Friese. The family moved to Bath where he owned two shops. It was in Bath that Friese-Green met John Arthur Roebuck Rudge (1837–1903), who had adapted the magic lantern to create the illusion of movement. Friese-Green thus became interested in moving pictures and in 1888 he developed a camera for taking a series of photographs. He then worked with Mortimer Evans, producing a patent for a camera that could take ten pictures a second. Because of his interest in inventing cameras he went bankrupt twice in 1891 and 1917. In 1905, Friese-Green perfected a system where successive images were taken through alternating filters and the printed frames dyed the colours of the filters. When projected at sufficient speed it gave the impression of colour. However, he died poor; on May 5th 1921 Friese-Green made a speech to film distributers in London, where he wondered what a film of his life would be like. He died a few minutes afterwards with only 1*s* 10*d* in his purse – all the money he had. (*Oxford Dictionary of National Biography*)

~ MAY 6TH ~

1939: The last tram ran in Bath on this day. Tram car No. 22 was driven by the Mayor, Captain Adrian Hopkins, and Chief Inspector Hale, and left the Guildhall at midnight with 100 passengers on board. Special tickets were issued for the final journey and placed in souvenir wallets. Progress was slow as the tram had to battle its way through the crowds that lined its route on the way back to the depot in Walcon Street. The trams were later broken up at the Glasshouse Sidings, located opposite St Martin's Hospital. (David & Jonathon Falconer, *A Century of Bath*, Sutton, 1999)

1954: Roger Bannister, a former pupil at the City of Bath Boys' School, became the first person to run a mile in under 4 minutes, during a meeting between the Amateur Athletics Association and the Oxford University Athletic Club. The exact time was 3 minutes 59.4 seconds. Thirty years later, to the day, in 1984, the University of Bath awarded Bannister with an honorary doctorate. (*The Times*; *Oxford Dictionary of National Biography*; David & Jonathan Falconer, *A Century of Bath*, Sutton, 1999)

─ May 7th ─

1870: Bath Green Park station opened. The station was then at the end of a 10-mile branch from the Midland Railway's Birmingham to Bristol mainline. The station façade was Georgian and two wooden platforms allowed for trains with up to nine carriages on the southern platform and eight on the northern platform. The platform, however, was not long enough for the summer specials that consisted of twelve or more coaches. The atmosphere of the station has been described as a 'perpetual Sunday afternoon', broken only by the summer specials and the arrival of the Pines Express – a train that ran from Manchester to Bournemouth, via Bath. Little was done to modernise the station or improve the services over the lines that served it. Although, for much of its life, it was known as Bath Queen Square, under British Railways it became Bath Green Park. The last service left the station on March 7th 1966. Closure of the station had been planned to take place two months earlier. However, since alternative road provision had not been made, an interim emergency service consisting of four trains leaving Green Park in the early morning and evening ran over the Somerset and Dorset line. (Robin Atthill, *The Somerset and Dorset Railway* Pan, 1970)

— MAY 8TH —

1907: Colonel George Vincent Fosbury (1833–1907), who had been awarded the Victoria Cross, died on this day. After attending Eton College, he joined the Bengal Army in 1952. His actions on October 30th 1863, whilst a lieutenant in the 4th Bengal Army, earned him the Victoria Cross: he led a party of his regiment to capture the Crag Piquet after his garrison had been attacked by the enemy, killing sixty men in hand-to-hand combat. He was the first man to reach the top of the Crag during the battle. When his commanding officer, Lieutenant Colonel Keys, was injured during the attack, Fosbury led a party to pursue the routed enemy. Fosbury was also an inventor and designer of firearms. In 1895, he patented a small self-cocking revolver. It was produced by the Webley & Scott Revolver & Arms Company. The gun known as the Webley-Fosbury Automatic Revolver was produced as a six-shot .455 calibre and as an eight-shot 0.38 calibre weapon. After his death, he was buried in the churchyard of St Mary the Virgin, Bathwick. (www.victoriacross.org.uk; www.nam.ac.uk)

~ May 9th ~

1848: 'In the large and populous parish of Tiverton containing, according to the last census, 3,342 souls, there has not been a death from natural causes since 9th of May last to the present time, a period of five months.' (*Berrow's Worcester Journal*)

———

2013: Councillors of the Bath and North-East Somerset Council approved a £5 million redevelopment plan to reopen the seventeenth-century Colonnades. The four-phase plan involves the building of cafés and restaurants and the council hopes that the project will bring in revenue of approximately £300,000 per year. The Colonnades, whose columns start just above water level, are located next to Pulteney Weir and run from there to the Parade Gardens. The Colonnades were built in around 1770 and were used for a number of leisure purposes; vaults were even built along the riverbank to stable horses. Gradually the area fell out of favour and many of the Colonnades' rooms are used as a store by the council. (www.bbc.co.uk)

~ MAY 10TH ~

1840: 'A most singular robbery' took place at the home of Mr Windsor of Park Street, Bath. The family were out attending church, when the cook, who was the only member of the household, answered the door to a man of 'gentlemanly appearance'. On hearing that Mr Windsor was at church, he requested that he be allowed to write a note for Mr Windsor, or to await his return. The cook showed the visitor into the drawing room, where he was left and the servant saw nothing more of him. When Mr Windsor returned from church, the cook told Mr Windsor of his visitor. On entering the drawing room, Mr Windsor discovered that his visitor was gone and the suspicion of robbery naturally arose. Nothing appeared to be taken. It was only much later, when Mrs Windsor returned, that it was discovered that a box belonging to Mrs Windsor, that contained a great deal of cash, had been smashed open. The box contained 536 gold sovereigns which had been taken, but £200 in bank notes and some gold watches, also stored in the box, had been left. No one heard the thief leave. 'The great imprudence of keeping a large sum of money unprotected', so owed to Mrs Winsdor who kept the money secretly, saving it for when her youngest daughter was married. It was suspected that a previous servant of the house might have provided intelligence about where the money was kept to the robber. (*The Times*)

‹ MAY 11TH ›

973: According to the *Anglo-Saxon Chronicle*, the Coronation of King Edgar (943/4–975) took place at Bath Abbey on Whitsun, which in 973 fell on May 11th. Edgar was the younger son of King Edmund (920/1–946) and his first wife Ælfgifu. Very little is known about the reign of Edgar. The *Anglo-Saxon Chronicle* contains only ten entries relating to him. This has led the historian Sir Frank Stenton to comment that his reign was 'singularly devoid of incident'. In 955, Edgar seems to have been made King of the Mercians, although historians are divided as to whether Edgar seized the kingdom from his elder brother Eadwig or whether they agreed to a partition. On the death of his brother in 959 Edgar became the king of all England. The delay in his consecration has also vexed historians. One suggestion is that the coronation was delayed until he reached the age of 30, which was the minimum age for a bishop. This seems likely, as the *Anglo-Saxon Chronicle* states that the coronation took place in his thirtieth year, when Edgar was 29. Another suggestion is that Edgar gained rule over all Britain, but this view is countered by the lack of evidence of territorial expansion in his reign. It seems unlikely that we will ever know. Edgar died aged 31/2 and is buried at Glastonbury Abbey. (*Oxford Dictionary of National Biography*; Bath Abbey website)

‑ MAY 12TH ‑

1660: Bath was the first city to proclaim Charles II as king, following the restoration of the monarchy bringing to the end the Protectorate and Britain's governance without monarchical involvement. (Tom Bradshaw, *Bath: A Pocket Miscellany*, The History Press, 2011)

——

1829: William Henry Smith, who went under the pseudonym John Bailey, was executed at Ilchester for passing forged bank notes of the Bank of Devizes, amounting to £10. He had managed to pass on twenty-seven of the thirty forged notes that were in his possession. The day before his execution, he spoke to his wife for two hours and 'the parting was most affecting'. He even stated that he was 'the happiest man in gaol!' He hoped that he would be able to walk to the execution drop unaided, but requested someone to be with him should that be required. In the event, Smith kept his eyes shut until he needed to ascend the stairs to his execution. Smith had been 'respectably brought up' and was a traveller in a commercial house for several years, but latterly had been living in reduced circumstances. (*The Times*)

⚊ MAY 13TH ⚊

1890: A prize-fight between Morgan Crowther of Newport and Hames 'Chaffy' Hayman of Bedminster took place at Brook Street Hall, Bath. The men, however, were later arrested for having taken part in the illegal prizefight. The trial, at the Bath Quarter Sessions, took place later that year on October 18th. Benjamin Hyams of Hackney also stood in the dock for aiding and abetting the pair. The trial was somewhat farcical: first, the trial was held up for half an hour because Mr Wilson, who was defending Hayman, missed his train (he was reprimanded by the Recorder as a result); then one of the jurors was asked to leave the box after admitting that he was present at the prizefight for which Crowther and Hayman were indicted. The case for prosecution argued that although the fighters were wearing gloves, they were too small – a poor attempt to comply with Queensbury Rules. (Queensbury Rules were first published in 1867 to promote fair play in the sport.) Furthermore, one of Hayman's eyes was forced shut after being punched in the face by Crowther. By acting as timekeeper, Hyams was aiding and abetting an illegal fight. Inspector Sutton of the Bath police was called to give evidence but had to admit that two officers of the Somerset constabulary were present for pleasure. He also denied that he combined business with pleasure. After retiring for an hour, the jury found the prisoners guilty of assault and Crowther and Hayman were each fined £25 and had to keep the peace for six months in sureties of £50. Hyams was fined £5. (*Western Mail*)

~ MAY 14TH ~

1784: On this day, four felons escaped from Bath Prison. They were: Michael Andrews, who shot two persons; James Grimes; William Hill and Thomas Wiltshire. After they escaped, they were seen heading in the direction of Warminster before they committed a robbery at Old Down. The jail keeper was deemed incompetent and lost his job following the escape. Three of the four men – Hill, Andrews and Grimes – were recaptured later that month. Hill was taken at the Griffin Horse Fair and Andrews and Grimes were taken at Elbroad Street in nearby Bristol. It is not known whether Wiltshire was ever captured. (*Bath Chronicle*)

———

2013: Bath Abbey began an exhibition of art by homeless people living in the city. The exhibition, entitled 'Think Different', includes film, photography, artwork and creative writing. The exhibition aimed to challenge perceptions of homeless people's potential. The art project is run by the social enterprise Clean Slate, and aims to give homeless people the chance to learn new skills and to express their opinions on alcohol and drug addiction, homelessness and mental health issues in different ways. (www.bbc.co.uk)

— MAY 15TH —

1836: A destructive fire took place at a clothing factory owned by a Mr Wilkins in Twerton. The fire destroyed the whole building and the property it contained, which was thought to have been worth around £50,000. The fire put 1,000 people out of employment from a factory regarded as one of the largest and most successful in the south-west region at this time. (*The Morning Post*)

2008: The *Bath Chronicle* reported that 'an anonymous expression of "art"' got 'people in Bath talking' when a red postbox was painted in sparkling gold paint from top to bottom in a guerrilla art attack. The box, situated on The Paragon, is used by many residents and businesses in the district. The identity of the 'artist' was unknown and people were divided over whether this should be seen as an act of vandalism or art. Royal Mail was unequivocal regarding the pillar box's 'facelift' as an act of vandalism and encouraged anyone with information to contact the police. Only one pillar box was affected. A spokeswoman from the Royal Mail commented that postboxes were sometimes 'customised' by members of the public. (*Bath Chronicle*)

~ MAY 16TH ~

1884: 'Shortly before nine o'clock yesterday morning a boiler explosion occurred at the works of the Bath Paper Mills Company (limited), Trevarno Mill, Bathford ... besides the personal injuries sustained, a portion of the premises was reduced to a complete wreck ... With such force did the explosion occur that the boiling room was reduced to a wreck, a portion of the fitting room destroyed and a part of the boiler fell through the roof covering the steam boilers and pierced one of them. Hobbs and Gardener, the former being the "grass-boiler" and the latter being his assistant, were seated on the floor of the boiling room, through which the top of the boiler protrudes, it is supposed at breakfast, and the floor being rent they fell through, heaps of debris falling around them. They are the most seriously injured of all, and must have escaped sudden death by little short of a miracle.' (*Bristol Mercury*)

1985: Lord Spencer, father of Diana, Princess of Wales, drew a glass of water from the Pump Room in Bath, when the fountain reopened for the first time in seven years. The fountain was closed in 1978 after the water was contaminated by an amoeba and led to the death of a girl. A pure new source had since been found and visitors to the Pump Room could taste the water for 25p a glass. (*The Times*)

‒ May 17th ‒

1881: in the southern part of Bath, a man named Tom Amos caused a 'sensation' when he tried to murder his sister, Emily Amos. It seems that Tom Amos, in the days prior to the attack on Emily, had started to exhibit unusual behaviour. On the day he attacked Emily, he was said to have been in a 'raving condition'. As Emily was returning home, Tom attacked her with a hatchet. Emily turned and ran but Tom caught her with a blow on the head. Fortunately, the weapon was blunt and Emily's thick hat that she had been wearing absorbed the force of the blow and almost certainly saved her life. Tom sought refuge in a grocer's shop and a policeman tried to secure him, but was unable to do so. A civilian beat Tom with a piece of timber which enabled him to be secured and taken into custody. What is remarkable about this affair is that Emily escaped with only slight injuries. (*Berrow's Worcester Journal*; *Bristol Mercury*)

- MAY 18TH -

1825: Peter Layng, aged 95, died after he fell down the steps at the bottom of Walcot Parade. He had been pushed down the steps by his wife, aged 57 – the couple had been married for less than one month. Peter Layng had previously been before the magistrates after he attempted to kill himself by cutting his throat. The verdict at the inquest was manslaughter and Peter's wife was remanded at Shepton Mallet Gaol to await trial at the next assizes. (*Bath Journal*)

2012: A painting which was left for over sixty years in the Victoria Art Gallery storeroom was authenticated as being by the artist, Maurice de Vlaminick (1876–1958). A research grant from the Art Fund allowed the painting, which was bought by the gallery for just £28 in 1938, to be authenticated by experts in Paris. The picture now takes pride of place amongst the gallery's collection. Maurice de Vlaminick was a leading member of the Fauve group of artists, who came to prominence during the first decade of the twentieth century. Members also included André Derain and Henri Matisse, and a characteristic of the group was their intense use of colour. (*The Western Daily Press*)

‒ MAY 19TH ‒

2008: A public art project was officially launched in the centre of Bath, which saw businesses sponsor over 100 of 'King Bladud's Pigs'. King Bladud was a legendary king of the Britons, and it is said that he studied at Athens where he contracted leprosy. He returned to Britain but his leprous skin would not allow him to inherit the throne, so he became a swineherd in the Avon Valley. Bladud's pigs also contracted the disease, but were cured when they were allowed to roll in hot mud around the Bath's springs. Bladud noticed this and he too immersed himself in the mud and was cured. Consequently, he was able to claim the throne. Since Bladud was grateful for his cure, he founded the city of Bath. One hundred and six model pigs were placed in the city's street and parks in 2008, and were displayed in Bath until the end of September that year. One month later, on October 31st 2008, the model pigs were auctioned for charity with the prices paid for them ranging from £1,250 to £21,000. The artists received 25 per cent of the sale price. The rest of the money helped to fund the Two Tunnels Project to reopen two disused railway tunnels into Bath and create a new cycle path into the city. (*Bath Chronicle*; www.kingbladudspigs.org)

— May 20th —

1977: Somerset County Cricket Club beat Australia, over three days, for the first time at Bath. Somerset elected to play this match away from County headquarters and enjoyed superb weather during the game. Australia batted first, and Greg Chappell made 99 runs by lunch, complete with 3 sixes and 14 fours. However only 55 runs were scored in the next 8 wickets and Australia made only 232 in their first innings. It was at least 100 runs less than expected. Somerset's opening batsmen put at least 80 runs on the scoreboard, with Denning scoring 39. However Somerset's next three batsmen fell quickly with Richards (18), Close (0) and Breakwell (23) making 141 for 4. Brian Rose eventually made a century and Ian Botham allowed Somerset to declare at 340 for 5. Australia got off to a poor start in their second innings and were soon on 18 for 2. Hopes for Australia were raised with David Hookes, who scored 85 runs in 90 minutes. Hookes went on to score 108 before being bowled out by Burgess. Hookes' second innings performance included 4 sixes and 15 fours. Australia was dismissed for 289, giving Somerset a target of 182 runs in 225 minutes. The opening Somerset batsmen, Rose and Denning, again made a good start gaining 50 runs and roughly a run per minute. Richards managed a quick 53 and Botham added 39 to give Somerset victory over the Australians. (Eddie Lawrence, *Classic Somerset Matches* Tempus, 2002)

— MAY 21ST —

1862: A case of arson poisoning occurred at No. 3 St George's Parade, Bath. The property was central to a legal dispute and a Mr Brinkworth claimed to be the landlord. The case had given Brinkworth considerable expense and the dispute had turned acrimonious. Indeed, Brinkworth had been brought before the magistrate several times charged with assault and had even threatened the solicitor representing the other party, whom Brinkworth believed was trying to deprive him of the property in some way. Mrs James occupied the lower part of the premises and, on this date, Brinkworth entered the property and went into one of the upper rooms. It was a considerable time before he left the property. A fire was reported shortly afterwards, and a hose truck was immediately dispatched to the scene and the fire extinguished. It was discovered that in one of the middle-storey rooms, some wood piled on a table had been set alight. The table had been pushed against a wooden partition and the window covered with a carpet. The room and the room above had been covered in turpentine. Furthermore, straw and rags had been spread around and soaked in the same liquid. The building was not insured and it was thought that Brinkworth was acting solely on spite. (*The Bristol Mercury*)

~ MAY 22ND ~

1973: Festivities began in Bath to celebrate 1,000 years of English monarchy. Sixty events were planned, including exhibitions, lectures, a tattoo and the European Chess Championships. The main exhibition was made by the Bath Festival Society and the Holbourne Museum, which illustrated the world of the Anglo-Saxon kings and the life and times of Edgar, with many examples of Anglo-Saxon artefacts. The other exhibition was staged by the Royal College of Arts which presented 1,000 years of the lives of the kings and queens of England. The date of the celebrations was chosen as it was 1,000 years since the coronation of Edgar, at Bath on May 11th 973. The discrepancy in the dates is the result of the 'loss' of eleven days when Britain changed from the Julian calendar to the Gregorian calendar. (*The Times*)

2012: Crowds up to eight people deep lined the streets of Bath to watch the Olympic torch relay. Torch bearers in Bath included Jason Gardiner, 2004 Olympic 4x100m relay champion, who was chosen for his contribution to athletics and inspiring young people in Bath to take up more sport. Modern pentathlete Kate Allenby also held the torch through Bath, as did Eleanore Reagan, who was nominated after setting up her Challenge Africa charity. (www.thisisbath.co.uk)

∼ MAY 23RD ∼

1754: John Wood the Elder was born in Bath and baptised in St James' Church on August 26th 1704. He was educated in the building trade by his father and became a joiner in Soho, London. Over the next six years he became a principal builder on the Cavendish-Harley Estate, a development to the north of Oxford Street. Woods acted as surveyor for a house being built by James Brydges, the 1st Duke of Chandos. It was through Chandos that Wood came back to Bath, in order to give the Duke better accommodation. Wood saw Bath as ripe for building and writing, and in 1725 his scheme proposed a number of visual centres, including the building of 'a grand Place of Assembly, to be called the Royal Forum of Bath; another place, no less magnificent, for the Exhibition of Sports, to be called the Grand Circus; and a third place, of equal state with either of the former, for the Practice of Medicinal Exercises, to be called the Imperial Gymnasium.' The Roman influence can be seen in his early buildings, namely Chapel Court and Queen Square, begun in 1728. Other projects include The Parades, begun as a speculation by Wood in 1740, and The Circus, begun in 1754, which is the earliest circus in England. He died in Bath on this date. He is buried in St Mary's Church, Swainswick, a few miles to the north of the city. (*Oxford Dictionary of National Biography*; Nikolaus Pevsner, *The Buildings of England: North Somerset and Bristol*, Penguin, 1958)

~ MAY 24TH ~

1862: Newspapers reported on a military accident that took place in Bath with fatal results. 'On Friday [23rd May] afternoon, while the Militia, who were undergoing their customary drill in the Sydenham-field, were standing at ease, one of the men, to show his agility, walked about upon the palms of his hands. Another private, named Creech, of Galloway-buildings, in this city, attempted a similar feat, but after throwing himself forward on his hands he fell backwards, and his bayonet dropping from its sheath at the same time the point of the weapon entered his back as he reached the ground, penetrating a depth of several inches. He bled most profusely, and, though he was promptly attended by Drs Wilson and Michael, surgeons of the regiment, who were in the field, he died soon after he reached the United Hospital, whither he was conveyed in a fly.' (*Bristol Mercury*)

1927: The Bath and West Show, which was to start the following day, marked the 150th anniversary of the society and, with one day to go, *The Times* promised its readers that 'if the level of the Oxfordshire meeting last week is an indication, the quality will be equally satisfactory'. (*The Times*)

~ MAY 25TH ~

1828: A 'ranter's meeting' took place on Coombe Down today. They appear to have been a group of non-conformist Christians, apparently seeking a direct experience of the Holy Spirit. The meeting is recorded in Revd John Skinner's diary. Revd Skinner, who was rector of Camerton, does not portray them sympathetically: 'I understand from the Bath papers that a number of my parishioners attended the Ranters' Camp Meeting on Coombe Down last Sunday: there were three wagon and their female preachers ... A most barbarous scene was then exhibited, men and women ranting and roaring and bellowing till they were black in the face, calling upon the Spirit to come down upon them – I presume in allusion to the descent of the Holy Spirit on the Apostles, as recorded in the service of the day. Old Smallcombe, who staid to receive the Sacrament, on my asking whether he had been there? answered in the affirmative. On my expressing myself surprised that anyone who had the least sense should go such a distance to witness the exposure of folly, he replied, if I had heard them myself I should not have called it folly, since the Lord was indeed among them!'

~ May 26th ~

1889: Ann Paul died after being struck on the head with a poker by her daughter, Gertrude Georgina Paul. Mother and daughter had been quarrelling. Ann Paul was taken to the Royal United Hospital but died from her injuries. Her daughter stood trial and was found guilty of Ann's murder, but was declared insane and ordered to be detained at Her Majesty's pleasure. (*Berrow's Worcester Journal*)

1997: One hundred thousand yellow plastic ducks were released into the River Avon at Bath, with the aim of raising money for Water Aid. It was expected that the event would raise £50,000 for projects in Ethiopia. Hundreds of onlookers lined the banks in the hope that their £1 sponsored duck would cross the finish line first to win an eleven-day holiday in Iceland. Wessex Water sponsored the race and ensured that all the plastic ducks were safely gathered back in to safeguard the environment. The current record for the largest duck race took place on the River Thames over a 1km (0.6mile) stretch on September 6th 2009. The event was organised by the Great British Duck Race (UK) and raised over £100,000 for various charities including the NSPCC. (*The Times*; www.guinnessworldrecords.com)

~ MAY 27TH ~

1874: A man named Weeks, a labourer in a glass factory, travelled to Bath from Bristol to visit the races. Whilst there, he went into the boxing tent, put on some gloves and tried his hand in the ring. He was dealt a severe blow that sent him to the floor. The man who accompanied him picked him up and offered him brandy, but was unable to persuade his friend to go with him back to Bristol. Weeks was later found lying 'insensible' in Landsdown, and was taken to the Royal United Hospital. He died from his injuries. A post-mortem examination found that he had suffered 'concussion of the brain and a broken blood vessel in the head.' (*Bristol Mercury*)

1987: *The Times* reported on Bath Abbey's surprising decision to ban applause at its concerts there, instead instructing audience members to stand after each performance to show their appreciation. The rector, Revd Geoffrey Lester, stated that 'some people like applause and some don't – we don't. Neither did Sir Adrian Boult. That is enough said.' Bath International Festival stated that it accepted the conditions. However, the audience defied the ban, following a recital by organist David Liddle. He stated that 'I'm glad they all applauded; it would have been horrible if the end had been met by silence.' Indeed, had the audience followed their programme instructions to stand at the end of the recital, Liddle would be unaware of their appreciation – he is blind. (*The Times*)

~ MAY 28TH ~

1938: Alice Park was officially opened. The park was a gift from Herbert Montgomery MacVicar, a Bath philanthropist of The Elms, London Road. The park is named after his wife, Frances Alice Harriet, who had died eighteen months previously in November 1936, aged 53. They were a devoted couple and Herbert was left devastated by her loss. After her death, he set about transforming the piece of meadow at the back of their home. The park was to be for local people to enjoy and included a playing field for children. It was endowed in perpetuity to ensure that it would not close for lack of funds. Very little is known of the MacVicars. Herbert was born into great wealth, in Rochford, Essex, in 1872 and the couple moved to Bath in the early 1930s to The Elms, but did not venture out very much. Herbert seems to have been well connected and a great fan of cricket. The famous cricketer W.G. Grace was a family friend and infrequent visitor to his Bath home. Herbert MacVicar also met Queen Mary the Queen Mother twice during the Second World War when she visited Alice Park to plant fruit trees. Herbert MacVicar died in July 1957 at the age of 85. (*The Times*; Bryan Chalker 'The Hero of Alice Park' in *The Larkhall News* August 2009)

~ MAY 29TH ~

1811: The Duke d'Angouleme and his wife, Marie Thérèse of France, arrived in Bath during the evening. Marie Thérèse was the daughter of the former king of France, Louis XVI, who was executed during the French Revolution. The following morning the couple walked about the city and since they were little known, they excited little attention. It was only when news of their arrival had circulated the city that the public began to identify them. By the afternoon a crowd had gathered around the White Horse Inn to witness their departure. (*The Times*)

1828: The rector of Camerton, Revd John Skinner, described the following journey towards Bath: 'Mrs William Skinner and Anna [John Skinner's wife] went to Bath in my phaeton. In their way through the plantations they dropped Owen's military cloak, and a poor man brought me. As he was a stranger to the place and, I believe, much distressed, I rewarded him so that it was an altogether a lucky occurrence to him, and he was well repaid for his honesty.' (John Skinner, *Journal of a Somerset Rector*, Howard Combes & Arthur N. Bax (eds), John Murray, 1930)

~ MAY 30TH ~

1805: Sir William Pulteney (1729–1805), politician and property developer, died at Bath House in Piccadilly, London. He was born William Johnson Westerhall in Dumfriesshire, educated at Edinburgh University and admitted to the Scottish bar in 1751. In 1759, he moved to London where he gained £400 per annum in customs and excise. In 1760 he married Frances, the daughter and sole heir of Daniel Pulteney MP. Lord Bath's immense fortune was passed to General Harry Pulteney in 1764 and when he died the estate passed to Daniel, and then on to Frances. From this point, William and Frances adopted the Pulteney name and spent considerable time developing his wife's estate. The estate in Bath was developed by the building of Pulteney Bridge linking the city with Bathwick. The bridge was designed by Robert Adam, who also drew up plans for development in Bathwick. However, only the bridge was built according to his plans. Development around Great Pulteney Street proceeded over the next thirty years. It is perhaps his most tangible monument to his work. Pulteney also served as an MP, beginning with Cromarty in 1768. He did not make a will and died intestate. His personal estate passed to his widow and daughter, whilst that English estates went to the Countess of Bath. The Scottish estates were inherited by his nephew, Sir George Johnstone of Westerhall. Pulteney was buried at Westminster Abbey. (*Oxford Dictionary of National Biography*)

~ MAY 31ST ~

1884: William Jay Bolton (1816–1884), who was born in Bath, was a pioneer revivalist of the 'cinque cento' style. Bolton's earliest artwork was a Bath panorama. Bolton rose at 4 a.m. and climbed Beechen Cliff to get a good view of the city, before it was obscured by chimney smoke. The resulting picture is now in the Victoria Art Gallery, Bath. The family moved to America in 1836–37, and it was here that he produced many of the stained-glass windows for Christ Church in Pelham, New York. In 1848, he returned to England and settled near Cambridge, where he studied theology. He was commissioned to undertake the large east window of St Peter's Church, West Lynn, and undertook many other smaller commissions. His artistic career ended when he entered the Anglican Church. He held a number of posts before coming back to Bath to the parish of St James. Bolton was now aged 65 and he was hoping for a quieter living. However, Bolton found his small parish a 'hotbed of vice' with twenty brothels nearby. Bolton went to brothel owners, remonstrated with them and when that failed to produce the desired result, he brought legal action against the women. If convicted, he asked that the women were pardoned on the condition that they swore to reform their lives. He died on May 28th and was buried in St James' cemetery on this date. (*Bristol Mercury*; Willene B. Clark, *The Stained Glass Art of William Jay Bolton*, Syracuse University Press, 1992)

– JUNE 1ST –

1853: Sir Charles Abraham Elton (1778–1853), poet and theologian, died in Bath on this day. On leaving Eton, he went into the 48th Regiment of Foot and rose to the rank of Captain. In 1804 he married Sarah Smith and had five sons and eight daughters. Tragedy struck in 1819 when two of his boys, aged 14 and 13, decided to explore Birnbeck, a small rocky island connected to Weston-Super-Mare at low tide by a causeway. The boys were exploring the rock pools but did not realise they were in danger of being trapped by the rising tide, even when a young woman, who was passing, shouted a warning from the mainland. By the time the boys realised the danger, the causeway was already underwater. The boys made desperate attempts to reach the shore, but the younger was swept away by the incoming tide. The elder boy swam after him and he too drowned. The bodies of both boys were never recovered. The following year, in 1820, Elton published one of his more memorable poetical works, born out of the tragic events of 1819, entitled 'The Brothers: A Monody'. In 1818, he published *An Appeal to Scripture in Defence of the Unitarian Faith*. In 1827, Elton recanted his Unitarian Faith in favour of the established church, publishing *Deuterai phrontides: Second Thoughts on the Person of Christ, on Human Sin, and on the Atonement*. (*Oxford Dictionary of National Biography*)

~ JUNE 2ND ~

1972: The ceremonial opening of the Bath weir scheme took place. Sir Edward Howard, Lord Mayor of London, cruised in a 35ft red and white admiral's barge up the River Avon. The Lord Mayor, with several other dignitaries all in ceremonial dress, came ashore for the ceremony. The Lord Mayor was accompanied by the Lady Mayoress, the Aldermanic Sheriff, the Chief Commoner, the high officers of the Corporation of London and Alderman Alec Ricketts, Mayor of Bath. The most striking feature of the weir, located just below Pulteney Bridge, is its v-shape. The weir was constructed following yet another heavy flood in 1960. In addition to the weir, between 1963 and 1972 the Avon was dredged, its banks raised and reinforced with sheet piling. The scheme was carried out by the Bristol and Avon River Authority under the direction of the Authority's engineer, Frank Greenhalgh. The works also received the Civic Trust Award and the commemorative plaque can still be seen in the parapet of the Grand Parade, which overlooks the weir. (*The Times*; www.bath-heritage.co.uk)

~ June 3rd ~

1871: The stationmaster of Bath received a telegram that the Duke of Edinburgh would pass through the station on the Paddington-Plymouth express. The mayor, on hearing the news, immediately convened a meeting of the aldermen, councillors, and representatives of the clergy and the legal profession and volunteers in order to greet the Duke. Various preparations were quickly put in hand: an address was drawn up, reporters were sent for, the Corporation regalia were cleaned and a special posse of police were detailed for duty. A great many people thronged the Guildhall, anxious to meet the royal visitor. Their hopes were dashed, however, when it was announced that the Duke had changed his mind and passed through, at 45mph, on a special train that did not stop at Bath. The crowd were infuriated and complained bitterly that they had been the victims of a cruel hoax. Blame was attached to the mayor and the council as it was felt that they had not properly ascertained His Royal Highness' intentions. The mayor tried to console the crowd, stating that short though the notice of Prince Alfred's passage through had been, Bath had at all events done its duty, and shown its readiness to testify its loyalty. (*Nottinghamshire Guardian*)

~ June 4th ~

1894: The country was severely affected by thunderstorms. At Bath, John Rymes, a corporation foreman, was struck by lightning whilst walking along the road and was taken back to his home 'insensible'. (*Morning Post*)

2012: A hot-air balloon was forced to land in the road near Green Park at 9 p.m. The newly restored balloon was passing over the city when it encountered difficulties. The balloon was not able to gain much height owing to the weather conditions and it is said to have passed a building with only 8ft to spare. Several attempts were made to land, but each time the balloon tried to land a small gust of wind blew the balloon off course. Residents in the Green Park area of the city contacted police at around 8.40 p.m., stating that a balloon appeared to be having difficulties. Police closed roads around Green Park and a number of officers grabbed the basket to stop it being dragged away. Around twenty officers attended the incident and all sixteen passengers escaped unhurt. Police were satisfied with the pilot's explanation and said that no further action would be taken. (*The Telegraph*)

~ June 5th ~

1739: John Wesley, preacher, argued with Beau Nash, Bath Master of Ceremonies, in this journal extract: 'There was a great expectation at Bath of what a noted man might do there, and I was much entreated not to preach; because no one knew what might happen. By this report I also gained a much larger audience, among them were many of the rich and great. I told them plainly, the Scripture had concluded them all under sin – high and low, rich and poor, one with another. Many of them seemed to be a little surprised when their champion [Nash] appeared, and coming close to me, asked by what authority I did these things. I replied, "By the authority of Jesus Christ, conveyed to me by the (now) Archbishop of Canterbury, when he laid hands upon me and said, 'Take thou authority to preach the Gospel.'" After further argument about the legality of the meeting, Nash replied. "I say it is [a conventicle]: And, beside, your preaching frightens people out of their wits." "Sir, did you ever hear me preach?" Wesley asked Nash for his name and finally Nash responded "I desire to know what this people comes here for": on which one replied, "Sir, leave him to me: let an old woman answer him. You, Mr. Nash, take care of your body; we take care of our souls; and for the food of our souls we come here." He replied not a word, but walked away.' (Elizabeth Jay (ed.), *The Journal of John Wesley: A Selection* Oxford University Press, 1987)

– JUNE 6TH –

1828: The public dissection of a man named Gilham, who had been executed on June 4th, continued. The body was taken to Bath United Hospital on June 5th, as executed criminals were one of the few legitimate sources of cadavers for medical study at the time. The dissection commenced at 4 a.m. on June 5th, under the direction of Mr Norman, the senior surgeon. It was overseen by sixty people, mainly other surgeons and students. The surgeons involved with the dissection 'only desisted for a slight breakfast'. By 2 p.m. the surgeons had dissected as far as the abdomen and Mr Soden, 'the next surgeon in eminence', gave a demonstration of the abdomen muscles followed by a demonstration of the 'auxiliary vessels'. In a further macabre twist, the following day (June 6th) the skin and thighs of the executed man were carefully removed and tanned. These pieces were given to others connected with the hospital. A contemporary newspaper report stated: 'Thus prepared the murderer's skin appears as thick as the leather ordinarily used for the soles of boots and shoes, and about the same colour.' Furthermore, some surgeons were disappointed that the brain was not going to be dissected. Those carrying out the dissection stated that this was in order to preserve the skeleton of the deceased. (*The Standard*)

~ June 7th ~

1947: The inaugural concert of the Bath Bach Choir took place at Bath Abbey, where Bach's *Mass in B Minor* was performed. The soloists at the concert were Isobel Baillie (Soprano), Eileen Pitcher (Contralto), Eric Greene (Tenor) and George Pizzey (Bass). The choir was founded by Cuthbert Bates, an established amateur musician. Bates was also a founding member of the Bath Bach festival. The original aim of the choir was to promote the work of J.S. Bach. The choir established a reputation for challenging programming and it was the first modern choir to perform Monteverde's *Vespers of 1610*. The choir continues to perform works from all eras. The current Director of Music is Nigel Perrin, who has held the post since 1990. (Bath Bach Choir website)

2009: Bath's new bus station in Dorchester Road finally opened at a cost of £14 million. The scheme, which formed part of the Southgate Development, had not been without opposition, as the new terminus was viewed as unsightly. Campaigners had also wanted the façade of Churchill House, an abandoned 1920s electricity company building, to be incorporated into the design. The campaigners were unsuccessful and Churchill House was demolished in order to make way for the new facility. (www.bbc.co.uk)

~ June 8th ~

1884: Edwina 'Winnie' Celia Trout was born in Newark Street, Bath. She became one of 713 survivors of the *Titanic* disaster. She was one of six children to Edwin Charles and Elizabeth Ellen Trout. Her father was landlord of the Edinburgh Caster (also known as the Lyncombe Brewery). One of Edwina's sisters had settled in Massachusetts, when she made her first visit to the United States in 1907. She crossed the channel no less than thirteen times during her lifetime. In 1912, she purchased her second-class ticket from Bell and Co. of Bath for £10 10s 10d for *Titanic*'s maiden voyage from Southampton on April 10th 1912. *Titanic*'s passenger list describes her as a 'shop assistant and domestic'. She berthed on E-deck, with two other women: Miss Susan Webster from Cornwall and Miss Nora Kean of Limerick. When disaster struck, Edwina made her way to Lifeboat No. 16 carrying a toothbrush, a bible and a small baby handed to her by a distraught (and ultimately doomed) father. The lifeboat had a capacity for sixty-five people but carried fifty-six to safety. Other lifeboats carried far fewer people. Her lifeboat was eventually rescued by RMS *Carpathia*, which, at 58 miles from *Titanic*, was the closest vessel to the stricken ship. Edwina eventually arrived in New York on April 18th. Edwina lived to be 100, dying in 1984. At that time she was the oldest *Titanic* survivor. (*Bath Chronicle*)

— JUNE 9TH —

1795: William White, a young man, was due to marry Maria Bally, a school teacher. However, Maria decided to break off their engagement when she found he had not been completely honest with her. On this day, William loaded a brace of pistols, walked coolly and purposefully into the school where Maria worked and shot her dead. The children ran out of the school, frightened by what they had seen, and cried out, 'Murder! The man has murdered Ma'am!' White came out of the school, discharged a pistol, crying out, 'I surrender myself to the justice of the law, for I have murdered her!' When White was brought before the justices, it was suggested to him that he might plead insanity. White replied, 'No,' and thanked them for the hint. He continued, 'I might play the hypocrite before men, but not before his maker.' (*The Times*)

1961: Bath (Green Park station) opened its doors to the 'Eleven o'clock Special' – a dance organised as part of the Bath festival with a shuttle service running over the Somerset and Dorset line to Wellow, where a barbeque was being held. Performances of *The Titfield Thunderbolt* were screened in the waiting room. (Robin Atthill, *The Somerset and Dorset Railway*, Pan, 1971)

~ June 10th ~

1846: 'James Hillier stood at the foot of a ladder whilst another workman ascended the ladder. The men were at work building a new church, St Matthew's Church, Cambridge Place, designed by G.P. Manners. One of the stones slipped as the workman climbed which hit Hillier on the head, fracturing his skull.' (Nicola Sly, *A Grim Almanac of Somerset*, The History Press, 2010; Nikolaus Pevsner, *The Buildings of England: North Somerset and Bristol*, Penguin, 1958)

2003: Cars gave way to cameras as Hollywood film-makers descended on Bath to make a film adaptation of William Makepeace Thackeray's novel *Vanity Fair*. Part of the city's historic centre was returned to its regency heyday, with 400 film extras wearing appropriate Georgian costume: top hats for the men, bonnets for the women and children decked out as street urchins. The film stars Reese Witherspoon as Becky Sharp, who defies her poverty-stricken background in order to ascend the social ladder. The script was written by Matthew Faulk, Mark Skeet and Julian Fellows, who is known for his scripts for *Gosford Park* (2001) and *Downton Abbey* (2010). However, drivers to Bath were forced to endure long diversions and shopkeepers on Pulteney Bridge complained of loss of earnings as the bridge led directly to the film set. (*The Times*)

— JUNE 11TH —

1875: The 10.01 a.m. Bath to Salisbury service derailed at Bathampton when the locomotive failed to take the points, causing it and the two leading coaches to overturn. One frightened passenger was killed when he jumped out of the train, only for a carriage to fall on him. A report in the *Bath Chronicle* stated that two men 'with much foresight took with them to the scene of the accident brandy and other stimulants which were found very useful'. (Colin G. Maggs, *The GWR Swindon to Bath Line*, Sutton, 2003)

———

1919: Bath Racecourse was sold by the Blathwayt family to the directors of Newbury Races for £12,750. Horseracing in Bath began at Claverton Down in the early eighteenth century. Meetings were infrequent until the 1770s. A few meetings were also held at Landsown, the current location of Bath Racecourse. After a gap of about fifteen years around the turn of the century, the Blathwayt family ensured that racing resumed at Landsdown in 1811, but for most of the nineteenth century, only one meeting was held. The Blathwayts continued to own the racecourse until the sale on this date. Under new ownership, the number of meetings was gradually increased. The racecourse is now owned by Northern Racing. Bath Racecourse is the highest flat racecourse in the country at 800ft (240m) above sea level and its course length measures 1 mile, 4 furlongs and 25 yards. (*The Times*; www.bath-racecourse.co.uk; Marion R. Halpenny, *British Racing & Racecourses*, Holmes & Son (Printers) 1971)

– JUNE 12TH –

1847: Shortly after midnight, firemen from a number of different insurance companies were alerted to a fire in the premises of Mr Long, a silk merchant. Police officers attended and a large crowd assembled around the building, apparently numbering in the thousands. The fire proved difficult to extinguish and threatened neighbouring properties. Burning embers spread out in all directions, descending on the roofs of houses and the abbey. Fortunately, fears that other fires may be started were not realised. The fire eventually burned out when Mr Long's premises, including most of his valuable stock, was destroyed. (*The Times*)

1881: 'A serious and extensive landslip has taken place and is continuing in a thickly-populated portion of Walcot parish, Bath, known as the Hedgemead district. Between twenty and thirty houses have already been rendered unsafe for habitation and are in course of demolition. The hill-side on which the slip has and is taking place was crowded with houses, but portions are now nothing more than complete ruin. The slip is moving towards the valley at the rate of one inch per day, and by disturbing foundations is wrecking all buildings on the affected area.' (*Daily News*)

~ JUNE 13TH ~

1889: The Duchess of Albany opened the Douche and Massage Baths. A general holiday was proclaimed, festivities arranged and the city decorated. The mayor, Dr Henry W. Freeman, who was also a Bath Royal United Hospital surgeon, led a tour of the new facilities, demonstrating the 'most modern appliances' that Bath now possessed. As medical science progressed, it was felt that Bath was lagging behind spas on the continent, such as Aix-les-Bains. As a result Dr H.W. Freeman and Major Charles Davis, the city surveyor, were sent on a tour of Europe to study the new treatments on offer. Their report encouraged the building of the Douche and Massage Baths on the corner of York Street and Stall Street. These baths contained a number of rooms including the Aix-les-Bains douche, Berthold vapour bath and an inhalation room. The new baths were very successful and doubled visitor revenue to the city. The baths claimed to cure a variety of conditions, from a stiff neck and muscular rheumatism to Scriviner's Palsy. The fashion for this type of medical treatment did not last all that long. By 1972, the baths were long derelict and consequently demolished in order to build an office block. (*The Times*; Barry Cuncliffe, *The City of Bath*, Sutton, 1986)

~ June 14th ~

1668: Diarist Samuel Pepys gives this account of his visit to the city: 'Up, and walked up and down the town, and saw a pretty good market-place, and many good streets, and very fair stone-houses. And so to the great Church, and there saw Bishop Montagu's tomb; and, when placed, did there see many brave people come, and, among others, two men brought in, in litters, and set down in the chancel to hear: but I did not know one face. Here a good organ; but a vain, pragmatical fellow preached a ridiculous, affected sermon, that made me angry, and some gentlemen that sat next me, and sang well. So home, walking round the walls of the City, which are good, and the battlements all whole ... So home to dinner, and after dinner comes Mr. Butts again to see me, and he and I to church, where the same idle fellow preached; and I slept most of the sermon. Thence home, and took my wife out and the girls, and come to this church again, to see it, and look over the monuments, where, among others, Dr. Venner and Pelling, and a lady of Sir W. Waller's; he lying with his face broken. So to the fields a little and walked, and then home.' (*Diary of Samuel Pepys*, George Bell, 1893)

~ JUNE 15TH ~

1843: At this time, in the major cities in Britain, considerable competition over man-powered vehicles raged. Local craftsmen often built complicated treadle-driven machines. In Bath, a tricycle working on a similar principle is described: 'It has three wheels, placed like those of a Bath chair. To the axletree of the two larger wheels are affixed a pair of treadles, which move on a hinge close to the small front wheel. By pressing down these treadles a few inches alternately with each foot the machine is propelled. The small front wheel is only for guiding. From it a handle passes to the rider, who is seated between the two larger wheels, and who does not move his body as well as his legs, as in the locomotive carriage. The present vehicle travels on level ground, with ease, at the rate of six miles an hour, and, with exertion, it will do eight. It will also ascent slight hills. The inventor lately came on it from Bath to Bristol in an hour and a half.' The tricycle is similar to the first true bicycle, which first appeared in 1839 and was made by Kirkpatrick Macmillan, a Scottish blacksmith. His machine involved the rear being driven by two treadles connected by rods to the crank arm on the back wheel. (*Berrow's Worcester Journal*; John Woodford, *The Story of the Bicycle*, Routledge & Kegan Paul, 1970; Serena Beeley, *A History of the Bicycle*, Studio, 1992)

— JUNE 16TH —

1920: James Farbrother made his first appearance in court charged with obtaining money to the value of £200 by false pretences. Farbrother rented a room in Brighton and appeared to be a man who dealt in typewriters. A Mr Booth agreed to buy some typewriters from him and paid two sums amounting to £200 by way of deposit. Sometime later, Booth expressed his concern that the typewriters had not yet arrived, to which Farbrother replied, 'The only fear you run is in the event of my death. Doesn't it seem the wisest plan would be to insure yourself against any possible loss if my death takes place before these machines are actually taken over?' Booth took out insurance and later stated that a claim had been made. Meanwhile, in Bath, a man named Jesse Gibbons Farbrother had died, who not only had the same surname, but also a remarkable resemblance to James Farbrother. In order to begin afresh, he assumed the identity of the deceased man, letting it be thought that it was he who had died. After several court appearances, he was found guilty of obtaining money by false pretences and sentenced to four months' imprisonment. (*The Times*)

~ JUNE 17TH ~

1871: At the Bath Guildhall, James Wheeler had been summoned by the Revd William Williamson for a violent assault that took place on the aforementioned clergyman. Wheeler had beaten Williamson around the head with an umbrella, causing several serious wounds. Since Revd Williamson was unwilling to pursue the case further, Wheeler was bound to keep the peace for six months. However, Wheeler was not able to raise any sureties and was about to be put into prison when he threatened to kill any policeman that approached him. Several police officers approached Wheeler but he drew a sharpened chisel and attempted to stab two of the officers, Inspector Sutton and Constable Davis. It was with much difficulty that the prisoner was subdued. Sutton and Davis managed to parry the blows, whilst the magistrates and other policemen went to the aid of Sutton and Davis. They were eventually able to hold Wheeler down and wrestle the chisel from his grasp. Wheeler was conveyed to the cells below and taken to the City Gaol with an escort of policemen to prevent any further violence. (*Western Mail*)

— JUNE 18TH —

1835: A singular case of double robbery was heard at Bath Magistrates around this time. John Lane stole a cart containing 28cwt of coals. He sold the stolen goods, left the cart and horse in the street and went on his way. That same night, Lane was accosted at Bradford on Avon by a man named Turner, who robbed him of the money he received from the stolen coals. Both men appeared in court for robbery and both were imprisoned. (*Berrow's Worcester Journal*)

1864: Sarah Susan Coles married John Tooling at Bath. However, the marriage was bigamous since Sarah was still married to her first husband, John Coles, who she had left because he had abused her. On being told of his apparent death, Sarah assumed she was free to marry. She was not, since John Coles was very much alive. Consequently, Sarah was remanded in prison to await trial at the Somerset Assizes. At that trial it was decided that the only harm done was to John Tooling for being subject to scandal for marrying a woman he was not entitled to marry. Sarah was apologetic and the judge relatively lenient. He took into consideration the time spent in prison and sentenced her to a month's imprisonment with hard labour. (Nicola Sly, *A Grim Almanac of Somerset*, The History Press, 2010)

~ June 19th ~

1875: An English bulldog that was accustomed to seeing trains took great exception to them. No more so than when out with its owner in the vicinity of the Somerset and Dorset Railway between Midford and Wellow station. The early train from Bath was approaching and the dog ran after it, oblivious to the calls of its owner. Fearing that the dog would be killed by the train, the owner ran after the dog. The gentleman-owner ran towards the track only to see his dog charge the cowcatcher of the train and disappear. Not wishing to see his dog be torn to pieces by the train, he closed his eyes for a moment. On opening them he saw the dog under the passing carriages waiting for an opportunity to dash between the wheels. The velocity of the train caused the dog to wait until all the carriages had passed over him. The dog emerged wagging his tail, having sustained only a few cuts and the loss of hair from the side of one tail. (*Bristol Mercury*)

1937: Nelson Ashton, Chief Constable of Bath, was killed in a motor accident at Congleton, Cheshire. Ashton had conducted a successful campaign at Bath aimed at reducing the number of motor accidents. He introduced accident black spot maps and had increased motor patrols in the city. (*The Times*)

~ June 20th ~

1873: J. Charles Cox stood as an alternative Liberal candidate in the by-election at Bath, standing for educational reform to ensure compulsory elementary education for all children. He was about to address the electors when men wearing the colours of Captain Hayter, the other Liberal candidate, attempted to throw him out of the window. When this failed, cayenne pepper was thrown in Cox's eyes and those about him, causing much suffering and leaving Cox temporarily blind. Cox later withdrew from the contest after Capt Hayter made concessions regarding the reform of education. Throughout the period 1868–75 Cox supported a number of radical causes. Cox was best known as an antiquary and an ecclesiologist. He was ordained into the Church of England, first as deacon in 1880 and then as priest in 1881. He held numerous ecclesiastical posts before moving to Sydenham, Kent, where he concentrated on writing, becoming an authority on the English parish church. As a churchman, he loved ancient ritual and abhorred the iconoclasm of the reformation. His book *The English Parish Church*, published in 1914, became a recognised handbook on the subject for many years afterwards. Controversially, he was received into the Roman Catholic Church on April 25th 1917 by Revd Ethelbert Horne, OSB, of Downside Abbey at St Benedict's Church, Stratton-on-the-Fosse, Somerset. He died on February 28th 1919 at his home in Kent. (*The Times*; *The Daily Gazette*; *Oxford Dictionary of National Biography*)

~ JUNE 21ST ~

1834: 'On Saturday evening, as Mr Bartlett was proceeding from Bath to his residence at Twerton, between 9 and 10 o'clock, he was accosted by two men, who sprang from the field over the hedge between the Turnpike and Brougham Hayes Buildings, and demanded if he had any money; but on Mr Bartlett remonstrating with them on the danger they were incurring in attempting a robbery so near where assistance could be obtained, and two men appearing in sight at that instance, they made off across the field from whence they came. We understand that Mr B. was well armed, had they proceeded in any acts of violence.' (*Bristol Mercury*)

2013: The museum at No. 1 Royal Crescent was officially reopened by food writer and broadcaster, Mary Berry. The museum exhibits how middle-class people lived in the eighteenth century. Following the purchase of No.1A Royal Crescent, which was the former servants' wing of the house, the museum's operators, the Bath Preservation Trust, can now also show what life was like for those living below the stairs. With No.1A now joined back to the main house, the museum's dressed floor space has doubled. (www.bbc.co.uk)

– JUNE 22ND –

1919: A large crowd assembled to witness the freeing of Cleveland Bridge from tolls by the Marquis of Bath. The bridge was designed by Henry Goodridge and construction was completed in 1827. When built, the bridge consisted of a single cast-iron span with limestone ashlar abutments. The bridge was the third to be built across the Avon in Bath. The bridge gave another access to the Bathwick estate, which was owned by the Earl of Darlington. The earl paid £10,000 to erect the bridge. The bridge contains toll houses which flank the approaches to the bridge. At road level, the buildings appear to be only single storey. In fact, the buildings extend down a further three storeys, through plinths of horizontal rustication down the banks of the River Avon. William Hazeldene, the contractor, was responsible for the building of the bridge. Hazeldene had also worked considerably with Thomas Telford on the design of many of his bridges. In 1928, the bridge's iron structure was rebuilt but maintained the architectural features of the bridge. Further restoration was carried out in 1992-93. Currently the building is Grade II* listed. (www.list.english-heritage; Nikolaus Pevsner *The Buildings of England: North Somerset and Bristol*, Penguin, 1958; David & Jonathan Falconer *A Century of Bath*, Sutton, 1999)

– June 23rd –

1666: Joseph Glanvill, philosopher and Church of England clergyman, was born in Plymouth, the son of a puritan merchant, Nicolas Glanville, and educated at Oxford. (Joseph Glanvill seems to have dropped the last 'e' in his surname.) He was ordained into the Church in 1660 and, in 1661, he published *Scepsis Scientifica, or The Vanity of Dogmatizing*. This book praised the philosopher Descartes and was critical of Aristotle and Cartesian physics and astronomy. In the book, some have seen that Glanvill imagined a form of electric telegraph when he states: 'That men should confer at very distant removes by an extemporary intercourse, is another reputed impossibility; but yet there are some hints in natural operations, that give us probability that it is feasible, and may be compast without unwarrantable correspondence with the people of the air.' Glanvill then goes on to describe how communication over long distances may be achieved by using magnets. Glanvill was also interested in witchcraft and was particularly concerned with the reality of spirits and their interaction with matter. He became rector of Bath Abbey on June 23rd 1666 and retained the living until his death. As a churchman, he was tolerant of a broad range of opinion within the established church, yet despised non-conformity. He died on November 4th 1680 and was buried at Bath Abbey. (*Oxford Dictionary of National Biography*; *The Times*; Joseph Glanvill, *Scepsis Scientifica, or The Vanity of Dogmatizing*, 1661)

— JUNE 24TH —

1890: The centre of Bath was, for the first time, lit by electric light on this day. One newspaper report claimed that 100 lights were lit 100 yards apart. An opening ceremony was held at the works of the Bath Electric Light Company, on Dorchester Street, at 9 p.m., when the lights were switched on for the first time. The mayor, Mr Bartrum, was in attendance, and after the opening ceremony, invited guests retired to enjoy supper at the Grand Pump Room Hotel, courtesy of Henry George Massingham, the proprietor of the Electric Company. Massingham's trade was as a shoe and boot dealer, but he regarded himself as an engineer. By February 1st 1889, he had signed a contract with the council to generate and supply electricity to the central area of Bath. Soon afterwards, the Bath Electric Light Company was formed. The contract was to provide eighty-one electric lamps of 1,200 candle-power. Massingham was to be paid £21 17s 6d per annum for each lamp. A private consumer could expect to pay £2 per annum for a lamp of ten candle-power burning from dusk until midnight each day. The consumer was also responsible for ensuring that his premises were wired correctly. (*Reynolds' Newspaper*; William E. Eyles, *Electricity in Bath 1890–1974*, Bath City Council & South Western Electricity Board, 1974)

~ JUNE 25TH ~

1961: Suffragette Mary Blathwayt (1879–1961) died at her Bath home, Eagle House, on this day. Blathwayt became involved with the suffrage movement after attending a meeting in 1906. She joined the Women's Suffrage and Political Union (WSPU) in 1908 and became treasurer to the Bath WSPU. She was persuaded by Annie Kenney, a fellow suffragette and organiser of the West of England for the WSPU, to join her in Bristol to engage in a full-time propaganda campaign. Thus between May 1908 and October 1909, Blathwayt distributed leaflets, chalked pavements, took part in demonstrations and arranged meetings in support of the WSPU. Her parents were also supportive and the family home, Eagle House, became a place of hospitality for visiting speakers and a place for suffragettes to rest. Suffragettes who visited Eagle House were encouraged to plant a tree in the garden which became known as 'Annie's Arboretum'. The increasing violence of the WSPU's campaign led to Blathwayt's resignation in May 1913, but she still supported the WSPU from the sidelines by attending meetings and helping out in the WSPU shop in Bath. She lived quietly after her resignation and took no further part in politics. (*Oxford Dictionary of National Biography*)

~ June 26th ~

1847: Reported in a newspaper under the section headed 'Miscellaneous', an unidentified Bath shopkeeper apparently had the following printed on his bills:

> My books are so crammed, and bad debts I've so many,
> I'm resolved that in future I'll trust not a penny:
> Giving credit to friends often friendship endangers,
> And I hope ne'er again to be cheated by strangers.

> (*Leeds Mercury*)

1859: Hailstones 1½in in diameter fell on Bath, causing considerable damage to glasshouses. Mr Drummond and Mr Griffin, both nurserymen, lost in excess of 5,000 panes and a Mr Turgett lost 300 panes in his greenhouse. The cost of the all the damage was put at £900. (Nicola Sly, *A Grim Almanac of Somerset*, The History Press, 2010)

⁓ JUNE 27TH ⁓

1877: The Revd Richard Marsh Watson stood trial at the Central Criminal Court charged with sending a letter demanding money with menaces. The circumstances go back to 1855 when he married the sister of the complainant. Sometime afterwards, Watson succeeded in seducing the complainant. In order to conceal the affair, he demanded considerable sums of money from the complainant. By 1875, the complainant could no longer bear to pay Watson any more money. The blackmail came to light when in March 1876, Watson wrote to the complainant, who lived in Queen Square, Bath, to demand £200, knowing that the complainant had inherited money following her father's death a year previously. Although Watson was only prosecuted for this crime, other letters found at his address hinted at the extent of his crimes with other young women. A letter dated September 23rd 1876, bearing the name of a young lady, stated in the following terms: 'I Emily —, take you Richard Marsh Watson, from this day forth to be my wedded husband, and I now swear to live with you as your faithful wedded wife, and shall lawfully marry you as soon as you are free, but in the meantime live with you as your lawful wedded wife, and swear this in the name of the Father, Son, and Holy Ghost.' The judge sentenced Watson to twelve years' penal servitude. (*Bristol Mercury*)

~ JUNE 28TH ~

1847: On this date, two railway navigators quarrelled at Bathampton, near Bath. The quarrel soon turned into a fight when the two men adjourned to a field to fight out their differences. A large crowd soon gathered around the men and formed a ring around them. The fight soon caught the attention of two policemen who attempted to separate the combatants. Both policemen were knocked down, one of them so savagely that he died only a few minutes later. On August 9th, Maurice Perry was put on trial for the wilful murder of John Bailey, the policeman that had tried to prevent the fight between the two railway navigators at Bath. The jury found Perry guilty and the judge, Chief Justice Wilde, pronounced the sentence of death for his crime. (*Manchester Times*)

1879: William Skeates, a blacksmith of No. 66 Lorne Terrace, was loading some household furniture onto a cart. However, a passing storm frightened the horse to which the cart was attached. The horse raced off at full speed. Skeates ran after the animal for some distance, caught up with the horse and seized its reigns. He failed to stop the horse and was dragged to the ground. One of the wheels of the cart went over his body, causing his death. (*Bristol Mercury*)

~ June 29th ~

1102: John of Tours, the Bishop of Bath and Wells, was given permission by Henry I to hold an annual fair on this date, which coincides with the patronal festival of Bath Abbey, dedicated to St Peter. The fair was probably held in the High Street, created much wealth for the abbey and was more than likely a continuation of an older fair. (Peter Davenport, *Medieval Bath Uncovered*, Tempus, 2002)

1764: Ralph Allen, postal service pioneer and philanthropist, died at his Prior Park mansion in Bath. Originally from St Columb Major, Cornwall, he bought the rights to the cross-post system in 1720. Prior to 1696, all mail travelled via London on six main post roads. From a successful experiment by Joseph Quash, Bristol mail was sent direct across the main post roads. Allen joined the Exeter post office in 1708, and moved to Bath in 1712 as the cross-system was extended around the country. Allen, recognising the system's potential, further extended the network and reaped the rewards. During the 1730s he built his own mansion, Prior Park, designed by the celebrated architect, John Wood the Elder. He was Mayor of Bath in 1742. As a philanthropist, he helped to build Bath General Hospital by providing funds and building stone. He died June 29th 1764 and is buried nearby at Claverton Church. (*Oxford Dictionary of National Biography*; Nilokaus Pevsner, *The Buildings of England: North Somerset and Bristol*, Penguin, 1958)

— JUNE 30TH —

1840: The first train from London to Bath operated following the completion of the section of line between Chippenham and Bath. At 3 a.m., Isambard Kingdom Brunel, Great Western Railway engineer, and Sir Frederick Smith, railway inspector, went over the line from Chippenham to Bath on a locomotive and tender, and Smith agreed that the line could be opened. The line duly opened to the public without ceremony. The first train from London Paddington left at 8 a.m., bedecked with flags and carrying the directors of the company, arriving at Bristol at noon. The first public train travelled from Bristol Temple Meads at 7 a.m. for Paddington. In order that services could commence, Daniel Gooch, the locomotive superintendent, personally acted as pilot for the next two days to ensure that only one train could pass through Box Tunnel, near Bath, which only had a single line completed. The only mishap on the opening of the new railway took place near Bath when a down train derailed near Bath station. The train was rerailed after an hour and proceeded towards Bristol. (Colin G. Maggs, *The GWR Swindon to Bath Line*, Sutton, 2003)

~ July 1st ~

1801: A thunderstorm raged over Bath and its environs on this day. At Marksbury, near Bath, the house of a Mr Hill was struck by lightning and in a short time the house was reduced to ashes. At the time of the strike, only three people were in the house: Mrs Hill, her infant child and her sister-in-law. At the beginning of the storm, the women bolted the doors, closed the window shutters and gathered themselves by the fireplace. A lightning bolt travelled down the chimney and struck Mrs Hill's sister-in-law, accompanied by a sulphurous smell. She fell down dead with some 'livid spots' on the back of her neck as the only sign of injury. Mrs Hill fled with her infant child into the adjoining room and fainted. The lightning also set the house on fire, but fortunately it was quickly noticed. Great difficulty was had in rescuing Mrs Hill and her child owing to the locked doors and shutters. Nonetheless, both mother and child survived. (*The Times*)

1876: 'A train from Bristol and Salisbury ran off the line yesterday at the Bathampton junction of the Great Western Railway at the point where the accident happened last year. No one was hurt, but great damage was done to the permanent way. On receiving a telegram announcing the accident [the] inspector on duty at Bath station dropped down dead.' (*Pall Mall Gazette*)

~ July 2nd ~

1771: Richard Sheridan (1751–1816) fought a second duel with Thomas Matthews. The origins of the dispute go back to Matthews' infatuation with Elizabeth Ann (Eliza) Linley, a singer, despite Matthews being already married. Elizabeth was tiring of singing and was deeply troubled by Matthews' infatuation with her, and so came up with the idea of moving to France and living in a convent until she became of age. Sheridan, who was secretly in love with Elizabeth and willing to play the gallant knight, agreed to escort her there. Whilst en route, Sheridan confessed his love to her and the pair were married by a priest 'who was often known to be employed on such occasions' near Calais. Sheridan found a place for Elizabeth in a convent in Lille. However, it was not until the arrival of Thomas Linley, Elizabeth's father, in Lille, that Sheridan learned of Matthews' defamatory advertisement about him in the *Bath Chronicle*. In the advertisement Matthews complained of Sheridan's apparent 'insinuations degregating from my character' and called him 'a L[iar] and a treacherous S[coundral]' Sheridan was incensed and returned to England to challenge Matthews to a duel. On arrival in London, Sheridan went round to find Matthews, who claimed he merely put in an advertisement to enquire to his whereabouts. When Sheridan returned to Bath, he visited the offices of the *Bath Chronicle* and discovered Matthews' deception. The subsequent duel took place late in the evening. It had the desired effect and an apology by Matthews was published in the *Bath Chronicle*. (Linda Kelly, *Richard Brinsley: A life*, Sheridan Sinclair-Stevenson, 1997)

~ JULY 3RD ~

1933: 'A Bath tramcar ascending Wells Road yesterday afternoon had reached the steepest point on a bend when it suddenly ran backwards downhill for nearly 100 yards and crashed into another tramcar which was following. Mrs Ethelreda Louisa Pessell, of Kipling Avenue, Bath, was killed, and 15 other passengers were taken to hospital for treatment, mostly for minor injuries. Two ambulances, private cars, and lorries were used to take the injured to hospital … among those taken to the hospital was a small child who could not be identified and who called for its mother. It was found to belong to Mrs Violet Leem, of Combe Down, who was in hospital suffering from concussion. The runaway tram, which was going from the centre of the city to one of the suburbs on the hill, gathered speed in spite of the efforts of the driver, who remained at the wheel. The driver of the second car, seeing that a crash was inevitable, jumped clear immediately before the collision. His platform was crushed, the front of his vehicle and the back of the first car being telescoped. The driver of the runaway car stated that, owing to the heat, the tar had melted on the road and run onto the rails, and the wheels skidded on the bend in the hill.' (*The Times*)

~ July 4th ~

1899: Walter Allen Shepard appeared before Bath City Police Court for allowing a locomotive to go along the Lower Bristol Road without a third person to render assistance as necessary and for a similar offence, on the same date, near Claverton Building. Since 1865, the Locomotive Act, or as it was more commonly known 'the red flag act', required all powered vehicles to travel a maximum speed of 4mph (2mph in towns), have a crew of three, one of whom should walk 60 yards in front of the vehicle bearing a red flag to warn of its approach. The defence argued that the new Locomotive Act of 1898 considerably modified the previous law. In fact, it was the 1896 Locomotives on Highways Act that removed the need for a third person and increased the speed limit to 14mph. (The 1898 act contained various measures to do with the height, weight and operations on the highway.) After some consideration, because of differing opinions on the Bench, the magistrates dismissed both charges. (*Bristol Mercury*)

~ JULY 5TH ~

1643: The battle of Lansdown Hill was fought on this date. The Royalist army was headed by Sir Ralph Hopton, whilst the Parliamentarians were headed by Sir William Waller. Waller had chosen an almost impregnable position on the top of Lansdown Hill, which the Royalists were reluctant to engage. The Parliamentarians advanced unseen, under hedge cover towards the Royalist camp at Tog Hill, where the Parliamentarians were able to pour heavy fire into the Royalist cavalry, routing two bodies of cavalry. However, Cornish musketeers were able to hold up the Parliamentary army until a counter-attack by Royalist forces could be made, which forced a Parliamentarian retreat back to Lansdown Hill, where the Royalists were left with a tricky assault. The flanks of Waller's army could not be seen by the Royalists since woodland obscured their view. The Royalist infantry secured the woods, but the central area was relatively open, and this was where the Royalist pikemen and cavalry moved forwards. In doing so, the Royalists suffered from heavy losses from the Parliamentarian guns. The Royalists made it to the top of the hill but at heavy cost. The cavalry in the centre ground melted away, either through losses in the battle or because some fled the scene of the battle. Nightfall caused fighting to cease and allowed the Parliamentarian army to slip away unnoticed. (Alfred H. Burne & Peter Young, *The Great Civil War*, Eyre & Spottiswood, 1959)

– July 6th –

1738: The original aim of the Bath Mineral Water Hospital was for 'the reception of poor strangers to the city whose cases require the use of the Bath waters'. The foundation stone of the hospital was laid by the Right Honourable William Putney, Earl of Bath, and the inscription on the stone read: 'This stone is the first which was laid in the foundation of the General Hospital. July the sixth AD 1738. God prosper this charitable undertaking.' Ralph Allen donated all the stone for the hospital, together with the paving slabs and lime mortar from his quarries at Combe Down. All other materials were purchased from funds raised by voluntary donations. The architect was John Wood, the Elder, who was responsible for a great number of Bath's Georgian buildings. The hospital took great pains to advertise its services and also the rules for admission to the hospital. Patients were only admitted if the patient could be considered 'a proper object of charity'. A local doctor first had to send a letter describing the patient's condition together with a letter from a priest or churchwarden to vouch that the patient was deserving of charity. Today, the hospital provides NHS rheumatology services. (Roger Rolls, *The Hospital of the Nation: The Story of Spa Medicine and the Mineral Water Hospital at Bath*, Bird Publications, 1988)

‑ July 7th ‑

1898: Thomas Holmes appeared before Bath Police Court charged with assault on his wife. Both he and his wife Annie had been drinking before returning to their home in Avonmouth. Thomas, a rag and bone man by trade, demanded that Annie take off her dress so he could tear it up. Annie refused, since the evening before Thomas had torn all her dresses and this was the only dress she had left. Thomas became incensed and, grabbing a shovel, he hit his wife several times over the head. Annie was then kicked in the ribs as the shovel broke. Fortunately the neighbours intervened before Annie was too seriously injured and Thomas was arrested. Thomas pleaded guilty at court and was sentenced to a month's imprisonment. (Nicola Sly, *A Grim Almanac of Somerset*, The History Press, 2010)

2011: Stone conservation students from the City of Bath College successfully restored a nineteenth-century statue damaged by an IRA bomb in 1974. The project was led by students on the college's architectural stone conservation course led by Bath and North-East Somerset Council, the Bath Preservation Trust and funded by the city's World Heritage Enhancement Fund. The project enabled students to get experience of the type of work they would be doing in their future careers. (*Bath Chronicle*)

– July 8th –

1861: 'A person, styling himself "Parallax" delivered the first of a series of lectures at the Temperance-hall, Widcombe, on Monday evening, for the purpose of proving that the earth is not round but "flat" and likewise of "correcting" some of the theories of Newton and other ancient astronomers.' Parallax was, in fact, Samuel Birley Rowbotham (1816–1884), who was, in the late 1830s, managing a radical socialist commune in the Cambridgeshire Fens. It was here along the flat landscapes that he first developed the notion that the earth was flat, after conducting a series of experiments on a straight stretch of the Old Bedford River. During the winter, when the canal was frozen, Rowbotham had lain flat on the ice and with a good telescope could see ice skaters at Welney, 6 miles away. In summer, he claimed to have seen villagers getting in and out of the water, even swimming. If the earth was round, reasoned Rowbotham, then he should not have been able to see anyone that distant. Rowbotham integrated the results of his 'experiments' with appeals to scripture and some mathematics calculations, and toured the country on a series of lecture tours, hiding his identity under the pseudonym 'Parallax'. Despite his unusual ideas, Rowbotham's debating style and his ability to use controversy to his advantage ensured his tours were commercially successful. (Christine Garwood, *Flat Earth: the History of an Infamous Idea*, Pan Books, 2008)

— JULY 9TH —

1881: 'Henry Kitley, a boy, was summoned for damaging a marble vase to Victoria-park. [The] Defendant was seen by a gardener named Frederick Lloyd to throw a stone at one of the vases on the band lawn. The missile struck a portion of the carving, the damage being estimated at 5*s*. His father expressed regret for the lad's conduct, and defendant was fined 15*s* and costs.' (*Bristol Mercury*)

———

2013: The *Bath Chronicle* reported the antics of a 17-year-old student who made a video of himself skateboarding around Bath in Georgian costume. Ben Curd hired the outfit to wear to a sixth-form leavers' prom, but decided to make the most of it and make a film. The 3½-minute film sees Curd skating in a number of well-known Bath locations including The Circus, Royal Victoria Park, Great Pulteney Street and the Royal Crescent. As Curd skates through the streets he can clearly be seen doffing his hat to passers-by. Ben made the film with his friend Jake Matthews, 18, and uploaded the film, entitled 'Ye Olde Bath Longboardy' to YouTube. Since publishing the video on July 6th 2013, the video has been viewed more than 1,000 times. Curd hopes to pursue a career in film-making. (*Bath Chronicle*)

– July 10th –

1920: On this day, the discovery of an unpublished letter by Lord Nelson was made at the Bath Reference Library by the curator R.W. Wright. The letter was found amongst the Napoleonic collection of Col. S.B. Miles, recently donated to the library by his widow. The letter was addressed to Revd Beaver, of HMS *Defiance* and was written on board Nelson's flagship, the *Saint George*, on June 4th 1801, at the end of the Baltic expedition. The chief interest in the letter lies in the postscript, which reads 'I wish you would make our worthy knight of Bath well consider he has now to comfort widows and to succour maidens in distress.' The 'worthy knight' refers to Rear-Admiral Graves who was on board the *Defiance*. He had been invested with the Order of the Bath in a ceremony on the quarter-deck of the *Saint George*, a few days previously. (*The Times*)

1968: Bath was badly affected by flooding, as were large areas of Somerset. On this date, 5in of rain fell in less than twenty-four hours. In Bath, the floods particularly affected the Lower Bristol Road and the Parade Gardens. (www.bbc.co.uk)

— July 11th —

1845: 'A veritable sea monster has been for some days exhibited in this city, being no other than the "sword-fish" of the Indian ocean. It was caught on Friday afternoon on the coast near Burnham, where, as may be imagined, its appearance excited not a little curiosity, for we never remember having heard of one being found in this latitude before. It was first observed floundering on the sands, in the shallow water, by Dr Prew, late of this city, who directed the attention of a fisherman to it, who immediately put off his boat, and having with the assistance of others secured it by a rope, dragged it on shore. It measures just ten feet long, and weighs three hundred weight; and from the appearance of the formidable weapon with which it is armed for offence and defence, we can readily imagine that it is as much the dread of other "monsters of the deep" – even of leviathan himself – as it is represented by naturalists to be. The "sword" or horne projecting from its snout is about three feet long, and has all the appearance of a bar of iron; towards the end it tapers considerably and ends in almost a sharp point.' (*Bath Herald*)

~ JULY 12TH ~

1727: The rise of visitors to the spa water at Bath and the subsequent growth of the city led to the need for better sanitation. Consequently, construction on a sewer was begun in Stall Street and on this day one of the workman uncovered a bronze head detached from the body. The head was from a Roman statue of the goddess Sulis Minerva and would have stood in the temple by the sacred spring, looking out towards a large altar. The head is slightly larger than life size and has six layers of gilding. It seems likely that the statue dated from the original foundation of the temple in the late first century AD. Examination of the head showed that it had been damaged; there was a large dent by the right eye and it appeared that the head had been torn from the body. This may have been due to Christian iconoclasts who may perhaps have been acting on the orders of the Emperor Theodosius who, in AD 391, ordered the closure of all pagan temples. The other possibility is that damage was sustained by Barbarian raiders of late-Roman Britain, attracted by the temple's wealth. Nevertheless, the statue head was an exceptionally rare find. (Barry Cuncliffe, *Roman Bath Discovered*, Tempus, 2000; www.romanbaths.co.uk)

~ July 13th ~

1889: So numerous were the complaints regarding the state of Bath Spa railway station at this time, that when Princess Helena visited the city on this date, a temporary platform was constructed half a mile away in the more congenial surroundings of Sydney Gardens. (Colin G. Maggs, *The GWR Swindon to Bath Line*, Sutton, 2003)

1992: Dr Cicely Williams, paediatrician and nutritionist, died on this date. She was born in 1893 in Jamaica but was educated in England, firstly at the Bath High School for Girls and then going on to read history at Somerville College, Oxford. In 1912 she was summoned back to Jamaica after a hurricane had left her family in financial difficulties. In 1917 she returned to Somerville College to study medicine. In 1929 she joined the Colonial Medical Service and was sent to the Gold Coast. It was here that she first identified kwashiorkor, an illness caused by a diet of roots and cereals leading to protein deficiency in young children. Her findings formed the basis for the Oxford DM degree in 1935. She also reported her findings in *The Lancet*, but it was some years before her conclusions were accepted by British doctors, who thought Williams was misdiagnosing cases of pellagra. In 1948, Williams became the first head of the maternal and child health section of the World Health Organisation in Geneva. She travelled widely, organising conferences and campaigning, including a campaign against UNICEF, which was distributing skimmed milk deficient in vitamin A. (*Oxford Dictionary of National Biography*)

~ JULY 14TH ~

1865: An extraordinary balloon voyage took place when 'aeronaut' Joseph Simmons took a night-time flight from Bath to Nottingham. Simmons set out from Bath just before 7 p.m. in the balloon *Raven*. At 7.10 the balloon passed over Tetbury and at 7.35 he 'was heartily cheered by the inhabitants of Cheltenham'. The winds increased and at 8.10 Simmons heard the words 'Come down here' exclaimed from Stratford-upon-Avon. Soon after leaving the town, Simmons threw grappling irons into a tree, but they broke loose and the balloon continued to speed along. Another attempt was made with the grapples, and the balloon was brought lower to the ground but, as a reporter stated, *Raven* 'was not to be brought to earth in this manner, so getting rid of her burden and shaking herself off, she careered away into cloudland. The intrepid aeronaut, uninjured by his fall from the balloon, made his way by foot to the nearest town, Warwick. He took a train in the direction that the balloon had been travelling in and on reaching Leicester he was informed that the grappling irons had taken hold on a large elm tree at the farm of Mr Jeffrey, at Stony Stanton, ten miles south-west of Leicester. The balloon's recovery saved the owner £700.' (*Nottinghamshire Guardian*)

~ July 15th ~

1808: A storm which occurred over Bath was described as exceeding 'in awful phenomena any remembered for many years past. There was continuous thunder for an hour and a half, followed by successive, uninterrupted flashes of lightening.' Perhaps the most remarkable aspect of this storm was the size of the hailstones that accompanied it. These 'irregular polygonic shapes' measured between 3in and 9in in diameter. (*The Times*)

1850: 'On Monday afternoon a fearful storm of lightning, thunder, hail, and rain broke over this city and neighbourhood … at Bath the rain fell in torrents, accompanied with lightning and very heavy peals of thunder, and on Combe-down hailstones of extraordinary size were picked up. Two houses in Macaulay-buildings, the residences of Mrs Pasley and Captain M'Dougall were injured by the lightening. The electric fluid stuck the chimney, accompanied by a loud explosion, scattering large fragments of stone into the gardens. Descending the chimney at Captain M'Dougall's into the kitchen, it filled the room with burning soot, scattering the fire from the grate in all directions. The walls in some of the rooms were discoloured, and the ceilings were cracked. Fortunately the servants had just left the kitchen with a child. Similar effects were experienced at Mrs Pasley's. The lightning injured a servant in the neck and arm.' (*The Bristol Mercury*)

~ July 16th ~

1953: A breakdown in telecommunications occurred between Bath Racecourse and the Bath telephone exchange, half an hour prior to the 2 p.m. race. The horse Francasel won the race with the odds at 10/1. Large numbers of bets had been placed on the horse in the minutes prior to the race. In the normal course of events, this would have been communicated to the course so that an adjustment could be made in the price of Francasel. Off-course bookmakers had no choice but to stick to the odds of 10/1. However, given the large number of bets placed on the horse Francasel, suspicion was aroused. The telephone line was sent away for analysis, and the majority of bookmakers held off paying out on Francasel. On July 21st, the police reported that a witness had seen a red lorry, an extendable ladder and two men with a cutting torch near to where the wires came down. Also a similar horse, together with the winning racehorse, was found on Sonning Common near Reading. It was suggested that the real Francasel had been substituted with another better horse. The following day, the racehorse owner, William M. Maurice, was interviewed by police. Enquires continued and the first arrest was made on August 5th when Leonard Phillips of Dinas, South Wales, was arrested on suspicion of cutting the cable. The following year, five men stood trial for conspiracy to defraud and four of the men were later convicted. William M. Williams and Gomer Charles received two years; Henry George Kateley, three years; and Victor R. Colquhon Dill, nine months' imprisonment. (*The Times*)

~ July 17th ~

1903: Buffalo Bill visited Bath to give a performance of his 'Wild West' show. Buffalo Bill was born in Iowa as William F. Cody. He gained the nickname Buffalo Bill from his skill as a buffalo hunter. His shows depicted life in the west and became so popular that a number of world tours were organised. From December 1902 and throughout 1903, the show once again came to Britain. The show started with a long run at London Olympia, with shorter runs in Manchester and Liverpool, before a series of one- and two-day performances in smaller town and cities. Bath was one of almost 100 locations that Buffalo Bill's show played at in Britain. The press gave good reviews and noted that Buffalo Bill could still draw in the crowds despite it being ten years since his last visit. The show first came to Britain in 1887 as part of the American contribution to Queen Victoria's Golden Jubilee. Queen Victoria was, it seems, most definitely amused – she saw the show again in 1892. Buffalo Bill returned to the United States in 1904, dying in 1917 from heart failure. (Alan Gallop, *Buffalo Bill's British Wild West*, (Sutton, 2001) www.buffalobill.org)

~ July 18th ~

1996: Prior Park Garden opened to the public, following a £650,000 restoration. Prior Park is regarded as one of the most beautiful landscape gardens in Britain. Restoration of Prior Park began after the National Trust was given the 28-acre gardens by Prior Park College, an independent Catholic school, and the Order of Christian Brothers. Money for the restoration came from a variety of sources, including the National Memorial Fund, Bath City Council, the European Commission and English Heritage. The gardens were designed by Capability Brown and are well known for the Palladian Bridge built in 1755. The bridge is one of only three built at this time, the others being in Stowe, Buckinghamshire, and Wilton, Wiltshire. Initially, the gardens were only granted planning permission to be open for two and a half years, owing to the National Trust's 'green' policy of encouraging people to visit the park by coming on foot, cycling or by public transport. Local residents feared that this policy would lead to the local area being full up with visitors' cars. The policy is still in place. Today, visitors can enjoy a 6-mile circular walk through woods, meadows, an Iron Age hill fort, Roman settlements and past eighteenth-century follies. (*The Times*; www.Nationaltrust.org.uk)

~ July 19th ~

1849: A cow and a calf belonging to Mr Shaul, a butcher, were driven from a field in Hanging-land to Bath, for the purposes of slaughtering the cow. The cow was separated from its calf and driven to a field near Englishcombe, some 4 miles distant from the city, and left to graze. About twelve o'clock at night, Mr Shaul's employees, who worked near the quay, were startled by a sudden attack on the door of premises and the loud mooing of a cow. They were surprised to discover it was the cow that they had driven to Englishcombe. Only after great difficulty did they manage to secure the cow, and in order to appease the animal, it was allowed to stay with its calf, until the offspring was slaughtered the following morning. What is remarkable is how the cow made its way from Englishcombe to the city. It seems that the cow must have forced its way through several hedges and either jumped over or taken a long detour around a set of turnpike gates. (*Bath Herald*)

~ July 20th ~

1834: 'A good reason why a prisoner should not take his trial was given at Bath Quarter Sessions … On the Recorder asking why James Berreman, against whom a true bill was found, had not been placed at the bar when his trial was called on, the gaoler, with much gravity, said he could not come. "Why not?" said the judge. "Because," answered the gaoler, "he died the week before last."' (*The Times*)

1874: The first Somerset and Dorset train left Bath Green Park station at 7.25 a.m. It carried only a few passengers as the Board of Trade Inspection of the line had only taken place a few days previously, on July 17th. Church bells rang out in celebration at Wellow; but at Evercreech and Wincanton, crowds that had turned out to meet the train severely delayed it. The *Bath Chronicle* commented: 'This is a bad beginning. May the Somerset & Dorset managers speedily mend their ways in the matter of punctuality or they will quickly find that would-be travellers will go by their longer and fairly punctual competitors, rather than by a route where the times of arrival are uncertain and delays not improbable, albeit the mileage may be considerably less.' Soon, the initials of the railway were referred to as the 'Slow and Dirty Railway'. (Robin Atthill, *The Somerset and Dorset Railway*, Pan Books, 1970)

~ July 21st ~

1662: Willem Schellinks (1627–1678), a Dutch landscape painter, visited Bath between July 19th and 21st 1662, and described his visit to the hot springs: 'It is the general custom to go there very early in the morning and in the evening after the meal. One undresses to the underskirt in one's lodgings, the men put on underpants under their shirt, the girls and women an entire shift; so prepared, one is carried to the bath in a sedan … chair; at the steps into the water, where men and women are waiting to help the strangers. All round and everywhere are seats in recesses, also rings to hold on to. If the seat is too low one asks for a cushion, so I was given a stone, soft and smoothed by the water. The water is fairly hot, so that one nearly breaks out in sweat. It is customary to drink some hot wine boiled up with sugar and herbs to prevent faintness. Some people stay in the water for two to three hours.' The baths also had people who would cut people's warts, corns and nails for a charge, and musicians. (Dr Catherine Spence, *Water, History and Style: Bath World Heritage Site*, The History Press, 2012)

~ JULY 22ND ~

1835: Two men, J. Challengar and Isaac Smith Flower, were committed by the Bath Magistrates to stand trial at the next Somerset Assize for stealing cloth from the factory, owned by Mr Wilkins of Twerton. The theft of cloth from the factory was a long-standing problem. The thefts could be carried out simply by wrapping cloth around their bodies as they left work. The originator of the thefts was a man called Isaac Nichols, who also worked for Mr Wilkins, and communicated the idea to a man named William Newman, another employee of Mr Wilkins who now lived in America. Nichols, in turn, gave the idea to Flower and Challengar, from America, where Nichols was safely outside British jurisdiction. As soon as it was known that Flower and Challengar were responsible for the latest thefts and this was known to the authorities, the two men scarpered. Flower was traced to London and brought back to Bath to face up to his crimes. (*Bristol Mercury*)

– JULY 23RD –

2002: Leo McKern, an actor known for his portrayal of Horace Rumpole in the television series *Rumpole of the Bailey*, died at his Bath nursing home, aged 82. He was born Reginald McKern in Sydney, Australia, in 1920. He had intended to become an engineer, but lost his left eye in an accident when he was 15, so turned to acting. He met his future wife when they worked at the same stage company, coming to England with her in 1946; they married two weeks after entering the country. A number of appearances for the Old Vic and Royal Shakespeare Theatre Company followed. In 1966, he was critically acclaimed for his role of Thomas Cromwell in a film version of *A Man for All Seasons*. McKern also played the role of Number 2 in three episodes of the cult television series *The Prisoner* – more than any other actor. In 1975, he played Rumpole for the first time in an ITV production, based on the novels by John Mortimer. A series was later commissioned and ran for forty-four episodes until 1992. Remembering McKern, John Mortimer said, 'He was a wonderful actor. He not only played the character Rumpole, he added to it, brightened it and brought it fully to life. He was a very private man who never failed in his public performances.' His last stage role was in *Hobson's Choice*, performed at London's West End. His last film was as a bishop in *The Story of Father Damien* in 1999. (*The Daily Mail*)

― July 24th ―

1856: Two juveniles, weary and footsore, entered the yard of the Greyhound Hotel, Bath. They asked if they could be accommodated for the night. Their polite manners and 'respectable dress' aroused the curiosity of the landlord, Mr Clarke. He asked further questions, but learned very little of their circumstances, and ultimately got in contact with the police. The children were then separated. One lodged with the police and the other stayed at the hotel. The mystery concerning the circumstances of the two juveniles was revealed the next morning when a livery servant arrived at the hotel in pursuit of the children. The juveniles were a brother, aged 14, and a sister, aged 13, who had left the family home, near Frome. The boy wanted to go to the sea and his sister's affection for her brother had determined to accompany him. She had dressed herself in some of his clothes and allowed her brother to cut her hair. The pair had been heading for Bristol, the nearest harbour. As soon as the children were missed, every effort had been made to find them again. They were conveyed back to their parents later that day. (*The Times*)

- July 25th -

2009: Harry Patch (1898–2009), soldier, plumber and longest-surviving First World War veteran, died in his Wells care home on this day. He was born at Coombe Down, near Bath. Patch joined the war in 1917 and was drafted into the 7th Battalion of the Duke of York's light infantry as a Lewis gunner. Lewis gunners worked in teams of five and Patch's job was to carry spare parts for the gun to allow quick repairs on the field of battle. Patch took part in the Battle of Passchendaele and, on the night of September 22nd 1917, Patch received a shrapnel wound to the groin. By August 1918 he was deemed fit enough to resume training and was on the Isle of Wight when armistice was declared. After the war, Patch was employed as a plumber until he retired in 1963. Patch never spoke about his war experiences until he reached 100 years of age. His memory of his wartime experiences was stirred when he noticed a flickering florescent light which reminded him of shellfire. Afterwards he took part in the television documentary *Veterans*, which led to appearances in other similar programmes, including *The Last Tommy*, broadcast in 2005. In 2008, he published *The Last Fighting Tommy*, his autobiography, and used the royalties to erect a memorial to his fallen comrades in the same place where they had fought, in Belgium, ninety-one years previously. He died on this date, aged 110. (*Oxford Dictionary of National Biography*)

~ July 26th ~

1797: Architect Henry Edmund Goodridge was baptised on this date at St Michel's Church, Bath. He was the son of James Goodridge, a leading builder in the city. He was apprenticed to John Lowder, architect of Bath, before establishing his own practice in the city in around 1820. Goodridge is noted for a number of buildings in Bath. Goodridge designed several buildings in the city and of particular note the Lansdown Tower (now better known as Beckford's Tower), built for William Beckford in 1827. The building consists of a 154ft tower attached to a small two-storey house, with a one-storey extension at its foot. An octagonal lantern on the square tower was inspired by the Lysicrates Monument in Athens and is perhaps the building's most striking feature. The building was later converted into a cemetery chapel and both William Beckford and H.E. Goodridge are buried within its grounds. Goodridge was also responsible for the design of Cleveland Place and Cleveland Bridge. The bridge was completed in 1827 as a second approach to the Bathwick estate and is a single-span structure with Greek Doric prostyle lodges. Goodridge died on October 26th 1864. (*Oxford Dictionary of National Biography*; Nikolaus Pevsner, *The Buildings of England: North Somerset and Bristol*, Penguin, 1958; Barry Cuncliffe, *The City of Bath*, Sutton, 1986)

– JULY 27TH –

1827: Goldsworthy Gurney's steam carriage set off today on a return journey from London to Bath as an official demonstration for the benefit of the Quartermaster General of the Army. The journey was not without mishap. After completing just a mile, the steam carriage collided with the Bristol mail coach and repairs had to be carried out at Reading. The steam carriage was then attacked by Luddites in Melksham and so the last few miles to Bath were covered under guard. After four days in Bath the return journey was made. The average speed of the round trip was 15mph, which was faster than the mail coach. Steam carriages did not take off in this country owing to the prohibitive tolls levied on them by turnpikes and in some instances active resistance on the part of mail coach owners. For example, a steam carriage run by Sir Charles Dance during 1831 that operated between Cheltenham and Gloucester closed down after just five months after the carriage was sabotaged by mail-coach operators. Gurney's own business folded in 1832, costing him £232,000. Gurney also had a number of more commercially successful inventions including his Bude lights, steam jets and the Gurney Stove. (Adam Hart-Davis & Paul Bader, *The Book of Victorian Heroes*, Sutton, 2001)

– July 28th –

1883: Major Charles Davis, antiquarian and architect, gave a tour of the newly discovered Roman baths to the Bristol and Clifton Junior Architects Society. Major Davis stressed the importance of these discoveries and the importance of the work in trying to keep the Roman baths uncovered. Davis was particularly noted for his archaeological work on the mineral baths. In 1869, he started excavating the site of the old King's Bath and discovered several Roman remains. These included a Roman well beneath the King's Bath in 1877–78, the Great Bath in 1880–81 and the Circular Bath in 1884–86. As the city surveyor, Davis did not always get on with his council paymasters, entering into a vitriolic public debate over who had discovered the baths. In 1886, Davis began work on the Queen's Bath and douche and massage baths, which the council wanted erected as cheaply and as quickly as possible. Davis, as an antiquarian, wanted to preserve the Roman remains beneath. Davis' solution was a slender south end to the baths, which at the time was heavily criticised for being unstable and for destroying the Roman Archaeology. An independent review by Alfred Waterhouse was carried out and concluded that Davis had struck the right balance between utility and preservation of the past. (Barry Cuncliffe, *The City of Bath*, Sutton, 1986; Nikolaus Pevsner, *The Buildings of England: North Somerset and Bristol*, Penguin, 1958; *Oxford Dictionary of National Biography*; *Bristol Mercury*; *Daily Post*)

~ July 29th ~

1936: A freight train overran the signals at Writhlington, near Radstock, and the crew, thinking that a collision with a tank engine hauling a rake of eight wagons was imminent, leapt from the footplate of their locomotive. The driver of the tank engine, however, was able to take evasive action by reversing his locomotive. The driver, seeing that the freight train was now only moving very slowly, jumped off his footplate, climbed on board the freight locomotive and was able to bring this train to a standstill. However, the fireman of the tank engine mistook the motive of his driver and he too jumped from the footplate of tank engine. The driver's triumph at stopping the freight train soon turned into despair when he realised that the tank engine, together with its eight wagons, was now being propelled back towards Bath with nobody on board to stop it. Miraculously, the tank engine had an almost clear road all the way to Bath. At Midford, most of the eight wagons derailed, littering the line with debris, partially demolishing the signal box and the 'signals and telegraph poles fell like ninepins'. The runaway train, with its one remaining wagon, passed through two single-track tunnels before finally derailing at Bath Junction. (Robin Atthill, *The Somerset and Dorset Railway*, Pan Books, 1970)

~ JULY 30TH ~

1568: The earliest record of Bath's Coat of Arms appears on a map dated July 30th/31st 1568. The shield depicts the city walls, and two way lines at the top of the shield refer to the River Avon. Running down the centre of the shield is a sword, which is the symbol of St Paul, one of the patron saints of Bath Abbey. The motto 'Aquae Sulis' is the Roman name for Bath. The shield is flanked by two bearers – a bear and a lion – and at the top is a crown referring to the coronation of King Edgar in 973. The keys on the bearers refer to Bath Abbey's other patron saint, St Peter. The bearers are standing on oak branches, which recalls the legendary foundation of Bath by Bladud. The legend states that Bladud was studying in Athens when he contracted leprosy. He returned to Britain, but realising that his leprosy was a barrier to him becoming king, he took a job as a swineherd in an untraveled part of the country. His pigs also suffered from leprosy, but Bladud noticed that they were cured after they rolled around in the hot, murky springs of Bath. Bladud decided to immerse himself in the waters and he too was cured. He was able to return home and claim the crown. (www.thecityofbath.co.uk)

— July 31st —

1925: Colonel Longhurst's 17-year-old daughter, Cynthia, eloped with Francis Ferdinand Friend, a former Roman Catholic priest, who had been asked to give Cynthia maths lessons, when she was then aged 13. Friend gained her affections and asked her to marry him. On July 23rd, Friend went to Winchester Register Office and filled in a declaration stating that Cynthia was 22. In the small hours of the morning of July 30th, the couple eloped and were married the following day. The couple stayed together for about a month before Cynthia went back to her parents. The couple were still on 'affectionate terms' during Friend's appearance in court for making a false marriage declaration. Colonel Longhurst appealed for leniency and the judge, Ernest Charles QC, sentenced Friend to three months' imprisonment, which was the least he could have passed and hoped it would not jeopardise the couple's future happiness. (*Bath Gazette*)

2007: An evacuation from the centre of Bath took place and an army bomb disposal squad was called to deal with a suspected Second World War device. The bomb was discovered close to Widcombe Infants' School in Archway Street. The bomb disposal squad took the device away from the scene and police cordoned off the area for two hours. (*Western Daily Press*)

⁓ August 1st ⁓

1953: Sydney Gardens, which date from the late eighteenth century, reopened to the public after restoration and improvements. Thousands of people walked down Great Pulteney Street during the evening to watch the illuminations, dancing and fireworks. Citizens paid 1*s* 6*d* to wander amongst the grounds. Earlier in the gardens' history, a critic once remarked that a concert due to be held would have more than its usual charm, since 'the gardens are large enough for me to get pretty well beyond the reach of its sound'. Even the building of the Kennet and Avon Canal, which reached Bath in 1810, was made into a water feature and two cast iron bridges were built over it. (*The Times*; Barry Cuncliffe, *The City of Bath*, Sutton, 1986)

⁓

2012: Michael Jamieson gained the silver medal in the 200m breaststroke during the 2012 Olympics held in London. He took 2:07:43 seconds to complete the distance. Jamieson trained at the University of Bath with coach David McNulty. The University of Bath is home to one of five British Swimming Intensive Training Centres. Jamieson was narrowly beaten by Hungary's Daniel Gyurta who set a world record with a time of 2:07:28. (www.bbc.co.uk; www.teambath.com)

~ AUGUST 2ND ~

1788: Thomas Gainsborough (1727–1788), artist and printmaker, died today. He was particularly noted for his portraits, landscapes and 'fancy pictures'. He showed particular talent for drawing at an early age and around 1740 he moved to London where he studied with Hubert-François Gravelot. By 1752, he had set up as a portrait painter in Ipswich, although Gainsborough also painted a number of landscapes at this time. A move to Bath in 1758, which was announced by the *Bath Advertiser* (October 7th), was probably motivated by financial reasons, providing Gainsborough with a stream of wealthy clients and easy access to print dealers. Gainsborough continued to paint landscapes but less often than before, since he was extremely busy with portrait commissions. In December 1768, Gainsborough accepted an invitation to become a founder member of the Royal Academy of Art and was the only portraitist from outside London to be so honoured. Gainsborough seems to have tired of living in Bath and moved back to London in 1774. Fellow artist John Warren stated that Gainsborough was 'uncommonly rude and uncivil to artists in general and was even haughty to his employers, which with his proud prices caused him to settle in London'. Developments at the Royal Academy may have also have contributed Gainsborough's decision to move. Here, Gainsborough became a favourite portrait painter of the Royal Family. Although he regarded himself as a portrait painter by profession, landscapes were his passion. (*Oxford Dictionary of National Biography*; Ian Chivers, *Oxford Dictionary of Art and Artists*, OUP, 2009)

⸺ August 3rd ⸺

1874: A bicycle race was held between Bath and London, a distance of 106 miles, for the captaincy and sub-captaincy of the Middlesex Bicycle Club. The competitors started the race outside Bath Abbey, and Mr Sparrow, who himself took part in the race, set the competitors off at 5.08 a.m. Some difficulty was had in passing through Bath owing to the numbers who had assembled to see them off. The unsurfaced and often weathered roads would also have caused problems for the competitors, particularly as the bicycles at the time were heavy, had no gears and the pneumatic tyre had not yet been invented. It is no surprise that many of the competitors had to dismount when ascending Box Hill. The machine of one competitor, a man named Goulding, 'gave way' after striking a large projecting stone whilst descending a hill near Hungerford. He attempted to repair the damage and made it as far as Thatcham, another 12 miles further on, where he was compelled to take a train back to London. Walker, who had led for much of the race, arrived at the club house in Kensington at 3.13 p.m., 10 hours and 5 minutes after the race began. Walker completed the journey in one hour less than the fasted recorded stagecoach. Mr Sparrow, who had started the race, and who was himself over 50, completed the journey, with stoppages, in fifteen hours. (*The Times*; www.victoriancyclist.com)

~ AUGUST 4TH ~

1806: On July 7th, Mr W. Turner, a butcher in the Grove, Bath, bought four bull-calves to the slaughterhouse in Boatstall Lane. However, two of the calves were missing the following morning. The butcher supposed that they had been stolen and offered a reward of thirteen guineas on the conviction of the perpetrators. No information was forthcoming until three weeks later, on this date, when a man saw one of the calves struggling in the water near Monk's Mill. A further search of the area was carried out and the second missing calf was found 300 yards upstream. The calves were both taken to a nearby mill and given quantities of milk. One of the calves improved rapidly, but the other calf sadly died. (*The Times*)

1864: 'The gallant act of a Bath Lady' was rewarded at a meeting of the National Lifeboat Station on September 8th 1864, where Miss le Geyt was presented with the silver medal of that institution. It was awarded in recognition for saving the lives of two boys from drowning, whilst at Lyme Regis on this date. Miss le Geyt was out in a rowing boat with a friend, when she spotted the two boys fall from the pier. She rowed immediately through choppy water to their rescue, throwing an oar to one and holding on to the other until further help could arrive. Miss le Geyt's actions undoubtedly saved the two boys' lives. (*Bath Chronicle and Weekly Gazette*)

‒ August 5th ‒

1936: Emperor Haile Selassie of Ethiopia arrived at Bath. He then spent the next couple of months in the comfortable surroundings of the Spa Hotel. Selassie had been forced to seek refuge in Britain after Italian dictator Benito Mussolini had ordered the invasion of Ethiopia. During that August, Selassie visited a number of Bath institutions including the new G.P.O. telephone exchange, the book-bindery of Cedric Chivers and the Guildhall. At his hotel, luncheon parties enabled Selassie to meet a number of Bathonians and many of these contacts proved useful to him. Selassie was also looking for a permanent place to live for himself and his family. The residence needed to be large enough to impress visitors but offer the emperor privacy and enable him to plan his future in exile. Fairfield House, set in 2.2 acres of grounds at the foot of Newbridge Hill, seemed to fit the criteria. A typical daily routine at Fairfield House began at 6 a.m. with prayers, then breakfast, followed by the dictation of his autobiography, dealing with affairs of state or dealing with correspondence. Selassie stayed in Bath until 1941, when he was allowed to return home to take part in the Ethiopian campaign against Italy. Selassie returned, once, to the city of Bath in October 1954 to receive the freedom of the city. In 1958, he gifted Fairfield House to the city. (www.bathintime.co.uk; Lutz Haber 'The Emperor Haile Selassie I in Bath 1936-1940', Anglo-Ethiopian Society News File, 1992)

~ August 6th ~

1864: Several newspapers relate how Henry Brine of No. 5 Howell's Cottages, Southgate Street, tried to murder his wife with a pistol. He had been out drinking for the past ten days and during that time he had threatened his wife several times. At the hospital, it was discovered that a tin tack had entered her ear, another entered her jaw and a smaller piece pierced her thumb. A small piece of lead had also entered her jaw. Fortunately these were removed without too much difficulty. (*Lloyd's Weekly Newspaper*; *London Standard*; *Dundee Courier*)

2003: Luciano Pavarotti appeared at a press conference in Bath to promote the Three Tenors concert in front of the Royal Crescent the following day. The free concert was to promote the reopening of the Bath Spa, delays in the project meant that it did not open for the next three years. The Three Tenors, Jose Carrearas – Placido Domingo and Luciano Pavarotti – performed in front of a seated audience of almost 13,000 people. A further 20,000 people watched the concert from large video screens in a nearby park. (www.bathintime.co.uk; *The Times*)

~ August 7th ~

2006: Bath's new thermal spa finally opened to the public following a refurbishment that began six years previously. The spa was closed in 1978 after a young girl died of Legionnaire's disease, giving concerns over the purity of the water. Five attempts were made to reopen the spa from the 1980s to the mid-1990s. In 1996, Bath and North-East Somerset Council applied for lottery funding to reinstate the spa, and in 1997 the council was awarded £7.78 million by the Millennium Commission. The total projected cost was estimated at £13 million. Work started in August 2000, with the hope that the spa would open in 2002. Delays in construction meant that the deadline was missed. Indeed the Bath Spa project was not still ready for the official reopening by the Three Tenors in 2003. In September 2003, a row broke out between the council and Mowlem, the contractor for the project. Of particular contention was the peeling paint in the spa pools. The following year, the council learned of the cracks in the foundations and leaks in the steam room. Vandalism also became a problem. In 2005, the council ploughed another £3.5 million into the project and paid for two new boreholes to safeguard the water supply at the spa. In April 2005, the council fired Mowlem and a new contractor, Capita Symonds, was appointed. Costs continued to rise to £35 million and the council offered tours of the site to locals, to prevent further disenchantment. (www.bbc.co.uk)

— AUGUST 8TH —

1848: Three boys were out playing with an old pistol, with a flint lock. They amused themselves by pouring powder into a pan and flashing it. On putting more powder in, one of the boys, aged 12, pointed the weapon at a young boy named Willies, who happened to be passing. The pistol went off, killing Willies. At the subsequent inquest, the verdict of death by misadventure was returned. It was also noted that had loaded pistols been kept out of the reach of children, then this tragedy would not have occurred. (*The Times*)

1977: Queen Elizabeth II was treated to a floral welcome from the city of Bath, with petals used as falling tickertape over a distance of a quarter of a mile, from the railway station to the Parade Gardens. At the Parade Gardens, a Union Jack had been made up from red, white and blue flowers and an 8ft high floral crown had been constructed. During her 40-minute tour of the city, the Queen received her first bouquet from Abigale Barker, granddaughter of Bath's mayor. The Queen was also entertained by the music of the 93rd (City of Bath) squadron's band, air training Corps, a demonstration of judo and a giant chess game in which the pieces were children in fancy dress. Throughout the city, people lined the streets on her route to the next stop at Keynsham. (*The Times*)

‑ August 9th ‑

1794: *The Times* reported: 'Bath charter – A further degree of power; to be vested in the Magistrates, being deemed necessary, a new charter was, a short time since, granted for that purpose. It was sent by the mail coach, and, for want of care in the packing, the impression of the Great Seal was knocked into atoms. Mr Barker, the solicitor for that city, on Thursday presented it to the Lord Chancellor to be re-sealed; this was refused by his Lordship, unless the Mayor and Corporation would petition the court, setting forth the reasons. The charter of Bath conveys the exclusive privilege of the electing two members to the British House of Commons, to the select Corporation of 26, excluding all the other inhabitants'. In the coming decades, the restricted franchise would come under increasing pressure to be amended as part of the countrywide call for parliamentary reform (*see* October 7th). (*The Times*)

1973: Queen Elizabeth II, accompanied by the Duke of Edinburgh, attended a thanksgiving service in Bath Abbey to mark 1,000 years of monarchy in England. The first king of all England, Edgar, had been crowned at Bath Abbey, a millennium previously at Whitsun in 973, by Archbishop Dunstan of Canterbury, assisted by Oswald, Archbishop of York. (David & Jonathan Falconer, *A Century of Bath*, Sutton, 1999)

⁓ August 10th ⁓

1841: 'A wedding was appointed to take place on Tuesday [August 10th], at Walcot church, Bath, and the lady with her bridesmaids and father arrived in a carriage at the hour fixed. They were however, after waiting a considerable time, not a little astonished at the non-arrival of the bridegroom. At length the father set off on horseback in search of his expected son-in-law, whom he found busily employed in his usual avocations, quite unconscious of his presence having been required on that particular morning! The mystery however was soon solved: the fixing of the day for the celebration of the happy event had been confided to the ladies, who sent the bridegroom (that was to be) a note, informing him of the result of their deliberations. The luckless note never reached his hands, and hence the disappointment we have named. The remainder of the day was spent in jollity, and the following morning saw the eventually happy couple united, much to the satisfaction of both, who thought it was "better late than never".' (*Berrow's Worcester Journal*)

— AUGUST 11TH —

1857: Richard Warner (1765–1857) was interested in antiquity from a young age. He attended Christchurch Grammar School and became familiar with the New Forest and its antiquities. Warner even excavated some of the barrows. He entered the Church and served a number of curacies, before coming to Bath to become the first minister of All Saints' Church, in 1794, and St James' Church, Bath, as well as taking up a curacy at Bath Abbey. He remained there until 1817. He became interested in Bath's antiquities and published frequently on the subject. These included *Illustrations of Roman History of Bath* (1797) and a full-scale *History of Bath* (1801). Warner was also a frequent contributor to the *Bath Journal*. In 1796, his summer vacation was spent walking from Bath to Caernarfon and back, at an average rate of 26 miles each day! His tour included visits to various antiquities and he wrote about them in *A Walk through Wales*, published in 1797. Warner served in a number of rectories after Bath and continued to publish widely on religious and historic antiquities. His books were more commercial than scholarly and as a result contained some inaccuracies. He died on July 27th 1857 and was buried on August 11th. (*Oxford Dictionary of National Biography*)

~ AUGUST 12TH ~

1837: 'Albion suspension bridge – The chain bridge, upon an entire new principle of suspension, discovered by Mr Motley, Engineer, unites the Upper Bristol road, near the Gasometer and the new Church, with the lower road at East Twerton. At the particular request of a friend, we called to look at it this morning, having learnt that in about a fortnight or less it would be open to foot-passengers, and would be wholly completed at the latter end of September. The river-span is 120 feet, and the whole dimensions of the suspension machinery is 230 feet. It presents to the view a very slight curve, or such a segment of a circle as would be given by a rise of 3 feet in 230. This arch gives it such a power of compression as to avoid any undulation or vibration until that power is overcome by superior weight, which nothing that is ever likely to pass over this bridge can effect. It is this, in reality, what has been a desideratum in bridges of this character – viz, an inflexible suspension chain.' The Albion Suspension Bridge is better known as the Victoria Bridge, which brewer James Dredge apparently had built so that he could take his beer more easily from one side of the city to the other. At the time of construction, suspension bridges were a very new design; the first permanent structure being the Saint Antione Bridge in Geneva, built in 1823. (*Bristol Mercury*)

— August 13th —

1853: An excursion train, returning from London to Bristol, was derailed near Box station, owing to the stubbornness of one man. The train became derailed shortly after leaving Box station when the driver, seeing a railway repair worker on the line giving a danger signal, let off steam and applied the brakes. The train left the rails and travelled on for another 200 yards before coming to a halt. The cause of the train's derailment owed much to a man named George Ford, a ganger in charge of five men and all in the employ of a Mr Brotherhood who were engaged in repairs of the Great Western Railway between Bath and Box. Although Ford was aware that an excursion train was expected at any minute, he obstinately persisted in raising the line, asserting that he could complete the repairs long before the train came. However, the train appeared and one of the men ran to meet it to give the danger signal. The derailment could have had potentially serious consequences; however, no one was hurt and the train was rerailed in an hour. Ford was immediately apprehended and a few days later he appeared before magistrates. The magistrate, on seeing that the prisoner was of good character, sobriety and of good previous conduct reduced his sentence from the usual £10 to £2. The amount was immediately paid and Ford expressed gratitude for his leniency and promised not to make the same mistake again. (*The Times*)

~ August 14th ~

1847: The 2:50 p.m. train from Bath was stopped after two men named Quasick and Thomas hailed the driver of the train by waving a red handkerchief. The driver stopped the train just near the Twerton tunnel, as he expected that the line was blocked further ahead. When the guard asked of the two men the cause of the train coming to a halt, one of them replied that he had no money and wanted a lift to Bristol. The guard humoured their request, allowing the two men to sit in his guard's van and the train proceeded to Bristol. The men congratulated themselves on having obtained such a cheap trip. However, on arrival at Bristol, the guard handed the men over to the police superintendent of the line. Two days later, on Monday, the men were brought before the magistrates. They were fined 40*s*, plus costs, or one month's imprisonment should they default on paying the fine. (*Daily News*)

~ August 15th ~

1876: 'Another accident occurred on Tuesday morning on the Great Western Railway near Bath. As the 1.40 goods train for London was passing the level crossing near Bathampton, one of the vans in the middle of the train left the rails, and, breaking away from the rest of the train, crossed the metals. The van, which contained several casks of brandy, was smashed and the contents spilled. The line was blocked for two hours.' (*Jackson's Oxford Journal*)

1906: James Dredge was born in Bath on July 29th 1840 and was educated at Bath Grammar School. Following in his father's footsteps, Dredge trained as a civil engineer, and in the early stages of his career, spent several years working on the Metropolitan District Railway. From 1866, a weekly periodical, *Engineering* magazine, was published and Dredge helped with illustrations and occasional articles. Following the founder Zerah Colburn's death in 1870, Dredge and W.H. Shaw took over, becoming joint editors and proprietors. Dredge remained active with the publication until May 1903, when he was disabled by paralysis. He wrote several books on engineering during his time with *Engineering*. He died, on this date, at his Middlesex home in Piner's Wood. (*Oxford Dictionary of National Biography*)

— AUGUST 16TH —

1818: John Palmer (1742–1818), theatre proprietor and postal reformer, was born in Bath, the son of a prosperous tradesman. His father's business interests included a brewery and a theatre. Palmer resisted family pressure to become a clergyman and consequently worked in the family's brewery for a short time, before becoming heavily involved in the running of the Orchard Street Theatre. Palmer was able to secure the position of the theatre by royal patent in 1768. It was the first theatre outside London to gain this status. During this time, Bath's Theatre Royal was home to well-known actress Sarah Siddons who would travel between there and Bristol to perform. This experience convinced Palmer of the need for improved communications along turnpikes. Palmer was also responsible for the introduction of mail coaches to improve the speed and security of the post; hence why mail coaches contained a strong-box and the coach had an armed guard. The coaches travelled overnight, stopping only to change horses and attend to the needs of any passengers. A faster service was helped by exemption from tolls and right of way over other vehicles. For his postal reforms, Palmer was awarded the freedom of eighteen towns and cities. Palmer was active in Bath's civic life and was elected mayor in 1796 and 1809. He died in Brighton, on this date, in 1818, and was buried at Bath Abbey. (*Oxford Dictionary of National Biography*)

~ August 17th ~

1874: Mr Stanton wagered a £100 bet that he could ride from Bath to London in eight and a half hours. Stanton accomplished the 106-mile journey on this date, with 2 minutes to spare and so won his wager. The journey was not without its difficulties. On Maidenhead Hill he collided with a carriage, causing him a long delay. The accident injured his left shoulder so that he could only steer the machine with his right hand. Loud cheers awaited him in London for his pluck and endurance. A month later, Stanton attempted to ride form Bath to London in seven and a half hours (*see* September 19th). (*Manchester Times*; *Reynold's Newspaper*)

1895: Reports of a fraudster began circulating, regarding a young man who had cards printed intimating that he was a solicitor practicing in Trowbridge. Using these, he ordered from several establishments of Bath items of lavish description, including several large salmon, wines and other provisions. Before concerns could be expressed about the lack of payment, the mysterious young man disappeared. The fraudster was also believed to be responsible for similar crimes in Trowbridge. (*Bristol Mercury and Daily Post*)

⏤ August 18th ⏤

1833: In the eighteenth century, wife selling was a way of ending an unsatisfactory marriage. The custom released the husband from financial obligations to his wife, and the purchaser was often the wife's lover; the transaction also freed the lover from any prosecution. During the nineteenth century, prosecutions for wife selling increased and the practice declined. The *Berkshire Chronicle* gives this account of wife selling that occurred at Bath: 'In our market-place yesterday, a man named Stradling offered his wife for sale to the highest bidder. The lady, it appeared, had been sold for half a crown on Monday at Lansdown fair, but the bargain was not considered legal – first because the sale was not held in a public market-place, and, secondly, because the purchaser had a wife already. The lady was dashingly attired and had a halter, covered with silk, around her neck. The bidding amounted at last to five shillings, at which sum it was understood she was brought in. It happened, however, very unluckily for the husband of the fair one, that the police had an eye to this little transaction, for just as the affair had concluded he was apprehended for having caused a disturbance, and was politely handed to a temporary lodging in the Bath gaol. The above disgraceful exhibition assembled, an immense concourse of spectators.' (*Berkshire Chronicle*)

~ AUGUST 19TH ~

1987: A bomb scare delayed the start of the world premiere of *Beyond Reasonable Doubt*, the first play by Jeffrey Archer, author and former conservative MP and deputy party chairman. Archer and his wife, Mary, were in the audience. The play starred Frank Finlay and Wendy Craig. The plot concerns the character Sir David Metcalf, who is accused of the murder of his terminally ill wife. When the play premiered at the West End later in September, it ran for over 600 performances. No stranger to controversy, Archer was jailed in 2003 following a conviction for perjury. (*The Times*; www.jeffreyarcher.co.uk)

———

1998: A shooting enthusiast had an unusual send-off when his ashes were fired from the antique guns of forty friends. Tony Goldsworthy, a founder member of the Bath Muzzle and Historic Breach-Loaders Association, died from cancer, aged 70. Fellow members gathered at Kelston's shooting range, and poured a small amount of Goldsworthy's ashes into each barrel, before firing it into the air. His widow, Margaret, who was present at the firing, said, 'It was a terrific send-off – exactly what he would have wanted. He was very young at heart for seventy.' (*The Times*)

~ August 20th ~

1727: During July, workmen constructing the Stall Street sewer dug through the remains of a Roman building 4.9m below the surface. An annotated sketch, dated August 20th 1727, which was made by Bernard Lens, shows that the workmen discovered part of a hypocaust. A hypocaust was a hollow space beneath a floor in which the hot air from a furnace could be used to heat a house or a bath. It was therefore the first discovery of a Roman bath in the city. Records of the time also record that 'black stuff, very like soot' was also discovered on the uncovered tiles. (Barry Cunliffe, *Roman Bath Discovered*, Tempus, 2000)

1862: A newspaper of this date records the following unusual occurrence in Bath: 'A marble monument, recently erected in the Abbey Cemetery, Bath, attracts more than a usual share of public notice. This curiosity arises from the fact that the tombstone records the death of a gentleman who is now alive, and who may be seen any day walking in vigorous health along the streets of Bath. The marble monument recites the naval rank of the personage who is hereafter to be buried beneath it, states that he expired "much respected" but, of course, leaves a blank where ordinarily appear the date, and age of the occupant of the tomb.' (*Trewman's Exeter Flying Post*)

~ AUGUST 21ST ~

1874: *The Times* reported that eleven oxen were stolen from the farm of Mr Caple, located near to Lansdown Racecourse, Bath. Two men drove the cattle away, which were valued at £250. It was first thought that the cattle had strayed but when the oxen could not be located, it became apparent that they had been stolen. Unfortunately, by this time, the thieves had a two-day head start. Superintendent Rawle, of the Fishponds Division, succeeded in tracing the cattle. He found that the cattle had been driven across country roads for a considerable distance to Didcot railway station. The cattle were then loaded onto a train bound for London. One ox escaped from the truck and this was sent on separately. With the exception of the ox that escaped, the others were slaughtered and sent to Smithfield Market. Superintendent Rawle did take possession of the animal that was sent on afterwards and managed to gain a good description of the thieves. Francis Martin, aged 26, was arrested for the theft and stood trial at the following Gloucestershire Quarter Sessions, where he received five years' imprisonment. (*The Times*; *The Bristol Mercury*)

~ AUGUST 22ND ~

1778: Sir Charles Whitworth, politician and writer, was born in Kent in around 1721. He was educated at Westminster School (1730–38) and entered Lincoln's Inn, in 1738. In 1742, he inherited the family estate at Leybourne, Kent, and in 1749 he became MP for Minehead. He married Martha Shelley, who was niece by marriage to the Duke of Newcastle. Whitworth continually sought, from the Duke, a government post. Consequently, he was awarded an annual pension of £400 and, in 1758, he succeeded in persuading the Duke to appoint him Governor of Gravesend and Tilsbury. Whitworth also served as a major for the Kent militia from 1759. As a writer, Whitworth wrote a number of political and historical reference works. These include the *List of English, Scots and Irish Nobility* (1765) and *Public Accounts of Services and Grants 1721–1771* (1771). Whitworth was also vice-president of the Society for the Encouragement of Arts, Manufactures and Commerce from 1755 until his death. Whitworth died at Bath, on this date. (*Oxford Dictionary of National Biography*)

~ AUGUST 23RD ~

1727: William Croft (1678–1727), organist and composer, was born in Nether Ettington, Warwickshire. He was a chorister in the Chapel Royal under John Blow between 1686 and 1698. In 1700, Croft was installed as organist at St Anne's Church, Soho. In 1708, Croft succeeded John Blow as organist of Westminster Abbey from 1708. Although a skilled organist, Croft is well known for his compositions and his works are considerable. Croft composed a number well-known hymn tunes, including St Anne, often sung to 'Our God Our Help in Ages Past' by Isaac Watts, and the tune Hanover, often sung to 'O Worship the King' by Sir Robert Grant. Croft also wrote three settings for the Eucharist and a collection of his anthems, *Musica Sacra*, published in 1724. He also wrote a number of secular songs. In fact, his earliest publications were secular. These included *Twelve New Songs* (1699), *Courtship Alamode* (1700) and *The Funeral* (1702). In July 1713, Croft gained a DMus degree from Oxford University. Croft died on August 14th 1727, in Bath, and was buried on August 23rd, near Henry Purcell's tomb in Westminster Abbey. (*Oxford Dictionary of National Biography*)

~ August 24th ~

1837: The *Bath Chronicle*, critical of radical reformers, stated on this date: 'Some reformers of our city have turned informers against the sweeps for employing in their business boys under 14 years of age. If this were done out of humanity, we would be among the last in the world to say a single word against the proceeding, but as it arises from political rancour, because the persons complained against voted at the last election for the Conservative candidates … the pitiful meanness and utter hypocrisy of these Radical informers, who, if the sweeps had continued to vote for Roebuck [a radical reformer who lost his seat the election held a month earlier], would never have cared a single rush if children of the tenderest age had been employed. No informations were heard of in Mr Roebuck's heyday of popularity, when the sweeps allowed themselves to be deluded by that person and his hangers-on, but now that things are hanged, these Radicals, these clamourers for the ballot, on the ground that everyman ought to be allowed to exercise the franchise without control, are "liberally" persecuting their former allies for doing as they please with the privilege of voting.' The legislation that made it illegal to employ children under the age of 14 as chimney sweeps was passed in 1834; however, there was no means of enforcement and the legislation was ignored. Effective enforcement only arrived with the passing of the 1875 Chimney Sweepers Act, when police were given the necessary powers of enforcement. (*Bath Chronicle*)

~ August 25th ~

1880: An inquest was held at Bath to investigate the death of Albert Mills, aged 9, who drowned in one of the locks on the Kennet and Avon Canal. The boy fell into the canal accidentally and two of his companions, named Hillier and Vowles, jumped into the water to try to save him. However, a boatman named Thomas Ames was using the lock and opened the paddle of the lock gate, letting water in to fill the lock. In doing so, he put all three boys' lives in danger. When Ames was appealed to close the gate, he is reported to have callously said, 'Let him drown!' A woman, who happened to be passing, also remonstrated with Ames, shouting, 'Good God, if you open the sluice, you will drown all three.' Mills drowned, and it was only with much difficulty that Hillier and Vowles escaped the torrent of water. The inquest was adjourned until the following day when a verdict of manslaughter was returned against Ames. At the subsequent trial, Ames was tried for wilful murder but found guilty of manslaughter and received seven years' imprisonment. By contrast, the two boys, Hillier and Vowels, who attempted to save the life of Mills, were commended highly by the judge and were given each three guineas. (*Daily News*; *Bristol Mercury*)

~ August 26th ~

1871: Bath's citizens were becoming increasingly annoyed by the disappearance of that great emblem of civilisation – the door knocker. Indeed, so frequently had these thefts become, that the Watch Committee had decided to impose a fine of 5*s* upon a policeman if a knocker theft occurred on his beat. The culprit turned out to be Charles Loughman, the son of a highly respectable clergyman of the city. He was caught when a policeman observed him trying to wrench off the knocker of No. 13 Milsom Street, a house owned by a Mr Pearson. On failing to wrench off the knocker, Loughman knocked loudly several times before running off. He was caught by the policeman and taken back to Milsom Street, where he was made to apologise to Mr Pearson, who had been woken by the knocking. Loughman appeared before Bath Police Court on this date, where he was sentenced to seven days' imprisonment. The Bench said that it was with 'great grief' that they had to send Loughman to jail given his education and position, but they felt compelled to do so. (*Lloyd's Weekly Newspaper; Manchester Times*)

~ August 27th ~

1829: A boy named Joseph Shrine was throwing walnuts from the tree of a Bath tradesman. He was asked to stop, but Shrine ran into an outhouse to hide and escape potential punishment. Unexpectedly, Shrine died; it was assumed to be due to 'excessive alarm'. (*The Bristol Mercury*)

1864: 'A deplorable accident happened at the Lansdown College, Bath, which involved the death of one man and serious injury to a lad. It appears that a man named William Adams, of Twerton, and a lad named Bailey were employed doing something to the roof of the college, and whilst standing on a ladder, which was placed against an old spout, the spout gave way and they were precipitated from a considerable height to the ground. The sufferers were at once removed to the hospital, where it was found that Adams had sustained a compound fracture of the arm, and he died soon after his admission. The lad's injuries were not of a very serious nature.' (*The Bristol Mercury*)

~ AUGUST 28TH ~

2003: *The Times* announced that the search for Britain's oldest continually inhabited house was over. The winner was Saltford Manor House, located 5 miles from Bath. The search was led by Dr John Goodall, an architectural historian, carrying out the investigation for *Country Life* magazine. Dr Goodall narrowed the shortlist of possible candidates to three houses: Horton Court in Gloucestershire, which dates to the 1160s; the Manor in Hemingford Grey, Cambridgeshire, dated by Dr Goodall to the 1150s, and which also claims to be the oldest continually inhabited house in Britain; and Saltford Manor House, which was built before 1150. Dr Goodall decided on Saltford because of the diamond markings of a Norman arch which was similar to Hereford Cathedral, which was built in 1148. Dr Goodall used strict criteria to select his shortlist of possible candidates. Royal palaces, churches and former monastic buildings converted into homes were excluded. Furthermore, the house was not to have fallen into total ruin and should have dateable evidence of its age. The façade of Saltford Manor dates to 1645 but on entering there are huge ceiling beams and a Norman arch. On the second floor, traces of a wall painting depicting the Blessed Virgin Mary and a Wheel of Fortune have been discovered. The wall painting is believed to date from 1200. (*The Times*; Nikolaus Pevsner, *The Buildings of England: North Somerset and Bristol*, Penguin, 1958)

~ AUGUST 29TH ~

1503: Oliver King, Bishop of Bath and Wells, died. He was born in London and educated at Eton and Cambridge. He was ordained sub-deacon in 1467 and deacon in 1473. He then studied civil law at Orleans and Cambridge, gaining a doctorate in 1481. He served under Edward IV and consequently acquired a number of religious preferments. At Edward IV's death, he became secretary to Edward V, but Richard, Duke of Gloucester and Edward V's protector, dismissed King from his position and arrested him in 1483. For the next two years, his movements are largely unknown. However, after the ascendancy of Henry VII to the throne, King again entered royal service. He gained the Bishopric of Exeter in 1492, but was not resident within the diocese. In 1495, he was translated to Bath and Wells by papal bull. King spent more time in this diocese. Although King used a suffragan bishop to deputise for him in both the dioceses where he was bishop, he organised the restoration of Bath Abbey from 1500. King claimed that the rebuilding of Bath Abbey was inspired after he had a dream in which he saw the Holy Trinity with angels ascending and descending a ladder to heaven. At the top of the ladder an olive tree supported a crown. He heard a voice saying, 'Let an olive establish a crowne, and let a King restore a church.' In King's will, he asked to be buried at Bath, rather than the chantry chapel he built himself at St George's Chapel, Windsor. Here the oak panels depict his royal masters, Prince Edward, Edward IV, Edward V and Henry VII. At Bath, his memorial has carved ladders and angels, alluding to his dream. (*Oxford Dictionary of National Biography*)

1842: J. Holmes, a quarryman of Milk Street, Bath, was working at the Combe Down Quarry when he was killed as a result of a 3-ton weight of stones falling on him. The deceased was working with another man, trying to throw down a mass of rock resting on a foundation not more than 2ft square, over which height it projected several feet. Homes' death deprived a wife and four children of their support. The youngest of these children was only a few weeks old. The inquest held into Homes' death recorded a verdict of accidental death. Combe Down and Bathampton Mines are now an area of Special Scientific Interest, as the disused mine workings provide a suitable habitat for the endangered Greater Horseshoe bat. (*The Times*)

1864: 'The Sewerage of Bath – At a special meeting of the Bath Council on Tuesday, it was resolved, with only one dissentient to apply to Parliament for powers to construct sewers on each side of the river, from the city to Newton Meads, below Twerton, where it is proposed to deodorise the sewage matter. The expense is estimated at £23,000.'

~ AUGUST 31ST ~

1840: The first train arrived at Bath station (now Bath Spa) from Bristol Temple Meads. The train, consisting of three first-class and five second-class carriages, was hauled by the locomotive *Fireball*. Trains to London, however, did not start until June 30th 1841, when the Box Tunnel was completed. (Mark Oakley, *Bristol Suburban: Temple Meads Local Stations Halts and Platforms 1840-1990*, Redcliffe Press, 1990)

—

1972: In February 1968, 'important national issues' were raised by Bath City Council's decision to serve an enforcement notice under the Town and Country Planning Act (1968) to Miss Wellesley-Colley to repaint the door of her house in the Royal Crescent, which she had painted a shade of 'primrose yellow'. The council had also demanded that the yellow blinds she had installed be removed. Mr Walker, Secretary for the Environment, ordered an enquiry to look into the issue. Wellesley-Colley claimed that the door had been painted in 1968, before the 1968 Act had come into force and that the Act could not apply retrospectively. Mr John Oxley, Director of the Bath Preservation Trust, stated that the trustees 'considered the colours most regrettable'. The outcome of the inquiry was that since the front door had faded to 'such an innocuous shade' the colour need not be changed; however, the blinds should be taken down. On this date, Mr Walker overturned that judgement, stating that he had no power to have interior fittings, such as blinds, to be removed and brought the sorry dispute to an end. (*The Times*)

— September 1st —

1284: A royal charter of Edward I was granted to Robert Burnell, Bishop of Bath and Wells. The charter gave the bishop the right to hold a ten-day fair annually at his Bath Manor House. Robert Burnell was a favourite of Edward I and immediately after the king's coronation in 1274, he was appointed Chancellor. In January 1275, the king secured him the election as the Bishop of Bath and Wells. Burnell's chancellorship coincided with the passing of a number of statutes and Burnell had responsibility for the growing administration and the passing of legislation in Parliament. Burnell also enquired in each county the nature of royal rights and privileges. Chroniclers remark on Burnell's desire to fix a base in London for the chancery for more effective administration. Burnell, by reputation, had several illegitimate children. Because of this, the pope rejected attempts by Edward I to translate Burnell to Canterbury in 1278 and the rich diocese of Winchester in 1280. In 1285, Burnell was involved with the production of Westminster II – a statute detailing regulations about the writs obtained in the chancery and defining the power of the clerks to frame new writs. He died at Berwick on October 25th 1292, and was buried at Wells. (*Oxford Dictionary of National Biography*; www.thecityofbath.co.uk)

– September 2nd –

1866: A novel form of crime took place during the Sunday service at All Saints' Church. Two men placed their hats upon a bench in the 'free seats' section of the church. During the service, a man who had been sitting next to them got up and left. At the end of the service they had found that he had taken their hats. The thief wore a cloth cap which he put into his pocket when he entered the church, and was thus able to remove, without any suspicion, the hat of his neighbour. (*Dundee Courier*)

1891: Henry 'Harry' Dainton was released from prison after serving a month's imprisonment for assaulting his wife Hannah. During his absence, Hannah had been granted a separation order. Henry became violent when he saw Hannah drinking, as he felt it excessive. Six days after his release, an argument broke out between the couple and Hannah was seen with a bloody nose. At 10 p.m., the couple were seen arguing on the banks of the River Avon at Bath. Hannah was shouting 'Murder!' Soon afterwards, Harry returned home to his house, wet through, telling his 14-year-old son that he had tried to drown himself. Later, Hannah's body was recovered from the river and there were marks of a struggle on the banks. Harry was tried at Wells and found guilty of murder. The jury recommended mercy, owing to Hannah's conduct that night. (Nicola Sly, *A Grim Almanac of Somerset*, The History Press, 2010)

— September 3rd —

1806: On August 12th 1806, the trial of John Docke Rouvelett began at Wells. Rouvelett stood accused of attempting to defraud Mary Simeon, a Bath dealer in laces, by forging a bill for £420. On Saturday, August 16th, Rouvelett, calling himself Romney, came to the residence of Mary Simeon and bought a fan. Later, in the afternoon, he brought with him Elizabeth Barnet, who he passed off as his wife, and the pair bought 2 yards of lace at 4 guineas per yard. Although not married, Rouvelett and Barnet lived together as though they were man and wife. Rouvelett visited Mary again two days later with Barnet, but the pair bought nothing. Later that week, Rouvelett called again proposing to buy a quantity of goods, if Mary Simeon would accept a bill of long date. She did accept the bill, but when she sent the bill away to London to be cashed, she received communication that the bill was, in fact, a forgery. Rouvelett was apprehended and stood trial. On this occasion, he was found guilty and was executed on this date. (*Newgate Calendar*)

~ September 4th ~

1590: Bath was granted a royal charter by Elizabeth I. The charter defined the rights of the municipality. It stated that:

- Bath should be a sole city by itself
- Governance should consist of a mayor, aldermen and common council
- The mayor should be chosen annually, the Monday before the feast of St Michael and All Angels (September 29th)
- Powers would be given to impose by-laws and fines
- Two Sergeants-at-Mace are to be chosen annually to carry, before the mayor, maces of gold or silver engraved with England's Coat of Arms
- The city's boundaries are to be defined
- Powers would be granted to make inhabitants of Bath citizens or burgesses
- The mayor was made clerk of the market and any fines were to go to the mayor, aldermen and citizens with the power of seizure
- Two markets were to be held each week: on Wednesdays and Saturdays

(www.thecityofbath.co.uk)

~ September 5th ~

1768: *The Times* tells the story of 'a reverend divine', who lived near the city of Bath. He observed some young men busy in the fields next to his mansion house and saw that they were using nets. He concluded that the nets were to poach young broods of partridges. Outraged, he became determined to make an example of the poachers. The reverend hid himself amongst the corn and waited for an opportunity to catch the would-be poachers. When an opportunity arose, he ran forth, seizing the nets, but found he had only liberated a clutch of beautiful butterflies. (*The Times*)

1997: An evening memorial service to Diana, Princess of Wales was held at Bath Abbey. The service filled the abbey to capacity and loudspeakers relayed the service to large crowds in the churchyard. Over 1,000 people signed a book of condolence. A candlelit vigil followed the service, allowing the opportunity for private prayer and reflection.

~ SEPTEMBER 6TH ~

1872: An inquest was held at Bath to look into the circumstances of the death of Miss Courtney, the aged sister of Admiral Courtney. Miss Courtney had lived in a cottage, in the outskirts of Bath, living, what was considered, an eccentric lifestyle. Although she was financially secure, Miss Courtney occupied a part-furnished room and slept on a couch without changing her clothes. Twice a week, an old soldier brought her food, whilst another fetched coal and wood for her. Neither man entered her house. Three days previously, she was found wearing a ragged chemise and an old blanket. Death was attributed to natural causes, but no one could work out why a well-off lady should live in such a manner. (*Lloyd's Weekly*; *Hampshire Advertiser*; *Hampshire Telegraph*)

1878: After spending a night drinking with his friends in numerous pubs in Bath, Edward Adams, aged 27, bet for the trifling sum of 6*d* to jump off Newton Bridge. The bridge, also known as Newbridge, is 40ft high. When Adams was on the parapet, Mr James of New Street, Bath, urged him not to make the jump. Adams, however, made the jump and he was drowned. A search was made for his body, but it was never found. (*Bristol Mercury and Daily Post*)

— SEPTEMBER 7TH —

1867: A facetious prisoner left this 'advert' after serving a three-month sentence at Bath City Prison: 'To be Let, ready furnished, a very snug apartment in the Bath City Hotel, Twerton. The above hotel is replete with every convenience, and is situate on the rise of a lovely hill on the left of the Lower Bristol-road, within 10 minutes of the station, from which a Royal Bus will convey you. The hotel has a beautiful view of Landsdown, Beaconhill, Beechen-cliff, with the whole city of Bath like a panorama. The rustic village and mills of Twerton is within 10 minutes' walk and the healthful and soul-inspiring Combe Down. The manager of the hotel, or governor, keeps it that respectable that no one is admitted as a resident without a special recommendation from the mayor and magistrates of Bath. The hotel has a spacious chapel, with a visiting chaplain, and the responses are daily accompanied with about 70 nasal organs. This department, mark'd 26 on the plan, would suit any young man, or Bachelor of quiet and sedentary habits, who will find this a quiet retreat. The property is well looked after, as the doors are of iron and double lock'd; the windows have iron bars to keep thieves out. Apply to the Mayor and Magistrates – N.B. Good attendants, and a man cook is kept.' (*Daily News*)

— September 8th —

1777: Following an advert in the *Bath Chronicle*, twenty-two gentlemen met at York House in Bath for the formation of a society to encourage agriculture, the arts, manufacturing, and commerce throughout the counties of Gloucestershire, Dorset, Bristol, Wiltshire and Somerset. From 1780, the society published an annual volume of reports, correspondence and essays to keep farmers up-to-date with the latest agricultural techniques. These technically good reports were mixed in with other reports that reflected the prejudices of their authors, including one by Dr Fothergill who believed that tea-drinking led women to alcoholism. He stated that 'this relaxing beverage, poured down hot, as it generally is twice a day, tends to unnerve the female frame and produce universal languor. The natural spirits being depressed, recourse is imprudently had to artificial ones.' An annual show became part of the society's activities and when the society merged with the Devon County Agricultural Society, the shows became peripatetic, replacing the annual meeting at Bath. From 1965, the society acquired 200 acres of land near Shepton Mallet to provide a permanent showground, and it is the current location for the Royal Bath and West Show. (Kenneth Hudsonm, *The Bath & West: A Bicentenary History*, Moonraker Press, 1976; Royal Bath & West of England Society website)

1868: 'On Tuesday a cow, belonging to Mr Weaver, of Farmborough, ran into the shop of Mr Asprey, cheesemonger, Bath, and before it could be expelled a number of cheeses were destroyed to the value of £15.' (*Bristol Mercury*)

~ September 9th ~

1974: Bath Theatre Royal reopened tonight following a three-month restoration, which cost £50,000 – the last time the painters were in was 1904. The Georgian theatre opened in 1750 and was given a royal charter by George III in 1768. The Theatre Royal moved to its current location in 1804, into a building designed by George Dance, the Younger. The Georgian interior was destroyed by fire in 1862. The interior was rebuilt in 1863 and reopened to Ellen Terry playing Titania in *A Midsummer Night's Dream*. Ellen Terry went on to become one of the most famous actresses of her generation. In the eighteenth century, Sarah Siddons also established her reputation at the Theatre Royal. On reporting tonight's reopening, *The Times* commented that veteran patrons would note that the faint smell of gas associated with the theatre had gone, following the replacement of the emergency gas lighting. The theatre reopened to a performace of Noël Coward's comedy *Present Laughter*, which was attended by the Duke of Gloucester. (*The Times*; Nikolaus Pevsner, *The Buildings of England: North Somerset and Bristol*, Penguin, 1958)

~ September 10th ~

1847: The *Bath Herald* reports that the inhabitants of Bath Street were surprised when they saw a fox running at full speed through the neighbourhood, being chased by a number of men and boys. The report continues: 'Reynard, finding the chase too close for him, took refuge in the chequers public-house, to the great disquietude of the worthy landlady and family. Search being made for the varmint, he was found to have ensconced himself in the bar amongst the ginger beer bottles and with which he made some havoc. Some difficulty was now found in dislodging master Reynard from his quarters, but by the aid of rope and a pair of tongs he was ignominiously ejected and borne off by his captors. We understand that the animals escaped from the premises of Mr Knott of the Abbey Green.' The article refers to the fox as 'Reynard', a literary name given to the fox, which may have come from fables originating in France, the Low Countries and Germany where Reynard the Fox is depicted as an anthropomorphic trickster. William Caxton's translation of the Middle Dutch versions of the stories in the fifteenth century made the figure of Reynard the Fox popular in England. (*Bath Herald*)

— September 11th —

1745: The poet Mary Chandler (1687–1745) died on this day. Her spinal deformity precluded marriage, so she educated herself by reading the classics and contemporary authors. She set up a milliners' shop in Bath, before the age of 20. In 1733, she published, anonymously, *A Description of Bath*, consisting of 322 rhyming couplets about Bath. An elderly businessman proposed marriage when she was 54 but she refused and wrote the incident up a verse of 'The True Tale':

'ourscore long miles, to buy a crooked wife!
Old too! I thought the oddest thing in life.

(Oxford Dictionary of National Biography)

1811: Arthur Bailey was executed at Ilchester for stealing a letter from the Post Office at Bath. Bailey had long been in the confidence of the Bath postmaster and the law was slow to catch up with him when letters started to go missing. Bailey was convicted at the Somerset Summer Assizes for the theft of a letter containing the bills of Messrs Slack, linen drapers, and forgery of an endorsement for one those bills. Before the sentence was carried out he addressed the spectators, saying, 'I hope you will all take warning', and picking up a prayer book said, 'I beg you to look often into this book, and you will not come to shame. Be sure to be honest, and not covet money, cursed money! – and particularly money that is not your own.' (*Newgate Calendar*)

— September 12th —

1869: A lady by the name of M'Limont, who lived in Victoria Villa, Weston Road in Bath, went to church on Sunday morning, leaving only her cook, Marie Kikillers, at home. On her return, she found the house locked and surmised that Marie had disappeared with a plate and jewellery up to the value of £200. Superintendent Morgan took charge of the investigation. He found that a man of 'foreign appearance' had signalled Marie from a cab that had stopped near the house. The railway stations of Bath were visited next but no trace was found of the pair. The superintendent heard that there was a cab on the Bristol Road containing a man and a woman with some luggage. He traced the fugitives to Bristol and found them enjoying a cup of tea at the White Lion Inn, Bedminster. The fugitives stated that they were man and wife and denied that they had come from Bath. The woman became agitated, which convinced the superintendent that he had caught the thieves. Whilst the thieves were apprehended to Bedminster police station, a search was made of their luggage and the stolen plate and several articles of jewellery were recovered. (*The York Herald*)

‒ September 13th ‒

1847: About this time, Mr Dudfield, a carrier from Bath, dropped a spark from a candle into a drawer containing £300 in bank notes. He shut the drawer, ignorant of the mischief, and on opening it the next morning, found all the notes destroyed. This story was reported in a number of newspapers at the time. (*Bath Chronicle*)

———

1862: Bath's GWR railway station platform thronged with people who were waiting to get the train to take them on an excursion to London. Amongst them was Mr Hopkins of Bathwick, who was waiting for his wife. As the train from Bristol to London drew into the station, there was a great deal of pushing amongst the crowd towards the carriages. The result was that Mr Hopkins fell down the gap between the station and the platform edge as the train was still moving. Mr Hopkins sustained a very serious injury: his ankle was crushed beneath the train and he was taken from beneath the train 'insensible' to the United Hospital. His leg was amputated, but sadly Mr Hopkins died. He was 70 and was both well known and well liked in the district. (*Hampshire Telegraph*)

— SEPTEMBER 14TH —

1822: 'On Saturday evening the 14th instant, about a quarter past nine, as one of the Bristol Coaches was returning to Bath, it upset about midway between Newton Turnpike and Twerton; when one of the passengers, a poor Irishman, named Hambleton, was so seriously injured that he died on Wednesday. On Friday last, an inquest was held on the body, and a verdict given of manslaughter; it appearing that the accident was occasioned by the furious driving of the coachman, George Clark.' (*Trewman's Exeter Flying Post*)

1938: An AA patrolman was erecting signs on the banks of the River Avon, at Bath, when he heard shouts from a man struggling in the icy-cold waters. Although the patrolman had only recently recovered from a severe bout of influenza, he threw off his coat, dived in and pulled the man to safety. It transpired that the rescued man was short-sighted and consequently had walked into the river. Both men recovered from their ordeal. (*The Times*)

― September 15th ―

1865: Bath Magistrates' Court heard the case against William Fletcher, who was charged with assaulting two pupils, Emily Martha Read and Marie Louise Perrin, of Mrs Pearson's School, Bath. The assault took place when the two girls, along with Miss Moore, a governess, were walking across some fields to Weston. They happened to walk through William Fletcher's field and on being attracted to some blackberries, they left the path. Before they could get to the hedge, though, Fletcher accosted the group with foul language. Miss Moore offered to leave if they were trespassing, but Fletcher attempted to strike the governess. Miss Moore evaded the blow and ran to safety. The two girls were not so lucky and were struck several times by Fletcher. The girls were both examined by Mr Field, a surgeon, who found unmistakable evidence of heavy blows from a stick on Marie's right shoulder blade and the mark of a severe blow on the nape of Emily's neck. Fletcher claimed that some children had recently lit fires in his field and several of his ricks had only narrowly escaped being burnt. The Bench, however, was unimpressed and could not see how Fletcher could have imagined that these girls with their governess could have been a threat to his hay. Fletcher was fined 40s to include a guinea to the girls' solicitor and the surgeon. (*Hampshire Telegraph*)

— September 16th —

1875: Fredrick Angall Carter, described as a gentleman, who resided at the Christopher Hotel, was charged with stealing a door knocker (value 3*s*) from No. 20 The Paragon, the property of Mrs Dunning. Detective Weaver apprehended Carter at Clevedon, when in the company of another young man. On being told that the door knockers had been found in his hotel room, he told his companion that it was no use to say anything since 'they had the two knockers'. One of the knockers found was identified by Mrs Dunning's servant, sister and an ironmonger who compared it with the part that remained on the door. Mr Bartrum, defending the prisoner, said that 'felonious intent, which was the first essential of felony, was absent, and that if the case was fully brought home to the prisoner it was only a silly "lark". After consulting in the private room for a time, the Bench decided to dismiss the charge of felony; but the prisoner was almost immediately arranged on a new charge of wilfully damaging. At an early stage Mr Bartrum rose and applied for a remand, in order that prisoner might be tried by an indifferent bench. His conviction with the present magistrates would, he said, be a foregone conclusion. The Bench remanded prisoner to Saturday.' (*Bristol Mercury*)

— September 17th —

1841: Between thirty and forty men were working in the GWR tunnel at Box, adding sleepers to the track. Two trains met, at speed, in the tunnel and two of the workmen were unable to get out of the way; they were knocked down by the approaching trains. One of the men, John Burns, died from injuries one hour after being knocked down. The other man suffered severe injuries to his hands and his feet. (*The Times*)

—

1893: Alfred Button, aged 27, was admitted to Bath Hospital after he cut his throat in a suicide attempt. Button stated that the ongoing miner's strike had driven him to the act as he saw starvation staring him in the face. The second half of the nineteenth century saw the first national coal strikes. In 1893, many miners went out on strike as the price of coal had dropped and colliery owners wanted to pay the miners less in order to maintain a profit. Miners rejected this and were 'locked out of work', unable to return until they accepted a reduction in pay. (*The Standard*; www.wwmm.org)

— September 18th —

1823: 'A stout man, habited in singular costume, and whose manners corresponded with his dress, who, it appeared, is a dissenting preacher in one of the neighbouring villages, came before the Bath Forum Magistrates, accompanied by his wife, who is very far advanced in pregnancy, for the purpose of her swearing the child! The husband declared (which was admitted by the wife) that he had not cohabited with her for the last two years and a half, and that in consequence of the real father of the child industriously circulating a report that the child was the husband's, which he stoutly denied, he gained the great displeasure of the hearers; and the reason of his bringing her before the Magistrates was for the purpose of removing the odium of falsehood from himself, and to set him right with his congregation. The wife with great candour solemnly declared who the real father of the child was; but the husband was told by the magistrate, that he was bound to maintain it, which he agreed to do provided it did not live with him. The happy couple then walked off seemingly well satisfied, excepting the regret of the husband that the gay seducer could not be punished for his amorous intrigue. The husband during the investigation frequently quoted passages from Scripture; and expressed himself happy in knowing that his wife had turned from the error of her ways! The quaintness with which he related his story was extremely diverting!' (*Bath Herald*)

— September 19th —

1874: At about 2 p.m. on this day, 8,000 people assembled in Kensington High Street to cheer Mr Stanton, who was attempting to ride from Bath to London (120 miles) in 7.5 hours. Stanton had not arrived by 2.30 p.m. and the crowd began to slope off. By 3.30, the crowd had shrunk to 2,000 people. Stanton eventually arrived on a bicycle that was too small for him, 54 minutes late. Stanton had left Bath at 7 a.m. At Box, he crashed into a horse. He fell from his machine and a fork was bent, but not enough to stop Stanton continuing. Throughout the journey, people from the town and villages en route came out to cheer Stanton on his way. The journey proceeded without incident until he reached Colnbrook, which lies between Winsdor and West Drayton. Here, he was attacked by four 'rough-looking' men with sticks. The ruffians hit Stanton over the head and severely damaged his bicycle. After the ruffians had left him, he mounted his disabled machine but it collapsed after cycling a mile and a half. Stanton was forced to walk into Colnbrook, where he borrowed a smaller and much less powerful machine from a friend. It was this bicycle on which Stanton finished his journey. Stanton lost the £200 wager he had on himself being able to complete the journey in the allotted time. This may have also been the motive for the attack. (*The Times*)

– September 20th –

1850: A cheap day excursion, which ran from Bath to London, was returning towards Bath when it derailed at Wootton Bassett. The train collided with a horsebox which was not properly secured in its siding and had rolled onto the main line. The impact caused the train and the front four carriages to roll down an embankment. Policeman White (forerunner of the signalman) had been advised by Skull, the day policeman, that the horsebox was secure by triangular blocks on both sides of the wheels, but had not checked it himself. A public footpath crossed the line by the horsebox and anyone could have removed the blocks. Nevertheless, White was found guilty of neglect at the County Magistrates' Court and sentenced to two months' imprisonment. (Colin G. Maggs, *The GWR Swindon to Bath Line*, Sutton, 2003)

—

1882: Residents near the Salvation Army Church in Newark Street were increasingly fed up with the beating of a large drum during services which ran late into the night. Despite numerous complaints no resolution had been reached and so those living near to the church assembled next door and proceeded to drown out the service by using a steam whistle, beating gongs and ringing bells, attracting a large crowd to the neighbourhood in the process. As a result, on this date two of the men were summoned to appear before Bath Police Court for having 'wilfully and maliciously disquieted the congregation' assembled next door and were committed for trial. (*The Standard*)

⟶ September 21st ⟵

1865: An inquest was held at Bath, by the coroner Mr A.H. English, concerning the death of Dr Tristram, aged 81. His doctor, George Leighton Wood, prescribed a mixture of syrup of poppies, camphor and a solution of acetate of morphine. Dr Tristram took the prescription to Mr Steele, a druggist of Milsom Street. However, it was Mr Steele's apprentice, Robert Gane, who made up the prescription. After taking a dose of the medicine, Dr Tristram lapsed into unconsciousness. Despite the efforts of the best surgeons, Dr Tristram died. At the inquest, it was revealed that Gane had mistaken the bottle containing acetate of morphine with the bottle containing pure morphine. The bottles, although not on the same shelf, were quite close to each other. The brother of Dr Tristram appealed to the jury to show leniency towards the young apprentice. However, the jury returned a verdict of manslaughter against Gane. The case proceeded to the Somerset Assizes, where the question of whether Gane had been criminally negligent was pursued. The court concluded that Gane he had not and he was released. (*Leicester Chronicle*; Nicola Sly, *A Grim Almanac of Somerset*, The History Press, 2010)

— SEPTEMBER 22ND —

1864: William George Horner (1786–1837), mathematician and school headmaster, died on this day. Horner was educated at the Kingswood School, Bristol, which was established by Charles Wesley. He became assistant master here between 1800 and 1804 before becoming headmaster, aged only 19! In 1809, he left to set up his own school, The Seminary, at No. 27 Grosvenor Place, Bath. Horner encouraged bright pupils to stay on for an extra year of schooling. Although Horner had a high intellect, he was impatient and would use the cane freely to those pupils he considered diligent but dull. Horner's main contribution to mathematics was to develop a quick method of approximating the roots of a polynomial equation. His method was published in *Philosophical Transactions* in 1819. He died after a short illness, at his school in Grosvenor Place. (*Oxford Dictionary of National Biography*)

— September 23rd —

1787: By the 1780s, 400 Methodist preaching houses had been established in Britain. Charles Wesley had established himself as a popular orator and large numbers would come to hear him preach. This extract from the *Bath Chronicle* shows Wesley's enduring popularity: 'Churches: it will give great pleasure to the friends of that extraordinary man, the Rev. John Wesley to hear that in his last visit to Bath he preached 3 times on Sunday & administered the sacrament to over 200 communicants.' (*Bath Chronicle*)

2008: A gas canister explosion occurred on the construction site of the new Southgate Street shopping centre near Henry Street. Officers were called just after 5 p.m. and a large area cordoned off because of the risk of further explosions from other gas canisters on the site. Bath Spa railway station was also closed for a time. A rest centre was set up in the Pavilion in North Parade Road for those unable to get home. Witnesses saw large plumes of black smoke and a series of large explosions. There were no reports of any casualties. The blaze was put out by 6 p.m. but fire crews remained to cool the remaining gas canisters. (www.bbc.co.uk)

— SEPTEMBER 24TH —

1933: Writer Alice Murial Williamson, née Livingstone, was born in New York, USA, in 1867 or 1868. Very little is known of her early life, but she was privately educated. She was 15 when she published her first story. During the 1890s, she travelled to Britain and met her future husband Charles Williamson, a journalist. Her first novel *The Barn Stormers* was published in 1897 and was well received. Both Alice and Charles were keen travellers and enjoyed motoring. Cars often formed the basis for some of the novels they wrote jointly, including *My Friend the Chauffeur* (1905) and *The Car of Destiny* (1906). After the First World War, the couple moved to Combe Down, Bath, and remained there until the death of Charles. Alice then lived at the Milestone Hotel, Kensington. She returned to Bath each year on the anniversary of her husband's death. Alice maintained a belief in spiritualism and believed that their collaborative writing projects continued, as she claimed that she could feel her husband's presence as she wrote. On September 23rd 1933, she was found unconscious in her hotel room and died on the following day. Sleeping pills were found in her room and at her inquest a verdict of accidental poisoning was given. (*Oxford Dictionary of National Biography*)

— SEPTEMBER 25TH —

1790: The remains of a Roman temple dedicated to Minerva were discovered by workmen digging the foundations for the new Pump Room in Stall Street. Columns measuring 3ft 8in in diameter were uncovered. The Corporation had given orders that these columns should be converted into foundations. However, the 'timely interventions of connoisseurs who shuddered at the idea of so gross an affront to the Goddess of Wisdom' prevented this from happening. (*The Times*)

1889: William Luke Nichols was born in Gosport, Hampshire, on August 10th 1802. He studied at Queen's College, Oxford, and entered the Church. Between 1834 and 1839 he was minister at St James' Church and for one year at Trinity Church, both in Bath. After holding various clerical posts in Devon, he returned to live at Bath in 1851 in Lansdown Crescent, and stayed for seven years. He was a frequent traveller abroad to study the scenery and antiquities of Spain, Italy, Greece and Palestine. Nichols also published in a number of periodicals and was a noted figure in the Bath literary set at this time. In 1838, he published *Horae Romanae, or, a Visit to a Roman Villa*, a pamphlet about the Roman villa at Newton St Loe, near Bath, discovered during the building of the Great Western Railway. He died on this date and was buried in the family vault in Gosport. (*Oxford Dictionary of National Biography*)

– September 26th –

1878: Mr Walter S. Britters, of the Clarence Bicycle Club, rode from London to Bath and back to London again in a single day, a distance of 212 miles. Britters set off from Hyde Park Corner just past midnight and reached Bath at 11.30 a.m. After a visit to the General Post Office to despatch a telegram, Britters reached his starting point a few minutes before midnight. Britters had apparently taken it easier in the last few hours, since he had ample time to spare. The exploit was undertaken simply to discover what distance could be achieved easily and comfortably in a day. (*Manchester Times*)

———

1895: A series of archaeological discoveries were reported in a number of newspapers about this time, due to the construction of the Monkswood Reservoir. On this date, an Iron Age axe was found. The metal head was attached by wooden pegs to a bone handle. Previous discoveries on the site included Bronze Age weapons and jewellery. The reservoir at Monkswood is located in St Catherine's Valley, near Bath. It is a Site of Special Scientific Interest containing ancient woodland with rich ground flora and a wide range of invertebrates. (*Hampshire Advertiser*; *Gloucester Citizen*; *Bath Chronicle and Weekly Gazette*; www.wessexwater.co.uk)

— September 27th —

1819: The Duke of Wellington visited Bath from Earl Bathurst's seat near Cirencester. 'The intelligence was no sooner become public than crowds assembled to obtain a sight of this illustrious warrior.' The Duke of Wellington only stayed a few hours. He was received by the mayor and toured the city. He remarked that he was highly delighted with the beauty and uniformity of the buildings. The Duke also called at the North Somerset Yeomanry Office and he recognised Capt. Thornhill, whom he had served with in the 8th Light Dragoons, between the years 1794 and 1795. The Duke heartily shook Thornhill by the hand and enquired of his family and about the strength and establishment of the North Somerset Yeomanry and Rifle Corps. The Duke left the city on his way to Wellington. Arthur Wellesley became famous in 1808, after he assumed control of the British, Portuguese and Spanish forces in the Peninsular War (1808–14), eventually forcing the French to surrender. Napoleon abdicated and Wellesley returned home, a hero, and was created the Duke of Wellington. In 1815, Wellington again became commander of the allied forces and finally defeated Napoleon at the Battle of Waterloo in June 1815. (*The Times*)

— September 28th —

1944: The Little Theatre at Citizen House was extensively damaged by fire, destroying period costumes and other stage equipment. The theatre was established in 1913 by Helen Hope, a pioneering social reformer, at Citizen House, the former mansion residence of the Duke of Buckingham and Chandos. In 1915, Consuelo de Reyes set up a community group known as The Citizen House Players, with the aim of making theatre accessible to people with limited contact with cultural pursuits. She soon established regular drama courses and managed to create a 200-seat auditorium. De Reyes succeeded Hope in owning and running the theatre. In the 1930s, an architect was commissioned and a combined theatre and news cinema was built next door, with art deco styling. Emperor Haile Selassie, during his time of exile in Bath, would come to the cinema in order to watch news reports of the Italian occupation of Ethiopia. It was the second time in the theatre's history that it has been affected by fire – the first being in 1936 when severe damage estimated at about £100,000 was caused and many items of historical interest were destroyed. (*The Times*; *Bath Chronicle*)

~ September 29th ~

1853: Joseph Beal, William Overton, Jess Nicholls, Henry Weber, James Allway, Joseph Weber and George Wilcox, inmates of the Union workhouse, appeared before Bath Police Court for refusing to work at stone breaking because the master of the workhouse refused to grant them the liquor in which the meat and pudding were boiled instead of water. It was judged that the inmates' actions were not justified and Overton and Beal were sentenced to twenty-one days' imprisonment. The others were imprisoned for seven days, with hard labour. The case was later brought before the Board of Guardians, who agreed that the broth of the workhouse should be distributed to the aged, infirm and the children. (*Daily News*)

1883: 'Mr Oscar Wilde appeared for the first time before a provincial audience on Saturday [September 29th] at the Bath Theatre Royal, and delivered his lecture on "Personal Impressions on America". There was some curiosity to see the well-known thespian, but the popular parts of the house were sparsely attended, the only part where the attendance was fairly numerous being the dress circle. The lecture lasted two hours. Speaking of his personal impressions on landing on the other side of the Atlantic, he said the Americans were decidedly the most comfortably dressed people in the world. There was an absence of romantic unpunctuality in America – the people were all in a hurry. In all applications of the modern science to machinery the Americans were wonderfully successful; but they failed in architecture.' (*Bristol Mercury*)

~ September 30th ~

1771: Bath's Assembly Rooms, designed by John Wood, the Younger, opened with a ridotto (a combination of a dance and a musical concert). The Master of Ceremonies on that occasion was Capt. William Wade. The assembly rooms were built to replace the two assembly rooms near to the abbey which were seen as too small for the increased numbers of visitors, too old-fashioned and too far away from the more fashionable parts of the city. In 1765, the Bath Corporation invited designs for the new assembly rooms; two designs were proposed, one by John Wood, the other by Robert Adam. Three years later, the Corporation accepted a revised plan by Wood. Finance was by a 'tontine' subscription. Here, the shares of those who have died are added to those still living; the longest-living shareholder inherits everything. At £20,000, it had the highest building costs for any building built in Bath during the eighteenth century. The building consists of two oblong blocks containing the Ball Room, with capacity for 800 dancers, and the Tea Room. A Tuscan colonnade runs the length of the Ball Room, which turns and forms the main entrance in between two main blocks. Behind this is the Octagonal Card Room. (Dr Cathryn Spence Water, *History and Style: Bath World Heritage Site*, The History Press, 2012; Nikolaus Pevsner, *The Buildings of England: North Somerset and Bristol*, Penguin, 1958)

~ OCTOBER 1ST ~

1813: The annual election of magistrates and municipal officers took place at the Guildhall. The occasion demonstrates the privileges of municipal officers at this time. The Recorder of the City and the Bath Corporation were treated to a lavish dinner at York House by the mayor elect. The dinner and desert contained 'all the luxuries of earth could produce, displayed with taste, splendour and elegance.' (*The Morning Post*)

2009: Eddie Sedgemore, aged 67, a cyclist from Marshfield, set up a record for the longest journey made on a motorised electric bicycle. Sedgemore then spent twenty-eight days travelling the length and breadth of the country travelling 1,912 miles, beating the previous record of 1,612 miles. He visited the northern, southern, eastern and western extremes of the UK mainland. At a ceremony in Bath, the city's MP, Don Foster, presented a certificate to Sedgemore. Along the cycle ride, Sedgemore raised money for the British Heart Foundation. (*Western Daily Press*)

⟶ October 2nd ⟵

1803: An affray took place on Avon Street at eleven o'clock at night between some soldiers of the Army Reserve. When the watchmen attempted to restore order, a number of soldiers drew their bayonets and stabbed one of the watchmen through the heart and left another watchman severely wounded. (*The Times*)

———

1991: Sluice gates near Teverton, Bath, were jammed open, causing dozens of boats to be beached on the River Avon, after river levels fell to less than half their normal depth. (*The Times*)

———

2000: Joyce Bainbridge decided to retire from being a keep-fit instructor at the age of 83. She began teaching keep-fit at the age 21, after being trained by the Woman's League of Health and Beauty, which was founded in 1930. Bainbridge taught keep-fit in both Bath and Bristol until she moved to Naunton, Gloucestershire, in 1974 and founded a branch of the league in nearby Bourton-on-the-Water. (*Western Daily Press*)

~ October 3rd ~

1862: The inquest into the death of Isaac West, aged 14, took place at the Guildhall in Bath. Isaac died from glanders, a bacterial disease normally associated with horses. It was thought that the disease could have been transmitted from the horses that worked at the Camerton Coal Mine where Isaac worked. Isaac became ill and was admitted to the United Hospital the Saturday previously, but his condition deteriorated. His skin became thick with pustules and Isaac died the following Wednesday. The inquest was held two days later. At the inquest, Joesph Crew, the foreman, stated that all the horses at the mine were healthy. This was confirmed by Richard Mullins, shoesmith, and Mr G. Feare, the mining engineer. This evidence presented to the inquest exonerated the mine owners of responsibility for Isaac's death. The jury found that Isaac had died from glanders, but since there was insufficient evidence to show how the deceased caught the disease, it was not possible to say how the disease was transmitted to Isaac. (*Bristol Mercury*)

~ October 4th ~

1821: John Rennie was born in Phantassie, Haddingtonshire, and from an early age took an interest in mechanics. He was able to set himself up as a millwright in 1779. In 1873, he made a tour of England, making notes on canals, bridges and machinery he found there. An introduction to James Watt and Matthew Boulton led to Rennie taking charge of the Albion Mills in London and erecting the engines they supplied there. Rennie's reputation as an engineer increased and in 1790 he was appointed surveyor to the Kennet and Avon Canal, a scheme to link Bristol and Bath with London. Construction began in 1794. Delays and unexpected costs dogged the building of the canal. One particular problem was the use of unweathered Bath stone. In March 1803, Rennie wrote to the Kennet and Avon canal committee, advising that bricks should be used in the construction. However, the committee failed to heed this advice. Possibly this was because considerable trade in quarried stone from Bath and Bristol to London was expected. Another unexpected cost came from the proprietors of Sydney Gardens in Bath, who demanded 2,000 guineas for the right to take the canal through the property. Rennie became involved in a number of river and harbour improvement works. Rennie was also responsible for the building of three of the capital's bridges: Waterloo, Southwark and London. Rennie died on this date, at his Southwark home. (*Oxford Dictionary of National Biography*; Kenneth R. Chew, *The Kennet and Avon Canal*, David & Charles, 1968)

~ OCTOBER 5TH ~

1874: Soon after the opening of the Bath extension on the Somerset and Dorset line from Evercreech Junction, an accident on this stretch of railway line occurred, owing to subsidence. Soon after leaving Evercreech Junction, the fireman 'suddenly found the locomotive and tender jumping up and down'. The engine went down over a bridge, killing the driver. At the subsequent inquest, the coroner's jury recommended that inspecting the line before the first morning train should be included in the printed rules. The *Bath Chronicle* of October 8th reported that 'the line since its opening has not been considered too safe by more than one competent judge, and signs have not been wanting of the line having been properly set.' (Robin Atthill, *The Somerset and Dorset Railway*, Pan Books, 1970)

1989: The Attorney General dropped court proceedings against Mr Peter Mars, a Bath bookseller who refused to stop selling *Spycatcher* by Peter Wright. *Spycatcher* is a candid account of the author's work at MI5, including his attempts to prove that Roger Hollis, a former MI5 Director-General, was, in fact, a KGB spy. The book also gives a history of MI5. Several attempts were made by the British government to ban publication of the book in the UK. Ultimately, these all proved unsuccessful. In the case of Mr Mars, the Attorney General paid all of his legal costs, amounting to £1,725, and dropped legal action against another bookseller who was facing legal action on the same grounds. (*The Times*)

— OCTOBER 6TH —

1946: Protests during the 'High Mass' of St John's Church, Bathwick, were made to the Bishop of Bath and Wells, Dr H.W. Bradfield, following his sermon. Towards the end of his sermon the bishop stated: 'Before coming here I received by telephone information that an organised attempt would be made to break up our act of worship this morning on the part of people from outside this parish … The service as announced is one to which you have been accustomed for many years. I want to say, that any congregation in this diocese, of whatever churchmanship or theological outlook, will have the fullest possible protection of my pastoral office in the face of any that of that kind.' The protests concerned the belief that the church was too Catholic. Mr P.W. Petter, Governing Director of the National Union of Protestants, rose to ask a question, but left when asked to do so. The service was later interrupted by Mr Edgar Tozer, who declared, 'I am here to protest against the celebration of the Mass as being contrary to the will of God and the Prayer Book.' Mr Tozer was escorted from the church. Mr M.A. Perkins also made a protest at the end of the service. His voice, however, was partially drowned out by the organ voluntary and a scuffle ensued as he was taken out of the church. (*The Times*)

~ October 7th ~

1812: Before the passing of the 1832 Parliamentary Reform Act, Bath was obliged to send two MPs to the House of Commons. The franchise was restricted to the mayor, alderman and common council. Lord J. Thynne and Col. Palmer were duly elected by this process. However, Mr John Allen appeared in the hall and demanded a poll for himself and Mr W.C. Graves. Allen also insisted on the right of the freemen of the city to vote. He then appointed a young man to act as clerk, who took the votes of several freemen. The following day, a large crowd of Mr Allen's supporters assembled outside the Guildhall, which was shut. The mayor, who thought that the crowd was about to riot and perpetrate a number of outrages, read the riot act. One of the chief constables then seized Allen by his collar, but he was rescued by his friends and disappeared from the affray. All the front windows of the Guildhall were smashed and it was only after the arrival of the Bath Calvary, together with a party of Oxford militia, that peace was restored. (*The Times*)

1940: A special war hospitality committee was formed, in order to show members of the overseas colonial forces around Bath. An information bureau was established in the Pump Rooms and admission charges to the Roman Baths and the Pump Room were also waived to these men. (*The Times*)

⚊ October 8th ⚊

1811: *The Times* reported on this date that during the previous week 'a hair-dresser of Bath undertook to run from the Old Bridge, Bath, to the first house in Temple-street, Bristol, and return to Bath (above 24 miles) in 4 hours and 56 minutes, which wonderful task he performed in 3 hours 51 minutes.' (*The Times*)

⚊

1878: An inquest was held in the Guildhall, Bath, into the death of Mary Ann Mills of Corn Street, two days after she had died. Mary Ann had complained to her daughters that she had been 'ill-used' by her husband, showing them a bruise on her forehead. The next afternoon she was found unconscious and Dr Wills of the Royal United Hospital was called. She died later that evening. Her husband, John Mills, claimed that his wife had fallen and banged her head. Dr Wills refused to write a death certificate without first conducting a post-mortem. His conclusion was that Mary Ann had died from 'compression to the brain caused by bleeding'. This could have been caused either by a fall or from being struck by a fist. Thomas Viner, who lived in the same residence as the Mills', stated at the inquest that he heard Mary Ann being abused by her husband. The jury, however, recorded a verdict of death by natural causes. (Nicola Sly, *A Grim Almanac of Somerset*, The History Press, 2010)

~ October 9th ~

1913: Mrs Young of Bath was using petrol to wash her hair near an open fire. Her hair ignited and she was enveloped by flames and died, despite the best attempts of some nearby policemen who were on patrol. They rushed into her house and smothered the flames. The fire brigade, on its way to the scene, also suffered a misfortune as its fire engine collided with a lamp post, completely demolishing it. (*Bath Chronicle and Weekly Gazette*)

—

1927: Two men drowned in the River Avon after the boat they were rowing from Bristol capsized. A third man, Arthur Nibbett, aged 18, was rescued by T. Blesdoc, a 17-year-old boy scout. The men who died were E. Knight, 20, and S. Smith, 17. All three men were from Bristol and had taken a single-oared rowing boat to row to the Weston weir at Bath. (*The Times*)

~ October 10th ~

1845: An accident occurred on the Great Western Railway, which, 'though not very serious in its consequences, was within almost a hair's breadth of upsetting a train and doing the most frightful mischief.' A coal depot was being constructed between Bath and Twerton and a contractor was employed to remove spoil and wagons, which were towed by horses, from one side of the line to the other. Wagons were not supposed to cross the line when a train was due. However, at two o'clock on Friday afternoon, one of the workmen, Harry Salter, crossed with a load. He should have waited, since a train was due. The train's buffer hit the horse's hind leg, severing it completely, whilst two other men were thrown down the embankment. One of them suffered a broken collarbone; the other suffered severe contusions about the body. Fortunately neither man was severely hurt. The following day, Harry Salter, described rather unkindly by *The Times* as a 'loutish stupid looking man', appeared before magistrates. For his carelessness, Salter was fined the minimum penalty of £5. (*The Times*)

⁓ OCTOBER 11TH ⁓

1946: A commemoration was held at Bath Abbey, 208 years after the birth of Arthur Phillip (1738–1814), the first governor of Australia. The Bishop of Bath and Wells preached a sermon at which he said that they were commemorating the beginning of Australia's history. Arthur Phillip was born in London and educated at the Royal Naval Hospital School. In 1755, Phillip joined the navy and served in a number of posts under Capt. Everitt. In 1775, Phillip was loaned to the Portuguese navy, with the expectation that he would return with detailed knowledge of coasts, harbours, and fortifications of the Spanish colonialists in South America. Returning to England in 1778, he re-joined the navy and worked his way through the ranks, reaching the rank of captain in 1781. In September 1786 he accepted the post of governor of the new penal colony at Botany Bay. He took a fleet of eleven ships, which arrived on January 26th 1788. Phillip showed himself to be an able manager of people, encountering many difficulties, including crop failures. He gave convicts a stake in the new society, holding out inducements of freedom and land. His rule was egalitarian and humane. Ill health forced him to return home for recuperation, and between 1808 and 1814 he lived at No. 19 Henrietta Street, Bath. He died on August 31st 1814 and is buried in St Nicolas' Churchyard, Bathampton. (*Oxford Dictionary of National Biography*; *The Times*)

~ October 12th ~

1805: The Bath Theatre Royal opened its new theatre at Beaufort Square. The theatre was designed by George Dance. The opening performance of *Richard III* was not a success, as the title role was given (in the words of the programme) to 'A gentleman, his first appearance on the stage.' This unfortunate actor was overcome with stage fright and forgot his lines. It is not known why such an important role was given to an unknown actor. (William Lowndes, *The Theatre Royal at Bath*, Redcliffe, 1982)

1926: General Hertzog, Prime Minister of South Africa, paid a visit to the city. He paid the 6*d* admission to the Roman Baths without being recognised. Hertzog joined a tour party and appeared very interested, asking a number of questions about the Roman remains. He also visited the abbey. The General mentioned that although South Africa has hot springs, they are not developed. Hertzog later left the city by car and continued his aim of seeing much of the scenery of Britain as possible. (*The Times*)

— October 13th —

1797: Nathaniel Bayly, poet and playwright, was born in Bath on this date. His literary career started in Bath, where he published satirical verses under the pseudonym 'Q in the corner'. These poems were later collected under various titles. One such poem was published in *Rough Sketches of Bath* (1817) and sang the praises of his native city:

> I seize my pen, determined to rehearse
> The sports of Bladud in heroic verse;
> To sing of those who walk in fashion's path,
> And thus immortalise the charms of Bath.

In September 1829, Bayly left Bath for London, keen to establish himself as a playwright. His first play, a farce entitled *Perfection, or, the Lady of Munster* was very favourably received. Bayly claimed to have written the entire play on a stagecoach between his uncle's home in Sussex and London. During the 1830s, Bayly's income became entirely dependent on his writing and the burden of providing for his family was at the forefront of his mind. Consequently, he spent extended periods abroad for the sake of his health. Bayly later moved to Cheltenham for the Spa waters, but this brought no improvement and he died from jaundice, complicated by dropsy, on April 22nd 1829. (*Oxford Dictionary of National Biography*)

~ OCTOBER 14TH ~

1841: An accident occurred on the Great Western Railway near Bath. Passengers leaving by the up train, which left Bath at seven o'clock, stopped only 2 miles into the journey. The passengers made enquiries about the cause of the stoppage and were informed that the previous train, which had left Bath a five o'clock, was stopped ahead in consequence of an accident that happed to a luggage train. Enquiries were made of railway staff, who told passengers that an axle of one of the carriages attached to the luggage train had become broken and that the railway would remain blocked until repairs could be effected. After the seven o'clock train was delayed by a further two hours, it was announced that the obstruction had been removed and the two trains continued their journey to Paddington, both arriving shortly after midnight. (*The Times*)

~ October 15th ~

1862: Bath Magistrates investigated an attempt of infanticide against two women, Sarah Caseley and Mrs Nichols of Batheaston. Mrs Nichols did not live with her husband and became pregnant by another man. In order to hide her disgrace, it was agreed that Caseley would take the child from her. The previous evening, Caseley and Nichols were walking together near Victoria Park when Nichols went into labour, giving birth to a daughter. A witness claimed that she saw something thrown over the park railings. The witness gave chase and, with the help of a passer-by, apprehended Caseley. A search was made and the child found. Nichols did not appear before magistrates on this occasion as she was too ill. Both women appeared before the county assizes charged with the attempted murder of the infant. Both were acquitted, in part due to the fact that Nichols had with her some baby clothes which showed that she had intended to look after her newborn child. During the 1800s, infanticide was often treated leniently by the courts, as it was recognised that following childbirth a number of women were affected by a 'mania', which is some cases resulted in harm to their newborn. Judges often took a sympathetic approach and many of these women were sent to local asylums. Many of these cases that came before the courts were women of the lower social classes and the children that were born were often illegitimate. (*The Times*; *Bristol Mercury*; *Western Morning News*; www.bbc.co.uk)

~ OCTOBER 16TH ~

1796: James Lindsay preached at Monkwell Street, a Presbyterian congregation on London, in honour of James Fordyce, a celebrated preacher who had once ministered to the congregation there. Fordyce was born on June 5th 1720 in Aberdeen. He received a classical education at Aberdeen High School and attended Marischall College, also in Aberdeen, before entering the Church of Scotland. In 1753, Fordyce moved to Alloa, where his ministry was more successful and he became noted for his preaching. His address to the General Assembly of the Church of Scotland in 1760, on 'The Folly, infamy and misery of unlawful pleasures', secured Fordyce's position as an outstanding preacher. In 1760 he moved to London to join the Monkwell Street Presbyterian Church. From here, Fordyce became one of the most celebrated preachers in London and many thousands travelled to hear him. Both his *Sermons to Young Women* (1765) and his *Addresses to Young Men* (1777) found a wide appeal. However, in the 1770s Fordyce's popularity declined. The declining congregation took its toll on Fordyce's health and he resigned his ministry at Christmas 1782. He moved to Bath following the death of his brother in 1784, and died on October 1st 1796. (*Oxford Dictionary of National Biography*)

~ OCTOBER 17TH ~

1922: Miss Ellen Terry, an actress who made her name on the Bath stage, unveiled a tablet on the house in The Paragon where Sarah Siddonshad lived. Ellen Terry made her first appearance on the Bath stage in 1863 and her last in 1904. After the unveiling ceremony, Miss Terry was given luncheon at the Guildhall. Afterwards, she and Sir Squire Bancroft, who accompanied her, gave speeches. This was followed by performances given by the Bath Players. Rather appropriately, the Players included an episode from *Bath Ghosts* which tells of Sarah Siddon's three reasons for leaving Bath – namely her three children Henry, Sally and Maria. The inscription of the tablet simply stated: 'Here dwelt Sarah Siddons b.1755 d.1831'. Terry was a well-known and liked actress, who was awarded the Order of the British Empire in 1925, making her only the second actress to be honoured in this way. (*Oxford Dictionary of National Biography*; *The Times*)

~ October 18th ~

1815: 'The bells of the city of Bath rang at intervals throughout the day, in compliance with the eccentric will and bequest of the late Colonel Nash, that the day of his funeral should be annually celebrated in such a manner; and that on the anniversary of his wedding, a bell should toll, or a muffled peal be rung throughout the day.' (*Lancashire Gazette*)

1831: The Roman Catholic Bishop of Cork was travelling from Bristol to London when his coach stopped at Bath to change horses. A crowd gathered, demanding to know if the bishop was a passenger. The grievance of the crowd was that they believed the bishop had voted against parliamentary reform, despite his protestations that he was a reformer. They tried to pull him out of the coach, but the coachman whipped up the horses and made a speedy getaway so no harm should come to the bishop. (*The Times*)

1954: Haile Salassie, Emperor of Ethiopia, became an honorary freeman of Bath, where his family had spent the years of their exile. The emperor was presented with an illuminated scroll and a specially bound volume on Bath's Georgian architecture by the mayor, Cllr W.H. Gallop. (For further details of Haile Salassie's stay in Bath, *see* August 5th.) (*The Times*)

~ October 19th ~

1866: 'The *Western Morning News* reports a strange case of superstition in the west of England. About three weeks ago there died the Rev E.D. Rhodes, vicar of Bathampton, a village two miles from Bath, and on the borders of Somerset and Wilts. Mr Rhodes was a man of very remarkable powers; his teaching was far above the average of the county clergymen, and his parishioners were commonly supposed to be, so far as intellectual attainments are concerned, much above the level of an ordinary rural parish. Nevertheless, since his death the rumour has become current that his ghost has been seen in Bathampton churchyard, and has been heard groaning and sighing. The witnesses increased in number and in positiveness of assertation, and the report obtaining general currency, crowds of persons came over from Bath to verify it. Their testimony was abundantly confirmed, and one old parishioner, entering more into detail than the rest, said that he had seen Mr Rhodes with a crown of glory round his head and a trumpet in his hand. The matter now became serious, and the aid of the police was asked, Constables accordingly were sent over on Friday night. The ghost appeared as usual, pale and ghastly, groaning and sighing. He was captured, and turned out to be a great white owl, which is henceforth condemned to humiliating imprisonment in a barn, with hard labour in the shape of mice catching.' (*Trewman's Exeter Flying Post*)

~ OCTOBER 20TH ~

1759: The following extract is a letter to the Royal Society, probably the first scientific body in the world, from Josiah Colebrooke and describes the phenomenon of Halley's Comet, which was visible in the sky until this date: 'On Saturday the 20th October, between five and six in the afternoon, as I walked over the north parade, a ball of fire, of the bigness of a tennis ball, of a very bright colour, with a train of four or five feet in length, darted from north-west, and, describing the arch of a great circle on my left hand, sunk behind the hills to the south-east: just before it sunk, several large sparks of bright blue fire issued from it; but it did not seem to burst: it was not more than two seconds in its passage, and I could compare it to nothing, but the most glorious sky rocket I had ever seen ... I do not remember that I heard any noise or whizzing in the air as it passed; not did any sulphureous smell attend it, that I could perceive. I looked on my watch immediately after it was gone by, and found by that, it was just twenty minutes past five; but, as I could not be sure that went right, I chose to mention that time in more general terms. It was seen by vast numbers of people, and much talked of the next day.' (*Philosophical Transactions of the Royal Society*, vol. 51, 1759)

~ October 21st ~

1848: Mr Turner alighted from his horse at Twerton and gave care of it to a lad until his return. On a whim, the boy mounted the animal but the horse took off at full speed towards Bath. On reaching the Old Bridge, the horse stumbled, unseating its young rider. However, the boy's leg was caught in the stirrup and he was dragged along upside down as the horse regained its footing. They proceeded for some distance up Southgate Street until the horse was stopped by a passer-by. The lad suffered only some bruising for his ordeal. (*Bath Journal*)

1899: Lord Lister was staying at Bath and whilst being driven up Lansdown Hill in a cab, his sister-in-law, an inspector for the Society for the Prevention of Cruelty to Animals, stopped the cab and alleged that the horse was lame. On this date, the driver appeared before Bath Police Court and was fined £10. Lord Lister attended, giving evidence on behalf of the cab driver. Lord Lister deemed it undesirable that Bath's inhabitants should be subject to a great inconvenience that his sister-in-law had put them to. Consequently, Lord Lister paid the cab driver's fine, stating 'I believe him to be an honest man, and if his horse was lame, the driver did not know it, and, therefore, was not cruel. I'm sorry to intrude upon the court.' (*Wrexham Advertiser*)

~ OCTOBER 22ND ~

1749: Phineas Bowles died in Bath on this date. During his lifetime he served in a number of regiments in the army and rose to the rank of lieutenant colonel. In 1715, he was involved with the suppression of the Jacobite uprising. In March 1719, he succeeded his cousin as Colonel of the 12th Lancers which were stationed in Ireland. His marriage to Alethea Maria in 1724 brought with it a large Irish estate. However, portions of the estate were given to Bowles upon his marriage and the remainder if the couple were able to produce a male heir. It was an arrangement that was to cause a long-running family argument after his death. Between 1735 and 1741, Bowles was MP of Bewdley. His stanch support for the Whig government ensured rapid promotion in the army, becoming lieutenant general in 1745. (*Oxford Dictionary of National Biography*)

2012: Bath and North-East Somerset Council announced that it was asking artists to design a new cross for Haycombe Cemetery Chapel after the original was controversially removed during renovation works. This sparked a campaign culminating in a 5,000-signature petition to retain the cross. The new cross can be removed when requested by families. Haycombe Cemetery opened in 1937 and a crematorium was added in 1961. The cemetery chapel is not a consecrated space and has not been claimed by any church of any denomination. (www.bbc.co.uk; www.bathnes.gov.uk)

~ October 23rd ~

1999: A French restaurateur in Bath was reprimanded by the French government after he removed his native dishes from the menu in protest at the ban of British beef. Philippe Roy, owner of the Cloy de Roy French restaurant, was told that his actions were 'deplorable' in a letter from the French embassy in London. A worldwide ban on British beef exports had been introduced in March 1996 because of the threat of Bovine Spongiform Encephalopathy (BSE), but after three years of trade blockade, the European Commission, on the advice of its scientific committee, announced the easing of restrictions from August 1999. France, however, continued to defy the European Commission and retained the ban on British beef. M. Roy commented: 'I feel like a little schoolboy being told off by the matron, but I'm not going to let them tell me what to do', and that, 'their position on British beef makes me ashamed to be French. The quality of English beef is much better than French beef.' France eventually lifted its ban on British beef in March 2006, when the EU also lifted the ban on live beef exports. (*The Times*; news.bbc.co.uk)

~ October 24th ~

1778: Sarah Siddons (1744–1808) was a famous actress who established her reputation at Bath. She first performed at the Orchard Lane Theatre on this date, as Lady Townley in Vanburgh's play *The Provoked Husband*. The *Bath Chronicle* simply announced her debut, but two weeks later described her performance of Elvira in Hannah More's *Percy* to have 'established in the judgement of the town as the most capital actress that has performed these many years'. Her work schedule was hectic, as members of her company also performed at Bristol. Recalling her life at Bath, Siddons stated: 'Hard labour indeed it was; for after the Rehearsal at Bath on a Monday morning, I had to go and act in Bristol in the evening of the same day, and reaching Bath again after a drive of twelve miles, I was obliged to represent some fatiguing part there on the Tuesday evening … That I had strength and courage to get through all this labour of mind and body, interrupted too, by the cares and childish sports of my poor children who were (most unwillingly often) hush'd to silence for interrupting my studies.' The family lived at No. 33 The Paragon, but were unable to support themselves in reasonable comfort. Siddons asked for an increased wage, but this was refused. At the same time she was offered a contract to perform at Drury Lane, which she accepted and which propelled her to even greater success. (*Oxford Dictionary of National Biography*; William Lowndes, *The Theatre Royal at Bath*, Redcliffe, 1982)

~ OCTOBER 25TH ~

1890: An unusual case was heard at Weston (Bath) Police Court. Nelly Stone, 21, had been arrested for attempting to defraud the Midland Railway Company without paying for a valid ticket six days ago. She was discovered underneath a seat by Guard William Price, when the 8.40 a.m. train was stopped at Bitton station; she appeared tired and exhausted, as if she had walked a long way. Unusually, Stone was also in male attire. Stone claimed in court that she had walked a long way and that she could not recollect how she came to be found underneath the seat of the third-class compartment. Stone also offered her apologies. According to Stone, her decision to wear male dress whilst she was out walking in the countryside was for protection from being molested. Stone's brother also gave evidence that his sister left home in Plymouth and began wandering the countryside. He was only apprised of his sister's situation in Bath when he read about it in a newspaper. The court allowed the case to be dismissed, allowing Stone to return home with her brother as the railway company was no longer willing to pursue the matter further. (*Bristol Mercury*)

~ October 26th ~

1966: The bronze head of Minerva, one of the most well-known and precious artefacts, was stolen from the Roman Baths Museum. The theft was discovered by an attendant opening up the city's baths. A ladder was found that may have been used to reach the top of the wall and gain access to the premises. The statue was not missing for long and was soon recovered from the Reference Library in Queen Square. This statue was apparently stolen to publicise the Bath Youth Carnival. The gilt bronze head was discovered in 1727. It belonged to the statue depicting the Roman goddess Sulis Minerva and would have stood within a temple dedicated to the goddess located beside the Sacred Spring. The statue could be an original object from the foundation of Roman Bath in the first century AD. It would have then stood for 300 years until the fall of the Roman Empire. (www.romanbaths.co.uk; *The Times*; www.bathintime.co.uk)

~ October 27th ~

1750: The New Theatre in Old Orchard Street opened. The first performance was Shakespeare's *Henry IV*. John Wood, the Elder, the famous Bath architect responsible for many of Bath's Georgian buildings, selected the site, although it is believed that the design for the theatre was undertaken by Thomas Jelly. The New Theatre became the Theatre Royal in 1767, and moved to its present site in Beaufort Square in 1805. At the opening of the play, a prologue written in blank verse, by a man called Watts, was read aloud, outlining the forthcoming attractions and urging audiences to be tolerant. The final rhyming couplet read: 'Small faults excuse, with cordial smiles attend, encouragement will urge us on to mend.' (William Lowndes, *The Theatre Royal at Bath*, Redcliffe, 1982)

1888: The first derby match between Bath and Bristol rugby clubs took place at Gloucester's County Cricket Ground in Nevil Road, Horfield. Bath won the game 5–3 and the crowd was estimated to be 700–800. The notable try of the match was scored by Bath rugby player Frank White; he achieved this feat without his shorts, which were left in the hands of the Bristol full-back. However, as Frank White himself recalled: 'I wore bathing drawers underneath, Bristol was not unduly horrified.' (Kevin Coughlan, Peter Hall and Colin Gale, *Before the Lemons: A History of Bath Rugby Football Club 1865-1965*, Tempus, 2003)

~ OCTOBER 28TH ~

1823: Camerton rector John Skinner recorded his journey into Bath and described a balloon flight, then an unusual event: 'I walked to the gasometer on the Bristol Road, where a balloon was filling under the direction of a Scotsman of the name of Graham. I do not think the thing itself would have had sufficient attractions to draw me away, unless Burrard had agreed I should meet him there. On my arrival, having paid a shilling for admission into a timber yard where the aerial vehicle was suspended, we continued nearly an hour in the open air, most of the time under a heavy shower of rain, til the signal was given and the gigantic ball ascended – the wife of Mr Graham being his companion du voyage. Owing to the thickness of the atmosphere, the globe was soon out of sight; the course it took seemed to be over the Crescent, but there are so many currents of air it was impossible to determine where it would steer. For my own part I feel but little interest in these exhibitions, this being the third I have witnessed: the risque is certainly to great, and the benefits to be obtained too small to meet with encouragement from any but the inconsiderate vulgar.' (John Skinner, *Journal of a Somerset Rector*, Howard Combes & Arthur N. Bax (eds), John Murray, 1930)

— OCTOBER 29TH —

1928: William Bartlett, aged 23, a boot repairer with only one leg, was remanded at Bath for the murder of his young wife, Marjorie Aileen Bartlett, to whom he had been married for five months. Bartlett had walked into Paddington Green Police Station, London, and admitted to his crime. Further investigations found Marjorie bludgeoned to death in their sweet shop in Monmouth Street, Bath. The couple were facing financial ruin, for only the previous day Marjorie had sold some of the shop's fixtures and fittings in order to buy time from their creditors. The £11 she received for the items was missing. At his trial, held at the next Somerset Assizes, Bartlett recalled that his wife made some sharp remarks to him. He remembered little of what happened next and only 'came to' when the metal bar he was holding dropped to the floor, bringing him to his senses. Seeing his wife lying in their blood-soaked bed, he fled the scene. The prosecution argued that Bartlett had killed his wife for the money. The defence council, led by Mr J.D. Casswell, made the case that Bartlett had suffered from an epileptic fit when he killed his wife. Casswell, summing up, made an emotive speech which moved many of the jury to tears. Bartlett was found guilty, but insane, and was imprisoned at Broadmoor Criminal Lunatic Asylum. (*The Times*; Nicola Sly, *A Grim Almanac of Somerset*, The History Press, 2010)

~ OCTOBER 30TH ~

1909: Eagle House in Batheaston was owned by the Blathwayt family and, between 1909 and 1912, the house served as a refuge for suffragettes to recover from the harsh treatment inflicted on them when they were imprisoned. The women were imprisoned for their, often violent, support for women's enfranchisement. Whilst at Eagle House, suffragettes were encouraged to plant a tree in the grounds. The result became known as Annie's Arboretum after the suffragette Annie Kenney. Today, Eagle House survives as a Grade II listed building, but the arboretum was destroyed in the 1960s to make way for a housing estate; destroyed, that is, with the exception of an Australian Pine. This tree was planted by Rose Lamartine Yates on this date in 1909. Rose Lamartine Yates had been arrested on February 24th 1909 whilst on a deputation to the House of Commons. At her trial she made an impassioned defence of her actions, stating 'every woman must have the courage of her convictions and must not sink back when she has taken the first step.' The court took a different view and she was sentenced to one month's imprisonment in Holloway Gaol. (*Oxford Dictionary of National Biography*; www.english-heritage.org.uk)

~ October 31st ~

1831: Following disturbances in Bristol, military aid was requested from the Somerset Yeomanry, commanded by Captain Wilkins of Twerton. On hearing of this request, Capt. Wilkins rode, in his uniform, into Bath for the purpose of assembling his troop. He was recognised by some 'loose characters' who followed him, yelling at him, to the White Hart Inn (located opposite the Pump Room). His pursuers wanted Wilkins to promise not to go to Bristol. Capt. Wilkins replied, jocularly, that 'he was a reformer as well as they; but he must go to Bristol to preserve order.' His pursuers were barred from the inn and became infuriated. A crowd assembled outside the inn and began to attack the building with stone missiles until there were only a few panes of glass left. Some of the mob proceeded to the Guildhall, but this was protected by officers. The attack on the White Hart continued and at 8 p.m. some of the mass went and got sticks from a pile in the Upper Bristol Road. These were used to demolish the shutters on the inn to gain entry. On entering they were told that Wilkins had left the premises but the crowd did not believe it. Capt. Wilkins had already left the inn via the back door and had changed from his regimental uniform into plain clothes. By this time, magistrates had sworn in a body of 'respectable citizens' as special constables. However, it was not until the early hours of the morning that law and order was restored. Support for parliamentary reform to extend the franchise was strong throughout Britain, as were accompanying protests and riots in a number of cities. (*The Morning Chronicle*)

– November 1st –

1879: *Berrow's Worcester Journal* recorded: 'A largely-attended meeting was held on Saturday [November 1st] at the Assembly-rooms, Bath, at which it was unanimously resolved that tramways were uncalled for, injurious and calculated to injure Bath. A deputation was appointed to accompany the chairman (Dr Falconer) and present the resolution to the town council.' The objections to the trams were not upheld and the following year saw the introduction of the first tram service. The service was horse-drawn and, initially, consisted of one route only. This ran from the GWR railway station (Bath Spa) via Southgate Street, High Street, Walcot and Grosvenor. The service was electrified in 1904 but discontinued in 1939. Trams had met with similar opposition in nearby Bristol, where some members of affluent Clifton feared an influx of the 'lower orders of society', who would spoil the area's amenities. Sunday observance and temperance societies feared that it would lead more people into sin. In more recent times, the reintroduction of trams prospers as one way of easing Bath's chronic traffic congestion. (*Berrow's Worcester Journal*; Peter Davey and Paul Well, *Bath Tramways*, Middleton Press; 1996; D.G. Amphlett, *The Bristol Book of Days*, The History Press, 2011)

— November 2nd —

1878: The *Bristol Mercury* illustrated the 'uncertainty of life' by the death of 23-year-old James Hunt, an assistant master at Partway House Academy, who was playing a game of football with his students, in Weston, near Bath. Hunt suddenly collapsed on the field and Dr Hopkins was summoned to his aid, but without success. The doctor attributed the cause of death to 'heart disease'. The story was of interest to at least one other newspaper: *The Blackburn Standard* gives a more embellished account. It states that Hunt became fatigued whilst playing, and that before he died, he called out to his players, 'Go into it boys, I can't help you any longer.' (*Bristol Mercury*; *The Blackburn Standard*)

—

1878: Mary Guildford was summoned for being disorderly at the Newbridge tavern, Twerton, The husband of the defendant was drinking in the above house, and it appears that she went for the purpose of getting him home. She was more abusive than persuasive to him, and used bad language. Considering the object of her visit the bench inflicted the mitigated penalty of 2*s* 6*d* and costs. (*Bristol Mercury*)

~ November 3rd ~

1927: Field Marshal Lord Allenby unveiled Bath War Memorial. Lord Allenby stated that 'echoes of the War were still resounding through an unquiet and troubled world' and that 'many of the old problems remained unsolved and new problems every day were pressing for a solution'. After urging his listeners not to be despondent, Allenby went om to say that 'the dead had given their lives for mankind, and we, the inheritors of their bequest, must see that the cause in which they died was carried through to full attainment.' The memorial, which is situated at the main entrance to the Royal Victoria Park, was designed by Sir Reginald Blomfield. The memorial takes the form of a Cross of Sacrifice. (*The Times*)

2012: One of the more unusual lots at a property auction was the sale of St James' Cemetery Lodge. The Grade II listed former lodge used to house the council superintendent. The property was described as having 'the most peaceful back garden settings in the country'. Peaceful is correct, since the cemetery holds around 24,000 graves, the last burial having taken place in 1937. The cemetery opened in 1861. The property was sold to a property developerf or £164,000, considerably more than the guide price of £60,000–£80,000. It was sold by Bath and North-East Somerset Council who stated that the funds raised from the sale would be reinvested into local services. (www.bbc.co.uk)

~ NOVEMBER 4TH ~

1874: A prisoner by the name of Smith escaped from Bath Gaol. Smith was being held on remand after deserting the army. Major Preston, the prison governor, had been using prisoner labour to build a 'photographic house'. Smith had been given the job of painting the roof of this new building. The prisoner, finding himself temporarily without the prison officer in charge of his custody, removed a 29ft ladder from the photographic house and placed it against the wall of the prison. Although the ladder was 5ft short of the wall's height, Smith succeeded in getting over the wall and escaping. (*Bristol Mercury*)

1909: A fire broke out at Batheaston Mill, severely damaging the building. The mill had been built in 1844 by Ambrose Emerson, replacing a smaller mill that had once belonged to the monks at Bath Abbey. Pieces of sculpture from the original mill had been used in the 1844 building. Following the fire, these were taken to the abbey cloisters. The damaged building was repaired and is currently operating as the Old Mill Hotel. (Paul De'Arth, *Bath: the Second Selection*, Tempus, 1998)

— November 5th —

2005: Firefighters spent more than two hours trying to free a cat that had become stuck up a tree in Weston, Bath. The cat, called Purdy, belonged to Elaine Gilbert and had been missing for five days until neighbours spotted the cat up in a tree in a nearby field. The cat had climbed 30ft and was unwilling to come down, despite the owner calling for it. Elaine called the RSPCA, but it was getting dark and they said they would not attend until the following morning. Mrs Gilbert's husband used a ladder to try and reach the cat but it was not long enough to reach the stranded moggy. The following morning, the RSPCA told the Gilberts that the fire brigade would be the best people to get the cat down. On arriving at the scene, the firemen used ladders and poles, but the cat became frightened and climbed still higher. Eventually, it was decided to remove parts of the tree and take the branch down from which the cat was resting. However, as soon as the cat was on the ground, she ran off and disappeared for another three days. There were sightings in nearby fields but no one could catch her. In the end, Purdy returned home suffering from a broken paw, which, given rest, would heal naturally. (*Western Daily Press*)

675: A twelfth-century copy of a charter, held by the monks at Bath Abbey until the Dissolution of the abbey in 1539, states that, on this date, King Osric of Hwice gave land at Bath to a 'convent of holy virgins'. The first abbess was Bertha, who was probably Frankish, and it has been suggested that she was from a nunnery near Paris which was active in spreading the monastic ideal. However, it is possible that the charter represents a refounding of an older religious establishment on this site. Osric's motivation may have been to encourage the church to establish a bishopric for his kingdom. (Peter Davenport, *Medieval Bath Uncovered*, Tempus, 2002)

1564: John Daniel was a lutenist and a composer, who worked in a number of Elizabethan and Jacobean households. It thought that he was baptised, on this date, in Wellow Church, near Bath. In 1603, he received a bachelor's degree from Oxford for music. Daniel is best remembered for the collection of *Songs for the Lute Viol and Voice* that he published in 1606. From 1614, he became a court musician to Prince Charles. His death date is not precisely known, but he is thought to have died in around 1626. (*Oxford Dictionary of National Biography*)

- November 7th -

1817: The Queen consort, Charlotte of Muklenburg-Strelitz and wife of King George III, was staying in Bath, where she learnt the melancholy news of the death of her daughter, Princess Charlotte of Wales. Princess Charlotte had died, aged 21, in childbirth. The Times records that 'the Royal party had just sat down to dinner, when Fisher, the messenger, arrived with a dispatch to Her Majesty. The afflicting nature of this second letter was unexpected. When the Queen perused the dispatch, she rose from her chair, and covering her face, uttered a convulsive sob, and left the table. Her Royal Highness the Princess Elizabeth likewise retired to her chamber. The windows of the house were instantly closed, and for the remainder of the night a mournful and sad silence prevailed throughout the whole household.' The following day, several shops, in the city, were shut and the bells of three churches tolled their 'solemn knells.' The royal party had been in Bath since 3rd November. On 4th November, the Royal party were observed to take an 'airing' of the city accompanied by HRH Duke of Clarence, followed, on 4th November, by a visit to the Baths. (*The Times*)

– NOVEMBER 8TH –

1886: The opening of the Bath Telephone Exchange and of trunk lines between Bristol and Bath at the company's office, in Union Street, took place. The offices were decorated and suspended above the chairman's seat were the crests of Alderman Hammond, the Mayor of Bath, and Mr C. Wathen, the Mayor of Bristol. The chairman of the company, Mr C. Nash, made a speech in which he outlined the different towns that had already adopted the use of the telephone. Bournemouth was said to have approximately 100 subscribers. Meanwhile in Bristol, more representatives of the press had assembled at the city's telephone exchange and they were able to hear the ceremony taking place at Bath, making out the voice of their mayor and the voice of Mr Nash. A number of questions were asked of Mr Nash, including the longest (in terms of distance) that a telephone call had been heard. The answer was 214 miles, in which Mr Nash had an hour's talk with their offices in London from Exeter. (*Bristol Mercury*)

1805: 'An inhabitant of Bath (now retired from business) received last week the following rather extraordinary letter, containing a Bank Note value 10l – It is full 21 years since the firm alluded to existed; and the gentleman who then composed it cannot possibly recollect or trace the name of their conscientious customer: "Sir – Enclosed value ten pounds – use as under: many years since I purchased some goods from you under the firm of —. The want of cash obliged me to leave Bath without paying you. Almost ever since I have been out of the kingdom. I know not what terms you and your partner were upon, but shall leave it to you to give him his share of this bill. For although the debt is dead in law, it is not dead in honour or honesty; and I trust you will be as honest to him as I am to you. M."' (*The Lancaster Gazette*)

1829: A poor man was digging a well at Bathford when the sandy soil around the hole collapsed inwards, taking the man with it and burying him. Many people were procured to render assistance to the unfortunate man, and after seven and a half hours of labour they succeeded in getting him out. Remarkably, the poor labourer suffered no broken bones. (*Bristol Mercury*)

~ November 10th ~

1966: Lord Hinton of Bankside was installed as the first Chancellor of the Bath University of Technology by the Pro-Vice Chancellor Sir James Pitman at the Assembly Rooms. Prior to the ceremony a silver mace was given by Goldsmith's Company and handed over to the university's second warden, Sir Owen Wansborough-Jones. Lord Hinton was given an honorary doctorate of science by the Vice-Chancellor, George Moore. The university's origins can be traced to an informal meeting between George Moore, the principal of Bristol College of Science and Technology, and Mr H. Brand, the Director of Education for Bath, that took place during the interval of a play. Their discussion centred on the difficulty of finding a site with sufficient space to expand the college in Bristol. Brand suggested the college site at Claverton Down. The Robbins Report of 1963 had also recommended that the college should become a university. By 1964, the buildings of the new university were under construction, and the university gained its charter in October 1966, when the first students were admitted. In the university's first year the population consisted of 1,145 undergraduates, 115 postgraduates and 470 staff. In 1971 the university was renamed and became the University of Bath in order to reflect the broader range of work that the university was undertaking. (Bath University Website; *The Times*)

‑ November 11th ‑

1815: Thomas Dehany Bernard (1815–1904) was born in Clifton on this date. He studied at Exeter College, Oxford, and in 1838 he won the Ellerton theological prize with an essay entitled 'On the conduct and character of St Peter'. He was ordained in 1840, and was a strong evangelical, which, in turn, led to his appointment to the rectory of Walcot in Bath by Charles Simeon's trustees in 1864. He held the post until 1886, when he moved to Wimbourne, Dorset. He was a frequent speaker at the Islington Clerical Meeting, the most important gathering of Anglican evangelicals at that time. Bernard continued to publish on theological matters throughout his life and was responsible for the revival of Wells Cathedral Grammar School in 1864. He died on December 7th 1904. (*Oxford Dictionary of National Biography*)

1927: A dedication of a new war memorial cloister, next to the south transept, took place at Bath Abbey on Armistice Day. It was built by Sir Thomas Jackson, who was also responsible for the reordering of the Norman chapel as memorial to those citizens of Bath who had died during the First World War. The chapel is now known as the Gethsemane Chapel and continues its theme of reconciliation and commemoration, possessing an Amnesty candle that burns continually on the altar. (bathabbey.org; Nikolaus Pevsner, *The Buildings of England: North Somerset and Bristol* Penguin, 1958)

– November 12th –

1275: King Edward I granted a charter to the Bishop of Bath and Wells. The charter exempted 'men of Bath' from paying certain tolls. This was the fifth royal charter to be issued to Bath. Twenty-seven royal charters have been issued in total so far. The last was in 1974, when Queen Elizabeth II reconferred Bath's city status on the borough of Bath, following local government reorganisation. (www.thecityofbath.co.uk)

———

2003: Ronald Pugsley, affectionately known as 'Mr Shoe', died at the age of 86. He was the third generation of his family to be involved with the sale and repair of shoes. The family business started a repair shop in Walcot, which later moved to Cheap Street. Another store was added in 1934. Ronald joined the family firm, aged 16, after completing a six-month apprenticeship with Clarks. After a thirty-seven-year career at the shop, he retired in 1983. The shop's lease was sold to another company. (*Western Daily Press*)

— November 13th —

1880: 'Samuel Smith, James, Lary and William Derrick, three young men, on remand, were charged with having robbed Harry wise, a carpenter, at Twerton, on the night of the 13th inst. Mr E.B. Titley appeared for the prosecutor and Mr F.S. Clark for defendants. According to the statements of Mr Wise, he was returning home about midnight when the defendants, without any provocation, knocked his hat off, and afterwards struck him to the ground. On reaching home he found that he had been robbed of about 30*s* in money, a knife, and a piece of meat. Evidence was adduced to prove that the prosecutor had been drinking, and that he had before preferred a similar charge against some soldiers who were discharged. The Bench decided to treat the case as one of common assault, and fined each of the defendants 2*s* 6*d* and costs.' (*Bristol Mercury*)

— November 14th —

1680: Joseph Glanville, Anglican clergyman, controversialist and philosopher, was born in Plymouth, the son of a Puritan merchant. He was educated at Oxford and in 1661 he published *Scepsis Scientifica*, which attacked Aristole, praied Descartes and upheld the view that knowledge would not be able to comprehend the inner workings of the universe. In *Lux Orientalis*, published a year later, argued the case for the pre-existence of the human soul before birth. Granville also wrote on witchcraft. Here, Granville was more concerned with the interaction of spirits on the material world, rather than the practice of witchcraft. Consequently, Granville believed strongly in the reality of the devil and its effect on people. On June 23rd 1666, Granville became the rector of Bath Abbey and retained the living for the rest of his life, although he gained many other preferments including becoming chaplain in ordinary to Charles II, in 1672. As an Anglican controversialist, he spoke out against dissenters, but argued for a broad, inclusive established church. He died, on this date, in 1680 and was buried at Bath Abbey. (*Oxford Dictionary of National Biography*)

NOVEMBER 15TH

1837: Isaac Pitman was born on January 4th 1813 in Trowbridge, Wiltshire, and was the third of eleven children to Samuel Pitman, a manager of a weaving mill. He left school, aged 12, suffering from fainting fits. The lack of education led Isaac to become well read in order to compensate. In 1831 he trained at the Borough Road Teaching College, London, to become a schoolmaster and taught Taylor's Shorthand to his most able students. In 1836 he accepted a post as schoolmaster in Wotton-under-Edge, Gloucestershire, but was dismissed by the strongly Calvinist school board who were not happy with his increasingly outspoken Swedenborgian beliefs. He ran a rival school in the town for the next two and a half years. After writing a book on Taylor's Shorthand, his publisher suggested that a book with a new system of shorthand would sell better. Although sceptical at first, he worked on the project and published, on this date, *Stenographic Sound-Hand*. The book used a series of dashes, dots, pecks and curves to represent the letters which could be written phonetically. The book went through several editions during Pitman's lifetime. By 1842, Pitman was now living in Bath and he was a resident of the city for over fifty years. During his time in the city, Pitman established himself as a printer, publisher and editor. He died on January 22nd 1897, at his home of No. 17 Royal Crescent. (*Oxford Dictionary of National Biography*)

~ November 16th ~

1861: 'The Bath and Pump-room Committee have obtained the sanction of the Town Council for the reparation of the stone balustrade in the King's Baths. Only a portion of this balustrade is in existence, and, though it has been cemented many times, it is in a very dilapidated condition. It is rather an ancient piece of work, and owes its origin to the circumstances set forth in the following inscription, which is still to be seen in the bath: "Sir Francis Storer, of Storer, in the county of Oxon, Knight, troubled with the gout and aches in the limbs, received benefit by the bath, and having lived many years after, well in health, to the age of near ninety, in memory of the same gave the stone rail about the baths in the year 1607." It is gratifying to know that the curious relic will be preserved, and that the stone balustrade will be restored to its pristine condition.' (*Bristol Mercury*)

1999: After a bus was cancelled owing to a shortage of drivers, fourteen furious passengers 'hi-jacked' the driver and demanded that he took them back to Twerton, 3 miles away. At first, the angry passengers staged a sit-in at Bath bus station, before deciding to storm a bus. They refused to leave and police had to be called. Twerton councillor, Carol Brown, who was one of the fourteen passengers, stated that she had no regrets over her action, which was taken to avoid the walk back to Twerton. No arrests were made. (*Western Daily Press*)

~ NOVEMBER 17TH ~

1999: On this date, the miniature sculptures of Willard Wigan were first exhibited at Bath. The sculptures are so small that the exhibition could easily fit into a matchbox. These miniature masterpieces are carved from cocktail sticks and microsurgical scalpels. The collection included sculptures of the Royal Family, Sir Winston Churchill and a bird feeding its young in a nest. Wigan started creating his tiny sculptures at the tender age of 5, apparently to escape the ridicule of teachers who mocked his inability to read or write – Wigan suffers from dyslexia. He also states that his micro-sculptures began when he started to make houses for ants, as he thought that they needed somewhere to live. Then he made them shoes and hats. His fantasy world became a place of escape from the reality of day-to-day living. His talents were unknown until he was made redundant at the age of 42 and Wigan made art his profession. In 2007, Wigan was awarded an MBE for his services to art. (*The Times*; www.willard-wigan.co.uk)

~ NOVEMBER 18TH ~

1830: Grosvenor Suspension Bridge was completed. The structure was later rebuilt in 1929 by F.R. Sissons, the city engineer. The original abutments of the suspension bridge were used but the suspension bridge deck was replaced with a concrete one. The bridge currently takes a footpath/cycle track across the River Avon, linking Kensington Meadows and the Kennet and Avon Canal. (Paul De'Arth, *Bath: the Second Selection* Tempus, 1998)

———

1873: 'William Willbon, charged with begging in Queen's Parade this morning, was discharged on promising to leave the town.' (*Bath and Cheltenham Gazette*)

~ November 19th ~

1721: Samuel Chilton, of Timsbury, near Bath, a labourer of 25 years of age, fell into such profound sleeps that nothing could rouse him. His first sleep lasted a month, his second seventeen weeks, during which Chilton was subject to being bled and blistered, but to no avail. When the third sleep came upon him, it lasted three months, during which Chilton was visited by the celebrated Bath physician Dr Oliver, who tried various different experiments upon him. These included pulling Chilton by his shoulders, pinching his nose, stopping his mouth and nose together for as long as the physician dared, holding a vial of sal-amoniac to the patient's nose and pouring the same down his nose. (Sal-amoniac was, historically, used to give relief to sore throats.) A large pin was thrust into Chilton's arm, but this too failed to wake him. Some food was left for him and it was usually gone within a day or two, but he was only observed sleeping, until November 19th 1721 when his mother heard noises from his bedchamber, ran up to him and found him eating. She asked him how he did and he replied, 'Very well, thank God.' Overjoyed she left him to tell his brother what had happened, but when they returned he was asleep again, until the following January when he seemed to respond to hearing his name being called. Eventually after a few days he awoke and was able to go back to his profession. (*Philosophical Transactions of the Royal Society*, vol. 24, 1704)

~ NOVEMBER 20TH ~

1927: After passing through the Combe Down Tunnel, near Bath, a freight train, of thirty-seven wagons and a break-van became derailed at the entrance to Bath Goods Yard killing three people. Driver Harry Jennings was killed along with Inspector John Norman, who was in charge of the goods yard, and Jack Loader, a young LMS clerk from Gloucester who was taking a shortcut through the yard on his way home from work. Both the fireman and the guard said that the tunnel was hot and smoky when they passed through it. After a short time, the guard stated that he had to wrap a coat around his head and to sit down. Afterwards, he remembered nothing. Guard Christopher Wagner suffered compound fractures to both legs. *The Times* reported that the force of the collision was such that the locomotive had turned on its side and that the trucks were piled high upon each other. Furthermore, the goods yard shed, which measured about 100 yards in length, 'was to a great extent crumpled up' and only one room was left comparatively undamaged. The accident report which followed could only suggest that both the driver and the fireman were overcome by smoke and fumes as the engine, which was said to have been steaming badly, laboured its way through the Combe Down Tunnel. (*The Times*; Robin Atthill, *The Somerset and Dorset Railway*, Pan Books, 1970)

— November 21st —

1866: 'The *Western Morning News* mentions an amusing incident which took place a few days ago near Bath. The river Avon, where it passes through the property of one of the leading landowners, is strictly preserved. The other day the keeper of an estate came upon a gentleman who was fishing in the forbidden waters. "Pack up your traps and be gone," said the keeper. "Do you know who I am?" said the gentleman. "Yes, you are the Mayor of Bath," replied the first, adding in the utmost seriousness, "and if you don't make off this minute I will bring you up before yourself tomorrow." It need not be added that his worship beat a retreat.' (*Trewman's Exeter Flying Post*)

1884: An elderly plasterer, named Abraham Greenslade, of No. 2 Gay's buildings, was admitted to Bath's Royal United Hospital after suffering a fall from a building in which he was working. Although the precise age of Greenslade was not given, it would appear that he continued to work as there would have been no alternative. State pensions were not introduced until 1908 and then only to those aged 70 or more. (*Bristol Mercury and Daily Post*)

~ November 22nd ~

1897: 'At the Bath Police Court on Monday [November 22nd], Sir Charles Nugent was fined 40*s* and costs, the full penalty, for smoking in a non-smoking compartment in a train on the Great Western Railway. It was stated that the company, in consequence of complaints, had instructed their staff to enforce the bye-law.' (*Hampshire Advertiser*)

2011: Soldiers from the 21st Signal Regiment based at Colerne paraded through the city led by their commanding officer, Lieutenant Colonel Graham. The troops were given the freedom of Bath after six months' service in Afghanistan. (*Western Daily Press*)

2012: The *Bath Chronicle* reported on Bath's only brewery, Bath Ales, as it celebrated its fifteenth anniversary brewing beer in the city. The brewery has been awarded many prizes for its Bellringer Best Bitter. The company supplies beer to many pubs within a 15-mile radius of the city. To mark the company's fifteen years in business, a beer, Bellringer Maximus, which was brewed for the company's tenth anniversary, was brewed once again. The beer's name Maximus is a term in change ringing referring to bell-ringing methods that are rung on twelve bells. (*Bath Chronicle*)

1838: Between the hours of eight and ten o'clock in the evening, the resident of No. 14 Royal Crescent, Colonel Kaye, was robbed of jewellery to the value of £2,000. The robbery was discovered at eleven o'clock, and the police were informed. Hall, described as a 'chief officer', headed the investigation. Hall proceeded with two other officers towards Bristol where they succeeded in obtaining a clue to the location of the thieves. The thieves were said to have travelled along the Gloucester Road in a gig. The officers pursued the men and about 6 miles from Bristol, they arrived at an inn where the thieves were staying. Two of the thieves were captured after some resistance, but a third managed to escape. The jewels were recovered from a Mackintosh cape. Returning to Bristol, one of the thieves attempted escape and give further resistance, but he was quickly captured by a 'young gentleman' who happened to be passing. (*The Times*)

- November 24th -

1845: A policeman named Richard Sheane was accompanying a boy and both took their place on an evening train from Bristol to Bath. Soon afterwards, both he and the boy fell asleep and were conveyed beyond their intended destination. The rushing noise of the locomotive in the Box Tunnel awoke the policeman. On realising that he had been conveyed beyond Bath, his first thought was that the train would stop at Corsham, but it did not, and continued onwards at speeds of 40–50mph. At length, Sheane decided to jump from the carriage, so he opened the door, alighted onto the step and jumped from the moving train. The boy travelled to the next stop at Chippenham where he raised the alarm. A search was made of the line, but Sheane could not be found. Sheane remembered little after this, but believed that he was struck by a bridge during the jump, for he was knocked unconscious. On coming round, he crawled to a nearby house where he lodged for the night. The following morning, he was well enough to walk into Corsham to seek medical treatment for a dislocated shoulder. Sheane also suffered from a number of cuts and bruises but, save for his shoulder, was otherwise unharmed. Furthermore, it did not appear that Sheane was intoxicated in the least and bore a very good character. His rash act may, therefore, be put down to an uncharacteristic lack of judgement. (*Devizes Gazette*)

~ November 25th ~

1915: Two officers in the same regiment, who held the same rank and possessed the same initials, led to a mistake in the reporting of a casualty of war. Mr and Mrs Robertson of St Leonard's, Weston Road, Bath, were informed that their son, Second Lieutenant Lennox George Robertson of the Tenth Gordon Highlanders, had been killed in action. An obituary notice to this effect had already been printed in *The Times*, when, on the evening of November 24th and the morning of November 25th, Mr and Mrs Robertson received word from their son. One of these communications stated 'The other L.G.R. was shot on Thursday. Wasn't it sad?' (*The Times*)

1999: Santa Claus may be coming to town, but not to Bath, after Bath and North-East Somerset Council announced there were no suitable places for a grotto. The council had searched for a suitable venue, but with Christmas approaching, space was at a premium in shops which were crammed with Christmas goods. In previous years, the grotto had been staged at the Guildhall. (*Western Daily Press*)

— November 26th —

1906: *The Times* reported on the 'dangers attended with the amateur collection of old masters has never been better exemplified than in the recent somewhat sensational discoveries at the Holburne Museum, Bath.' Following a review of the collection, it was reckoned that about four-fifths of the collection were copies and in some cases were said not to resemble the work of their reputed painter. Thirteen years previously, on 3rd June 1893, the museum opened. The museum's collection was formed by Sir Thomas William Holburne (1793–1874). From 1830, Sir William lived at No. 10 Cavendish Crescent with his three unmarried sisters. Not much is known about the circumstances of his collecting. The collection includes porcelain, silverware, old masters, miniature portraits and miscellaneous smaller items including Roman coins. The collection of over 4,000 objects was bequeathed to the people of Bath by his sister, Mary Anne Barbara Holburne (1802–1882) to form the basis of a museum. On Sir William Holburne's collection of old masters *The Times* article goes on to state, 'It is interesting to speculate on the circumstances of in which Sir William Holburne came into the possession of the impudent forgeries. Living in the country and having little opportunity of studying the genuine pictures, it is said that his knowledge was derived from a library of books on art matters … a strange feature of this astonishing collection is the fact that it possesses a few very fine pictures.' (*The Times*)

— NOVEMBER 27TH —

1944: During the 1930s, developments within Germany had been viewed with a growing unease, since it was widely believed that air power would be critical to success in war. Protecting armaments from aerial bombardment was a priority. Just to the east of Bath, between Box and Corsham, a series of quarries, located 100ft (30m) underground, was thought to be the ideal location. Furthermore, they were connected by a short underground railway which emerged at the eastern portal of the Box Tunnel. Workers from South Wales and Durham were drafted in to start construction in 1936. Understandably on pay day, some of the men got drunk and brawls occurred. Sentencing two workmen for brawling, in 1938, the chairman of the magistrates stated: 'When they come to a place like Bath, they should behave as Bath people behave. Bath people do not get drunk.' During the Second World War, 300,000 tons were stored underground and the site was even used as a control centre for the No. 10 Group, RAF Fighter Command. On this date, a massive underground explosion occurred involving 4,000 tons of explosive and leading to the loss of dozens of lives. After the war, preparations were made to turn part of the site into government headquarters that were secure from the threat of atomic warfare. Conventional weapons were blown up on site during the early 1960s as they were thought obsolete against the nuclear threat. (Sally Watson, *Secret Underground Bristol*, Broadcast Books, 2002; David Brandon, *Haunted Bath*, The History Press, 2009)

— November 28th —

1980: Bath Magistrates heard the case against Miss Lisa Diane Demartino, 22, an American student at the University of Bath, following her arrest in a telephone box, as they believed that she was trying to avoid payment on an overseas call. However, Miss Demartino told magistrates that she had arranged for the cost of her call to be added to her sister's bill in the United States. The police were not able to provide any evidence against Miss Demartino. Consequently, the case was dismissed and the prosecution was ordered to pay costs of £168.91. The police arrested the student owing to the mistaken impression of a telephone supervisor who became suspicious when calls were made to the telephone box in Camden Road. Miss Demartino's defence accepted that the police were acting on information supplied by the Post Office, but were critical of the Post Office because of its delay in checking Miss Demartino's statement. Inspector Maurice Bailey, of Avon and Somerset Constabulary, offered his apologies to Miss Demartino. (*The Times*)

~ November 29th ~

1801: Ann Barry (née Street) was born in Bath on April 8th 1733 and, aged 17, embarked on a career as an actress. She first appeared in York where she was staying with relatives. In 1754, she came back to Bath to play the role of Cordelia in a production of Shakespeare's *King Lear*. She acted at theatres in London and Dublin and was regarded as one of the finest actresses of her generation. She performed for the last time in 1798, and spent her final years in comfortable retirement, dividing her time between London and Bath. She died on this date. (*Oxford Dictionary of National Biography*)

1824: Sutton, the Kentish Pedestrian, walked last week, on the Lower Bristol road ... 300 miles in six successive days, without making one turn in the performance of this great undertaking, but re-pacing backwards, his first mile, and so in succession taking every second mile backwards! The powers of this pedestrian on the backward step are truly astonishing; and that the inhabitants of Bath and its vicinity may have an opportunity of witnessing so rare a performance, he is matched (for a moderate sum to walk 250 miles backwards in six successive days in Sydney Gardens; to commence on Monday the 29th inst. And to finish each day by five o'clock!' (*Hampshire Telegraphy & Sussex Chronicle*)

~ November 30th ~

1774: John Rann, highwayman, was executed at Tyburn. The *Newgate Calendar* cites his place of birth as being in a village near Bath. His parents were poor but of good character. He entered service at a young age, becoming popular with his masters. He came to London and was coachman to John Montagu, the 4th Earl of Sandwich. At some point, Rann seems to have lost his good character and drifted into crime. On November 13th 1773, he was arrested, along with five others, for the highway robbery of the Hempstead stagecoach. One of the men, John Scott, agreed to testify against the others, but the case against Rann and the other men collapsed since neither the passengers nor the stagecoach driver could identify the robbers. Another acquittal for two accounts of highway robbery followed in April 1774. About this time, he gained the nickname 'Sixteen-string Jack' from wearing breeches with eight strings at the knee. At Bagnidge Wells, Rann appeared dressed in a scarlet coat, tambour waistcoat, white stockings and laced hat; and finding that he had lost a ring, stated that it was 'a hundred guineas gone, but that one evening's work would replace'. On September 26th, Rann robbed William Bell of his watch, which he gave to his mistress Eleanor Roache. Her attempts to pawn the watch led to his arrest. He was convicted at the Old Bailey in October and sentenced to death. (*Newgate Calendar*; *Oxford Dictionary of National Biography*)

- December 1st -

1851: A man named George Bush left his lodgings in Timsbury to attend an auction at Priston, just 3 miles away. After the auction, Bush spent quite some time drinking in the Ring of Bells pub in the village. However, Bush failed to return home and the next morning his landlady, Ellen Flower, sent her sons George and Isaac out towards Priston to find him. They found his body lying in a field. Bush's throat had been cut and the wound had been stuffed with grass. Bush had set out with a considerable sum of money which was now missing. Several people were arrested in connection with the murder. These included Ellen Flower, who had been aware that Bush had a considerable amount of money about his person; her daughter, Harriet; her son-in-law Jacob Windmill and their friend, Stephen Box. A few days later, the police arrested another man, James Evans, who was witnessed arguing with the victim in the Ring of Bells pub. The following year, Christopher Smith was arrested for vagrancy in the neighbouring part of Dorset. He confessed to the murder of George Bush and asked to be brought back to Bath. However, at his trial during the next Somerset Assizes, Judge Baron Platt had his doubts about whether Smith was guilty. He ordered that Smith be examined by doctors. Smith had confessed to a number of other murders and the doctors concluded that Smith was unable to plead. Smith was detained, but it is unlikely that he killed Bush. The murderer or murderers of George Bush were never caught. (Nicola Sly, *A Grim Almanac of Somerset*, The History Press, 2010)

~ December 2nd ~

1878: A public meeting was held, at which the Under Secretary for War, Lord Dury, defended the recent war in Afghanistan. Two motions were proposed at the meeting: one supporting the government, the other calling into question government policy. Neither was able to be put to the assembly owing to numerous disturbances at the meeting. The war in question was the Second Anglo-Afghan War (1878–1880) which was started after the Amir, Sher Ali Khan, was too slow in accepting British influence. The Amir had allowed Russia to enter the capital, Kabul, and prevented General Sir Neville Chamberlain from entering the country through the Khyber Pass. Afghanistan was important to the British as it provided a buffer between Russia and British territories. (*Reynolds' Newspaper*)

1898: Lord Kitchener made a brief visit to Bath. His train, bound for Cardiff, was allowed to stop at Bath railway station for 10 minutes so that he could be received by the Lord Mayor. Lord Kitchener was conducted from his train to a raised dais and the mayor thanked him for his recent military campaign in the Sudan, where he had succeeded in regaining Khartoum for the British. Lord Kitchener made his thanks to the assembled crowds, stating that 'it is a great pleasure to me, as it is to the troops who served with me to feel how fully our services have been appreciated in the country'. Kitchener returned to the train and bowed his acknowledgements to the crowds as the train steamed out of the station. (*The Times*)

‒ December 3rd ‒

1869: Newspapers of the time often put unfortunate coincidences together to make an interesting story, as is evident in this short article regarding a Bath resident: 'On Friday [December 3rd] week a man named Stockden, living in Holloway, near Bath, had been drinking at a beer-house in Union passage, Bath, when a dispute arose between him and some of his company. During the altercation he exclaimed, "May God strike me dead," and he had scarcely uttered the word "dead" when he became speechless and lost the entire use of his limbs. He was taken to his residence where he still remains in the same deplorable state.' (*Bristol Mercury*)

1896: An inquest was held into the death of Charles Weston, a 16-year-old labourer. He had been working on scaffolding at the Pump Room. A pulley was used to transfer fresh mortar to workers at the top of the scaffolding. When work ceased, Weston used the pulley rope to descend from the scaffolding. The rope, however, was not secured, sending Weston crashing to the ground. He died from a fractured skull and a verdict of accidental death was recorded. (Nicola Sly, *A Grim Almanac of Somerset*, The History Press, 2010)

1988: Police armed themselves with shields and riot gear after they came under attack from a under attack from a man with a bow and arrow. The man had been refused admission to a Salvation Army Shelter. (*Sunday Times*)

340

— December 4th —

1845: An Anti-Corn Law soirée was held at Bath's Guildhall, attended by many of Bath's 'influential inhabitants'. In total 700 people attended. The news of the government's announcement, that the Corn Laws were to be repealed, had come to the city that afternoon. Mr Hunt, a town councillor, in speaking to the assembled throng, remarked that 'the funeral of the Corn Laws was about to take place' and that 'no doubt some of the gentlemen on this platform were about to become its pall-bearers.' Others spoke in a similar manner, with cheers and applause from the audience. The Corn Laws were introduced in 1815 to protect the price of corn from cheaper imports. Opposition to the Corn Laws increased and legislation was passed in 1846 allowing for their abolition. (*The Times*)

1962: Flooding affected large parts of Britain and rescuers were out in the Wye, Severn and Derwent valleys, rescuing families from flooded homes, or distributing food to homes that were cut off by flooding. Villagers of Weston, near Bath, protested outside the Guildhall before that night's council meeting as villagers believed that flooding in their area could have been prevented if a scheme that had already been given the go-ahead had been carried out. Along St John's Road, flooding was reported to be 7ft deep in places. (*The Times*)

– DECEMBER 5TH –

1898: At Bath Police Court, 'a gentlemanly looking man', George Price Power, aged 61 from London, was charged with stealing by picking the pockets of women, and also of attempting to do so. Power had been detained the previous Saturday evening by Mr Oliver, an attendant at the Assembly Rooms. PC Crane, who was on duty in Milsom Street, duly attended the scene of the crime. On arresting Power, the prisoner told PC Crane, 'I think you have made a terrible mistake constable,' and 'Constable, you will get yourself into serious trouble.' When Power was searched, £8 9s 5½d, an imitation gold watch and chain, some stamps and keys were found on his person. It was not only the Pump Room that Power seems to have been 'at work'. Mrs Jane Anne Best, aged 37, was called to give evidence. She stated that having entered a GWR tramcar, she found the accused's hands upon her. Power was sitting at the entrance. Asked to identify if the prisoner was that man, she pointed to another man in court, giving rise to much laughter. She was questioned about his apparel before looking around the court again, this time identifying the prisoner. For attempting to pickpocket in the Pump Room, Power received a month's imprisonment and for pickpocketing Mrs Best, he was sentenced to three months' hard labour. The sentences were to run concurrently. (*Bristol Mercury*)

- December 6th -

1862: George Britton returned to his Manor Farm home in Englishcombe from Bath market with a considerable sum of money. On his arrival home, he followed his usual routine: first he went upstairs to deposit the cash in his chest, and then he had his tea and smoked his pipe. After tea, at about eight o'clock, he took a candle and a lantern to inspect his farm. However, Britton did not return. His wife made a search of the premises and found that the eggs from the fowl-house had been collected and his lantern was left nearby. These were the only traces of Britton from that night that remained. Several villagers scoured neighbouring lanes, ponds, ditches and woods, but Britton's whereabouts remained a mystery. Further enquires elicited that Britton was experiencing some financial difficulties and that the money that should have been in the house was no longer there. It would appear that Britton had absconded, although the value of the stock on the farm would have covered his liabilities. Newspaper speculation states that Britton may have gone to Australia where Britton had relatives who were thought to be doing well. Briton is also said to have visited Bristol and made preparations for going abroad. A couple of weeks later, Britton sent a letter postmarked from Dublin giving certain directions to his administrative affairs, but did not give any information as to his precise whereabouts or intended destination. (*Bristol Mercury*; *Western News*)

~ December 7th ~

1189: In order to pay for King Richard I to fight in the Crusades, charters were sold by the monarch as a way of making money from wealthy towns and cities. This particular charter granted that Bath should be free from tolls to encourage trade. The charter was limited to trade and because of this, the charter is said to have started the process of self-government for the city as citizens sought further charters to grant more powers. (www.thecityofbath.co.uk)

1832: Reports of thefts from coaches were a relatively frequent occurrence of the period. The *Bristol Mercury* reported: 'About 7 o'clock, on Friday night, a commercial gentleman lost, on the road from Bath to Bristol six acceptances to the amount of 376l., and two 5l. Bristol Branch Bank of England notes, from a portmanteau, placed on the roof of the coach. Two suspicious-looking individuals got up behind the coach as it was leaving Bristol, and left it again at Twerton, during which time they sheltered themselves from the observance of the front passengers by an umbrella; and the boisterous wind prevented their being heard while they opened the portmanteau, and replaced all the straps, &c., so as to leave the whole, to all appearance, untouched. As the numbers of these notes are known, and the acceptances are all advised, it is hoped that the passing of the notes will lead to the apprehension of the thieves.' (*The Bristol Mercury*)

– December 8th –

1837: Eleazer Pickwick was baptised in Freshford on February 2nd 1749. The Pickwick family lived in obscurity on the Somerset/Wilshire border before they moved to Bath. Pickwick married Susanna Coombs in St Michael's Church, in 1775. Pickwick started out as a postboy at the Bear Inn and used these skills to develop a reliable post coach service, which began operating from the end of the 1770s. This started with a service between Bath and London and operated from the Angel Inn. Services were later transferred to the White Hart Inn, Stall Street, and increased services to London Bath and the Oxford Cross post system. He thus made his fortune and was able to purchase land including a house in Bath Street, a manor house in Bathford and another manor house in Wingfield, Wiltshire. In 1830, he purchased a fine town house at No. 10 Queen Square, Bath. It is said that author Charles Dickens modelled his character 'Pickwick' on Eleazer Pickwick in *Pickwick Papers* after visiting the White Hart Inn. Eleazer Pickwick died on this date. (*Oxford Dictionary of National Biography*)

~ December 9th ~

1974: An explosion from a 5lb bomb went off in the centre of Bath, 20 minutes after a warning was given to the police. The Corridor shopping arcade was sealed off by sixty policemen. The bomb was later acknowledged to have come from the IRA. Fortunately no one was injured. (*The Times*; *Bath Chronicle*)

———

2010: BBC News reported on the improvement works at the 170-year-old Bath Spa station. First Great Western, who lease the station from Network Rail, said that the revamp would see extra entrances and access to the platforms improved. A number of historic architectural features would also be restored. Not everyone, it seems, was happy, since plans for the revamp were first unveiled ten years ago. Mr Kerr, representing The Federation of Bath Residents, claimed that they had not had enough time to have their say since there was no opportunity for consultation. The works were completed by the following summer. (www.bbc.co.uk)

~ DECEMBER 10TH ~

2002: The Jane Austen Centre in Bath displayed what it believes to be the definitive portrait of Jane Austen, despite it being painted 185 years after her death. The portrait was commissioned by David Baldock, director of the Jane Austen Centre, and was painted by Melissa Dring, a freelance forensic police artist, who has worked with a number of police forces in the UK. On seeing the painting, Jane Austen experts claimed that the portrait had 'captured her humour and sparkle as they had only imagined.' The main difficulty with the commission is the lack of contemporary portraits of the author. Instead, Melisa Dring had to rely on contemporary reports of Jane Austen's appearance that describe Austen as 'a brunette with full round cheeks and bright hazel eyes, an appearance expressive of health and animation.' In researching Jane Austen's appearance, Dring also looked at Jane Austen's dresses and the appearance of her family members. Thus, Dring's portrait includes features which all the family shared including bright eyes, long nose, and a small narrow mouth. One of the few contemporary portraits of Austen, and the most familiar, was painted by her elder sister Cassandra, when the author herself was 35. However, Austen's niece stated that Casandra's watercolour looked nothing like the author. Dring's portrait tries to capture Austen when she was aged between 26 and 31, which coincides with when Austen was living in Bath. (*The Times*; *Jane Austen's Regency World* magazine)

~ December 11th ~

1893: The remains of Elsie Adelaine, alias Wilkie, were interred at Bathampton parish church, at the expense of the parish since none of her relatives were able or willing to bear the cost. The service was conducted by Revd H. Girdlestone, vicar of the parish. The body had been found the previous September in a cave at Hampton Down. It was clear she was murdered. The domestic servant had gone missing two years previously, and it appears that no one was ever caught for her murder. (*Bristol Mercury*; *Reynold's Newspaper*; *Hampshire Telegraph*)

2003: *The Times* newspaper announces that worshipers would be able to log-on to the first on-line carol service from St Philip's and St James' Church, Bath. (*The Times*)

2011: 'Occupy Bath' protestors, who set up camp on October 30th in Queen's Square, Bath, moved on. The campaigners were protesting against financial inequality and the political handling of the banking crisis. (www.bbc.co.uk)

— December 12th —

1797: Lucy Anderson was born on this date in Bath, the daughter of John Philpot, a music seller. Her father, who was her first piano teacher, intended that she should go on to learn the harp. However, her progress on the piano was so great that she made her first solo performances in Bath from a young age. After playing in London, in 1818, she continued to perform regularly in the capital. In 1820, she married George Anderson, a violinist. Lucy became the first woman pianist to perform at a Philharmonic Society concert. Sir George Smart introduced her to royal circles and she was appointed pianist to Queen Adelaide in 1832 and pianist to Queen Victoria in 1837. Lucy also gave lessons to Queen Victoria when she was a princess from 1834 and taught all of the queen's children music. Lucy was also on good terms with many famous composers, including Chopin and Mendelssohn. She retired in 1862 after amassing a £40,000 fortune, and died on December 24th 1878. (*Oxford Dictionary of National Biography*)

1836: *The Times* reported that the Bath Corporation employed Mr Hancock to find water using divination. *The Times* sarcastically puts Hancock's appointment down to the 'great sagacity of new corporations'. (*The Times*)

~ December 13th ~

1846: An amusing article appeared in *The Era* magazine on this date: 'Two gentleman of Bath, having quarrelled, one went to the other's door early in the morning, and wrote "scoundrel" upon it. The other, upon this, called upon his neighbour, but was answered by the servant, that his master was not at home, but that if he had anything to say, he might leave it with him. "No, no," replied the gentleman quickly, "I only came to return your master's visit, as he left his name at my door this morning".' (*The Era*)

1878: Shortly after eight o'clock, a blockage in the Coombe Down Tunnel was reported. No one was injured during the partial collapse of the tunnel, but seventy labourers were employed in moving the debris. It took four days to clear the line. However, on resuming services through the tunnel that same day, a goods train carrying coal spilled part of its load and the locomotive became separated from its wagons. Damage was caused to the permanent way. During the blockage, the railway company provided numerous men to convey passengers' luggage. Services were resumed later that day. (*Bristol Mercury*; *The Pall Mall Gazette*)

– December 14th –

1874: A prizefight took place at Limpley Stoke, near Bath. The combat was between two Bristol lightweights whose names remained secret on account of the illegality of such bouts. The party alighted at Limpley Stoke station, from the first train to arrive there that day, with one of the combatants, the other combatant arriving by road. However, the fight was prevented by Inspector Maggs and his men of the Wiltshire Constabulary, after he received a tip-off, by telegraph, of the intended fight. The managers of the fight, by staging their fight near two police divisions, simply moved the party half-a-mile down the turnpike road to Somerset when the Wiltshire Constabulary turned up. A ring was formed by the joining of hands and the fight commenced, lasting an hour. The fight was severely contested and both men were heavily 'punished'. The loser especially so, since he was at last so violently hit, he was not able to recommence the fight within the specified time. The case illustrates a weakness of the police force at the time by only being able to move illegal activity into another area. (*York Herald*)

— DECEMBER 15TH —

1727: The River Avon was navigable to shipping for 14½ miles from its mouth to Hanham Mills, above Bristol, which was the tidal limit on the river. From the reign of Elizabeth I several schemes were put forward to link the Avon with the Thames. In 1619, the mayor and aldermen of Bath petitioned James I for improvements to the river, complaining of the expense of transporting goods to and from Bristol 'by reason of rockie and mountaynous ways.' The development of Bath as a spa spurred improvement on the Avon owing to the difficulty in transporting materials for the rebuilding of the city by packhorses over bad roads, since there was no alternative. A deed dated March 10th 1724 assigned parts of the River Avon between Bath and Hanham Mills to a number of proprietors who were collectively responsible for raising money to fund improvements. A month later, John Hore was 'imployed in the direction and chief management of the works'. The navigation from Hanham Mills to the city weir at Bath was fully opened and on this date, the first barge carrying 'deal-boards, pig lead and meal' arrived in the city, having travelled the length of the new navigation. (Kenneth R. Chew, *The Kennet & Avon Canal*, David & Charles, 1968)

– DECEMBER 16TH –

1926: An apology was given by the Mayor of Bath after the extraordinary scenes were witnessed at the Guildhall, on November 5th, which was dubbed by the press as a 'free flight for free tea'. Large numbers of people arrived at the Guildhall to hear Prebendary Wilson Carlile, the founder of the church army, speak. The event was also to allow the Church Army to solicit for donations. Wilson Carlile was an evangelist, working within the established church and founded the Church Army as a missionary organisation that seeks to share faith through words and actions – especially social works. Carlile had spoken twice at similar events before without incident. These events were invitation only and normally 1,050 invitations were sent out. However, 7,000 invitations were issued – 5,000 people replied and the caterers supplying the tea were simply told to do the best they could. Eight hundred people were crammed into the banqueting hall, with large numbers unable to gain admission. The error was put down to one of the Church Army clerks responsible for sending the invitations. Carlile conveyed his apologies to the mayor. (*The Times*)

— December 17th —

1891: 'A young woman named Alice Male, was taking breakfast, on Thursday morning, to her husband, who is employed at the depot of the Bath Tramway Company, when her clothes were caught in the machinery of the chaff cutting apparatus. Her head was terribly injured, and death was instantaneous. Her husband, in endeavouring to save her, was also caught, but managed to free himself.' (*Hampshire Advertiser*)

1935: Brian Langford, cricketer for Somerset, was born in Bath. He made his debut for Somerset Cricket Club aged only 17. As an off-spin bowler, he went on to claim 26 wickets in 3 matches. Five years later, he became the Somerset's youngest player to reach 100 wickets in one season and the youngest ever in the county championships. (*Somerset County Cricket Club*, Tempus, 1999)

1991: Using up the first of its nine lives, a 'kitten which climbed into a washing machine in Weston, Bath, was saved from drowning when its owner smashed the glass door with a hammer after spotting it spinning round with the wash.' (*The Times*)

～ December 18th ～

1847: Thomas Barker (1767–1847), artist and pioneer lithographer, was buried at All Saints' Church, Weston, on this day. He was born in Trosnant, Pontypool, the son of solicitor and minor artist Benjamin Barker (*c.* 1720–1793). In 1783 the family moved to Bath. Barker seems to have learned his trade by copying the paintings of his patron Charles Spackman, a Bath businessman. He was also heavily influenced by Gainsborough. His *Self-Portrait with his Preceptor Charles Spackman* of 1789 shows himself painting a landscape in Gainsborough's style and his *Woodman in a Storm*, also of 1789, is similar to Gainsborough's *Woodman*. His *Old Woodman* and *Old Man with Staff* helped to establish his reputation and Barker occasionally exhibited at the Royal Academy between 1791 and 1829, and regularly at the British Institute between 1807 and 1847. In 1805, he opened a gallery at Sion Hill. He became a pioneer of the newly invented process of lithography and contributed, in 1803, to the first set of lithographs published in Britain. In 1813 he published a book of forty lithographs, *Rustic Figures*, which was printed in Bath by D.J. Redman, followed by, in 1814, a series of thirty-two landscape lithographs. Barker also painted the *Massacre at Chios* fresco at Doric House in 1825–6. Despite his efforts he died in poverty on December 11th 1847 surrounded by pawnbrokers' tickets. (*Oxford Dictionary of National Biography*)

~ DECEMBER 19TH ~

1790: William Edward Parry was born on this date, in Bath. He is best remembered as a naval officer and as an artic explorer. Parry briefly attended Bath Grammar School before joining the navy on board the *Ville de Paris*. In 1810 he became a lieutenant and was in charge of the frigate *Alexandria*, charged with protecting the Spitsbergen whaling fleet and thanked by the admiralty for charting of the coast of Norway and the Baltic Sound. It was his expeditions to the Arctic to find a north-west passage that Parry is best remembered for. Knowledge gained on these expeditions proved invaluable, as Parry was able to solve practical problems of surviving artic conditions and set about his exploration of the Arctic with a meticulous scientific approach. Many of his officers, including James Clark Ross, went on to become explorers themselves. His third expedition was an attempt to reach the North Pole from Spitsbergen. Parry turned back when he found that the ice flows were drifting south almost as fast as they could travel north. It was, however, the furthest north that anyone had ever reached (lat. 82° 43' 32"N). Parry's record stood for over fifty years. Parry continued to climb through the navy's ranks, culminating with the rank of rear admiral. His health began to fail during 1854 and he went to Emms, Germany, for medical treatment, but died on July 8th 1855. (*Oxford Dictionary of National Biography*)

1815: A stump of a large tree, weighing approximately 6cwt, fell from its place in Smallcombe Wood, near Bath. It rolled down an incline for approximately 100 yards before crashing into a cottage below. The tree stump forced its way through a roof before coming to rest upon a bed. No one was hurt or injured, although the people living at the cottage – a mother, her two children and her daughter-in-law – had a narrow escape. (*Royal Cornwall Gazette*)

1913: Considerable damage was done to Westwood House, Lansdown, Bath, when a fire was deliberately started in the early hours of the morning. It was believed that the fire was started by suffragettes, since a quantity of suffragist papers were found in the grounds. *The Suffragette* newspaper described the fire as 'a beacon to all Bath'. The fire could be seen from many miles away. Firemen had difficulty extinguishing the blaze since the only available hydrant was unavailable to deliver water at sufficient pressure. The house had been unoccupied for some time prior to the blaze. (*The Times*; *The Suffragette*)

~ December 21st ~

1830: During this month, a 'singular coincidence of somnambulism' (sleepwalking) occurred in Bath. The first incidence occurred in the between three and four o'clock in the morning, on December 9th, at the Darby & Joan public house. James Watkins had arrived to spend the night there. The following morning, Watkins dreamt that he was letting himself out of the window onto some grass. However, he woke up to find himself holding onto an attic window frame. He could not maintain his grip on the frame and fell through a skylight 15ft below. Watkins suffered severe cuts inflicted by the glass but survived the fall. The second occurrence, on December 21st, took place at the Plough, on Southgate Street, again between the hours of three and four o'clock in the morning. Mr Durbin, a musician, dressed himself and lifted the sash window of his bedroom. He fell out of the window, hit the street below and was found by two nightwatchmen in a state of insensibility. Durbin also suffered from a fractured elbow and was very much bruised, but he too survived the fall. (*Bath Chronicle*)

~ DECEMBER 22ND ~

1821: The Earl of Liverpool was presented with a medallion which granted him the freedom of the city. Part of the inscription on the medallion read, 'In testimony of the high sense of his Lordship's public services, during a long and trying period.' The Earl of Liverpool was Robert Banks Jenkinson, who was also the Prime Minister. The 'long and trying period' may refer generally to the problems of government or perhaps an allusion to the death of his wife six months previously. The Earl made regular visits to Bath to alleviate a vascular weakness. (*The Morning Post*; *Oxford Dictionary of National Biography*)

1855: 'A few weeks or so ago, a woman, driving her cart along a way to a coal pit from Bath was stopped early in the morning a short distance from Twerton, by a man who demanded her money, threatening that if she did not render it he would take her life. The woman, whoever she was, quite a match for her antagonist in shrewdness, if not in strength, and, on being thus saluted rejoined "Bless'e sir, I got no money; my husband wouldn't trust I with it; he is coming on behind", or words to that effect. This reply was given with such apparent truthfulness as to induce her unwelcome visitor to let her pursue her journey without further molestation.' (*Berrow's Worcester Journal*)

‑ DECEMBER 23RD ‑

1941: The Ministry of Food, which was set up during the Second World War, was forced to intervene to ensure that thousands of Bath residents got their rations, after 450 employees of the Bath Co-operative Society (which had, at the time, 20,000 members) went on strike. The ministry took over the co-operative's meat supplies, and emergency food coupons were made available at other shops to ensure that people got their rations. Milk was distributed by voluntary services. The strike was over a dispute regarding the bonuses paid to branch managers and juniors. During the afternoon, the Ministry of Labour tried to bring the two parties together and it was not felt that the strike was likely to spread. Strikes were a surprisingly common occurrence during the war, and under the provision of Order 1305 and the 1941 Essential Work (General Provisions) Act, strikes and lockouts were illegal. However, throughout the war, few prosecutions under the act were made, as the government pursued a policy of conciliation in order to avoid the labour unrest that was experienced during the First World War. The number of strikes increased until 1944, and was particularly common in the mining sector, perhaps owing to conscription in this industry. It is reckoned that almost half the strikes were because of pay disputes and the rest were because of a deterioration in working conditions. (*The Times*; www.unionhistory.info)

~ December 24th ~

1891: *Berrow's Worcester Journal* records 'A Singular Incident at Bath' and goes on to tell the tale of a remorseful thief: 'The post on Christmas Eve brought to a lady in Bath a singular case of restitution of stolen money. Many years ago the lady in question was making purchases at a shop, when she missed her purse. Inquiries failed to trace its whereabouts, and the owner reconciled herself to her loss. In the lapse of years the incident faded from her memory, but it has now been revived in an agreeable manner, by the receipt of a letter, evidently written by a person in humble life, enclosing a postal note for 10*s*. The note reads as follows: "In 1855, when you were Miss —, you lost your purse. With sorrow and shame I confess I took it. I believe there was £2 in it. It is my great wish to repay it, and enclose the first 10*s*. Give me time and I hope to pay you all, and I humbly ask for your forgiveness. I have confessed this great sin to God, and know He has forgiven me. That is why I wish to pay you all, as you must think it strange to receive this letter after so many years."' (*Berrow's Worcester Journal*)

~ DECEMBER 25TH ~

1191: On June 23rd 1174, the consecration of Reginald Fitz Jocelin (*c.*1140–1191) as Bishop of Bath and Wells, by the Archbishops of Canterbury and Tarentaise, took place at St Jean-de-Maurienne. The enthronement took place in Bath in November of that year. Reginald is recorded in King Henry II's service from around 1167 and when Archbishop Thomas Becket was murdered in 1170, Reginald pleaded the king's case at the papal curia. For his loyal service to the king, he was rewarded with the bishopric of Bath and Wells. He was, by the standards of the day, a conscientious bishop who administered his diocese effectively. He regulated the relationship between monasteries and vicars of appropriated churches, often in the latter group's favour, to ensure they were sufficiently provided for. Reginald also built St John's Hospital in Bath to ensure that the poor had access to the mineral waters. He was elected Archbishop of Canterbury in November 1191, but died only a month later on Christmas Day. Just before he died he received the monastic habit from Prior Walter of Bath, with these words: 'God did not wish me to be an archbishop, nor do I. He wished me to be your monk, and so do I.' He is buried near the high altar of Bath Abbey. (*Oxford Dictionary of National Biography*)

~ December 26th ~

1122: John of Tours, the Bishop of Bath and Wells, died on this date. He was a priest of the Church of Tours and practiced as a physician in his early life. It is possible that John of Tours may be the 'Johannes Medicus' who attended William I on his deathbed. He was chaplain under William II and it was from here that he gained the episcopacy to Wells in 1088. Under his rule, the episcopal seat transferred from Wells to Bath Abbey, which became a cathedral priory after William II granted him the abbey and its buildings. Chronicler William of Malmsbury thought that the motive was simply one of greed for the abbey's wealth. However, it could be that the move was made to a site that was more secure. Other criticisms of John of Tours' rule include those by Orderic Vitallis for being given an ecclesiastical honour 'like hirelings wages'. His actions at Wells provoke further criticism for reducing the endowment, and giving much of its wealth to his brother and steward Hildebert. However, under his rule the diocese established a bishop's council and appointed three archdeacons. On Christmas Day 1122 he suffered chest pains and died the next day. He was buried in the middle of the choir at Bath Abbey. (*Oxford Dictionary of National Biography*; Bath Abbey Website)

~ DECEMBER 27TH ~

1875: A railway signalman was sentenced to a month's hard labour for neglect of duty. Mr Biggs was a signalman at Wellow station, on the Somerset and Dorset Railway line. He had left the signal box without notice and went on a drinking bout in a nearby pub. He refused to return when the stationmaster sent for him. Furthermore, Biggs had left his box during one of the busiest times for the railway – the week prior to Christmas. Biggs' absence was only discovered when an express train had to cross the slow train at Wellow and it was necessary for both the signalman and the stationmaster to be present for the safe passage of trains. The sentence reflected the Bench's belief that the offence was a serious one, since Biggs' actions could have had serious consequences. Wellow station was one of the most patronised stations on the line, since the main part of the village was situated at the bottom of breakneck hills in almost every direction. (*The Times*; Robin Atthill, *The Somerset and Dorset Railway* Pan, 1970)

- December 28th -

1853: Baronets are not above the law, as this case showed when Sir James Rivers was charged with riotous and disorderly conduct in Milsom Street and at the police station, when he appeared before the magistrate at Bath Police Court. Evidence given by PC 33 stated that whilst on duty in Milsom Street, Sir James approached him between eleven and twelve o'clock at night, stating: 'Peeler, you must take care of this horse and cart, for I can't get in anywhere.' The PC replied that he had other things to do and that Sir James should go to the Castle Hotel. Sir James and a friend took some dogs out of the cart and went away up Milsom Street, leaving the horse and cart unattended. The PC stated that if they did not come back and take care of the horse and cart, he should impound them. Sir James said to his friend, 'Come on, that's a greenhorn; never mind what he says.' His friend, however, returned to collect the horse and cart and began to lead it away. Sir James followed, but created a disturbance calling the PC a number of names including 'beast' and 'greenhorn'. As a result Sir James was arrested. The evidence of the PC was corroborated by another officer. Sir James was ordered by the magistrates to find bail of £20 and one surety of £20, and to keep the peace for one month. (*Bristol Mercury*)

～ December 29th ～

1853: The *Bath Chronicle* reported a singular accident of a servant girl who lived in one of the houses of the city. She was ordered to fetch a decanter from a cupboard in the drawing room. She stood on a chair in order to reach the decanter when she fell through a 'borrowed light' in the floor into the room beneath, a distance of 20ft. Several others in the house, alerted to the crash, rushed to her aid. They discovered the servant girl unconscious, but sitting upright in the chair. In her hand she was holding the decanter, which was unbroken. The servant was uninjured, sustaining only a few bruises on one hand and arm and a small scratch to the back of the head. The seat of the chair, into which the servant had fallen, had sunk a few inches. George King, the doctor who was called in following the accident, and was of the opinion that during the fall the girl suffered from catalepsy, a condition where the body suffers from a muscular rigidity so that the limbs remain in whatever position they are placed. The servant girl soon recovered. (*Bath Chronicle*)

~ December 30th ~

1871: Two young gentlemen took advantage of the extremely cold conditions to skate from Bath to Devizes and back, along the Kennet and Avon Canal, making for a distance of 45-mile round trip. The men set off at 11 a.m. and returned at 8.30 p.m., with considerable time given for refreshment and rest along the way. Skating along the canals in the 1800s, during the winter months, seems to have been a common occurrence in the area. The Revd John Skinner, writing in his diary for January 14th 1823, recorded: 'As it had frozen hard during the night, and the boys wished me to accompany them to skaite, I walked with them to the Dundas Aqueduct in the Claverton valley, and skaited for four hours on a fine piece of ice where the Combe Hay canal had not been broken. Some of the Catholic gentlemen from Downside [Abbey] had passed us, and said they had come on the canal the whole way from Camerton', a distance of about 8 miles. The 'Combe Hay Canal' that John Skinner refers to is the Somerset Coal Canal that ran from the Dundas Aqueduct on the Kennet and Avon to Canal to Paulton, Somerset, and was operational from 1805 to 1898. (*Western Mail*; John Skinner, *Journal of a Somerset Rector*, Howard Combes & Arthur N. Bax (eds), John Murray, 1930; www.coalcanal.org)

~ December 31st ~

1842: A newspaper report gives this account of an unusual umbrella for sale in a Bath shop: 'An optician of Bath named Braham, has for some time past exhibited in his shop an ordinary-looking silk umbrella, but which contains a telescope, microscope, a thermometer, compass and sundial skilfully packed away in the handle.' Sadly, such an invention does not appear to have caught on. (*The Bristol Mercury*)

1898: Police Sergeant Bates was assaulted when he tried to place William Rufus Crook under arrest for being drunk and disorderly. Crook, a fishmonger by trade, was fined 20*s* for the offence and fined 40*s* for assaulting Sergeant Bath. At his appearance before the Bath Magistrates' Court, he was warned that this was his fifty-second appearance before the Bench for similar offences and that his next appearance would result in a prison sentence. (Nicola Sly, *A Grim Almanac of Somerset*, The History Press, 2010)